'Estrangement is so common and yet so stigmatised, so to read a work on this subject is refreshing. Karl has managed to provide such a valuable insight for professionals and interested parties, with an intense and detailed study of the phenomenon. His own first-hand knowledge shines through and brings authenticity to a difficult and distressing societal reality. This book is a tool for anybody who wants to better understand estrangement and find ways of counselling and healing.'

Jo Spain, *bestselling author and screenwriter*

'In sharing his expertise on this important and often hidden topic, Karl Melvin's compassion shines through each page. This book will be helpful to so many people. Karl Melvin explores the complex topic of family estrangement with kindness and compassion. Whether you have personal experience, or support people in a professional capacity, or perhaps both – this book is a must read.'

Dr. Lucy Blake, *Family Estrangement expert and author of* No Family is Perfect

'An important and refreshing addition to the emerging estrangement literature, Karl Melvin writes with authority and heart.'

Dr Kylie Agllias, *University of Newcastle and author of* Family Estrangement: A Matter of Perspective

'Karl Melvin's book is essential reading for anyone navigating family estrangement. As an expert working in the field, Melvin's compassion and attention to detail provides a comprehensive and thoughtful guide to help them through this difficult experience. This is a must-read.'

Stella O'Malley, *Psychotherapist and author of* What Your Teen is Trying to Tell You

T0384960

Navigating Family Estrangement

Family estrangement and the stigma attached to it are complex phenomena affecting a great number of people in various ways. In response, *Navigating Family Estrangement* offers a deep dive into the reality of being estranged in contemporary society.

This practical guide looks at how to effectively help estranged adults achieve better outcomes from a variety of perspectives. The author explores the difficulties of working with estrangement, including professional roadblocks such as the six biases that prevent connecting with a client's experience. He delves into the unique seven-step Estrangement Inquiry Model that aims to provide important insight into a client's family history, map out the present estrangement dynamic, and highlight the types of interventions to support their needs. Combining research from a range of different fields with the author's decade of clinical experience, the book is supplemented with five comprehensive case studies to demonstrate the practical strategies that address estrangement challenges.

This book offers a clear and collaborative approach to a topic that will be relevant for a range of professionals, including psychotherapists, psychologists, counsellors and social workers.

Karl Melvin is a psychotherapist and Family Estrangement expert. As well as running a busy practice, he delivers training globally to both estranged adults and professionals who are seeking a comprehensive understanding of complex family issues. Originally from Dublin, he lives in the West of Ireland with his wife and two sons and can be contacted via his website for therapy, workshops and seminars, and media requests: www.karlmelvin.com.

Navigating Family Estrangement

Helping Adults Understand and Manage
the Challenges of Family Estrangement

Karl Melvin

Routledge
Taylor & Francis Group

LONDON AND NEW YORK

Designed cover image: © Getty Images

First published 2024
by Routledge
4 Park Square, Milton Park, Abingdon, Oxon OX14 4RN

and by Routledge
605 Third Avenue, New York, NY 10158

Routledge is an imprint of the Taylor & Francis Group, an informa business

British Library Cataloguing-in-Publication Data
A catalogue record for this book is available from the British Library

Library of Congress Cataloging-in-Publication Data
Names: Melvin, Karl, 1978– author.
Title: Navigating family estrangement : helping adults understand
and manage the challenges of family estrangement / Karl Melvin.
Description: 1 edition. | New York, NY : Routledge, 2024. |
Includes bibliographical references and index.
Identifiers: LCCN 2023058594 (print) |
LCCN 2023058595 (ebook) | ISBN 9781032423104 (hardback) |
ISBN 9781032423067 (paperback) | ISBN 9781003362203 (ebook)
Subjects: LCSH: Families–Psychological aspects. |
Interpersonal conflict. | Alienation (Social psychology)
Classification: LCC HQ519 .M45 2024 (print) |
LCC HQ519 (ebook) | DDC 302.5/44–dc23/eng/20240202
LC record available at https://lccn.loc.gov/2023058594
LC ebook record available at https://lccn.loc.gov/2023058595

ISBN: 9781032423104 (hbk)
ISBN: 9781032423067 (pbk)
ISBN: 9781003362203 (ebk)

DOI: 10.4324/9781003362203

Typeset in Times New Roman
by Newgen Publishing UK

About the Cover Image

I wanted to find an image which captures the far reaching and pervasive impact estrangements can have. The overlapping circles appear as ripples across a plane of water and represent how estrangements can similarly send ripples across entire families and propagate divisions over multiple generations.

The image also represents the rippling affect an estrangement can have on many aspects of an individual's life, such as their mental and physical health, identity and self-worth, close and intimate relationships, career and sense of purpose and place in world.

Finally, the image also visually captures the broader societal impact of estrangement and how the loss of family support could potentially affect healthcare, addiction and homeless services, education providers, cultural and religious institutions and countless other community groups which support estranged adults.

Contents

Biography

Karl Melvin is an Irish psychotherapist, researcher, and family estrangement educator. Prior to beginning his training in psychotherapy, he worked as a software developer, but his personal experiences of estrangement prompted him to seek therapy to help make sense of this situation. One year later, he returned to further education to study counselling and psychotherapy, and he loved every minute of it.

When he began practicing as a psychotherapist, he was quickly drawn to working with adults who were struggling in their familial relationships. His initial experience was working with adult children estranged from one or more parents, siblings, or both. Later, he was presented with the opportunity to work with estranged parents, and having heard countless stories from opposing perspectives, he strives to maintain a neutral and nuanced view of the many ways estrangement manifests.

As well as running a busy practice, he is a sought-out educator and delivers training globally to both estranged adults seeking to explore their family history and professionals who regularly work with estrangement and are seeking a comprehensive understanding of the complexity of family struggles. His approach is practical, putting the client's needs first and emphasizing their strengths while supporting them through the struggles they are facing.

Karl is originally from Dublin and now lives in the West of Ireland with his wife and two sons. He can be contacted via his website for estrangement therapy, workshops and seminars, speaking engagements, and media requests: www.karlmelvin.com.

Acknowledgements

A special thanks to my friend Lynn Fay for her endless support, keen proof-reading skills, and for keeping my biases in check.

To my original therapists, Pat Hanna, Liam McGrath, and Tony Buckley, who were there for me when I needed them, this was a priceless gift I will never forget.

A special mention goes to Linda Balfe and the Aspen Counselling team. Linda gave me my break as a therapist, and I spent nine incredible years there, where I began my real training both in psychotherapy and life.

I would like to thank my lecturers in psychotherapy at PCI College; their training and experience inspired me to pursue this new career path. I would also like to thank the team at ICHAS, where I completed my master's degree and original estrangement research, and in particular, my academic supervisor, John Hickey, for his support and guidance.

To my family and friends, thank you for your ongoing love and patience in listening to me endlessly discuss estrangement.

I wish to thank the many estrangement researchers whose dedicated work has helped to broaden our understanding of this complex phenomenon and hopefully reduce some of the stigma felt by many.

A huge thank you to Kylie Agllias and Lucy Blake for their constant feedback, support, and encouragement.

I want to acknowledge the many clients who allowed me into their world and shared their wisdom and courage, which never ceases to inspire me.

I wish to thank my wonderful mother, Stella, who had to be both mother and father to me many times in my life, and my incredible stepfather, Richie, who has been a positive role model to me in ways I still regularly discover.

Finally, I dedicate this book to my amazing wife Treasa, who has witnessed the pain of my own estrangement firsthand and met it with pure unconditional love, and our two beautiful boys, Eli and Jude, who have been my ultimate teachers in life.

Preface

Before we begin, I would ask you to put aside any preconceived ideas you might have about family estrangement. Our concept of family is heavily subjective and influenced by many experiences, both inside and outside the family home, but there is much for us to learn if we are to embrace the diversity of this phenomenon, which affects many families and individuals.

Learning about families and how they become estranged was one of my motivations for writing this book. As a psychotherapist working with estranged adults, I have sat with many sons, daughters, mothers, fathers, brothers, sisters, grandparents, and other family roles/positions, and it was evident they were all struggling in their own unique ways and for a wide range of reasons. It was also evident they had individual strengths and coping mechanisms that helped them endure and survive their family dynamic and eventual estrangement, although many did not feel like they were strong or coping well at all.

Having experienced estrangement from several family members myself, I felt an overwhelming urge to create something that spoke to all these perspectives, to acknowledge the uniqueness of their story that separates them from others, as well as find commonalities that bind them together. And one thing that was universal to all these perspectives was the need to be heard and validated.

To be clear, this book is not about taking sides in family disputes, and I wish estrangement was neither necessary nor considered the only option. However, as we will learn, the reasons for each estrangement are complex, and because of this complexity, there are some who can see no visible solution to their family problems and view their estrangement as the only choice; there are some whose estrangement is forced upon them and are then left to pick up the pieces of their lives; and there are those whose estrangement sits between these polarities. Irrespective of whether an estrangement is chosen or not, the need for support is inevitable, but the type of support needed can be equally complex to determine. Over time, I found my role in helping my estranged clients extended beyond just listening and validating, to finding practical ways of navigating the many challenges they faced, both with their estranged family and those directly or indirectly affected.

With this book, I wanted to document my own approach to working with estranged adults and provide a guide for those in a position to offer this support.

My aim is to show how diverse estrangements can be, both in their causes and consequences; to highlight the various ways estranged people have survived this possibly very painful reality; and to introduce professionals to the many ways we can help. This might mean helping them to reconnect with family after a period of reflection and personal development and perhaps confronting the issues that cause the rift; it might mean helping them to find ways to explain not just their situation but their needs to partners and friends; it might mean helping them to manage the overpowering feelings and emotions they carry as a result of their family history; or it might mean all of these and more at different points throughout the process.

This book is written for professionals of varying backgrounds, and I will address them throughout. However, I hope it will be accessible to anyone interested in or affected by family issues, and specifically estrangement, so please do not feel you are being excluded or that your own views are not valued.

Privacy Disclaimer

The names and identifying characteristics of individuals featured in this book have been chosen to create relatable narratives of how estrangements might look and feel and do not represent actual people. Any likeness to real stories is purely coincidental.

Glossary

Estrangement A process of creating distance from one or more family members.

Parental Estrangement Estrangement from one or more parents.

Adult Son and Daughter Estrangement Estrangement from one or more adult sons or daughters.

Sibling Estrangement Estrangement from one or more siblings.

The Estrangement Impact Triad The three aspects of a client's life that can be impacted by an estrangement, including the psychological impact, relational struggles, and other social challenges.

The Estrangement Inquiry Model A process of exploring a client's estrangement, using seven factors that shape the estrangement, including the estranged parties, the estrangement type, the estrangement nature, the estrangement approach, the estrangement method, the estrangement duration, and the estrangement radius.

An Estrangement Map The output of the Estrangement Inquiry Model that takes the form of a table, with seven columns for each of the seven factors, an eight column for notes, and a row for each of the client's estranged parties.

Estranged Party or Parties (EP) The specific family member(s) a client is estranged from, including parents, adult sons and daughters, siblings, aunts and uncles, cousins, grandparents, etc. EP can be used in the singular, for one estranged party, or in the plural, for more than one.

Estrangement Type (ET) The types of estrangement, of which there are eight, including physical, emotional, cyclical, absent, mutually-disengaged, inherited, secondary, and self-protective.

Estrangement Nature (EN) The nature of an estrangement, i.e., whether it was chosen by the client or not. There are three natures, which include voluntary/non-mutual, voluntary/mutual, and involuntary.

Estrangement Approach (EA) The approach of an estrangement, i.e., the manner in which an estrangement was or was not communicated. There are two approaches direct or indirect.

Estrangement Method (EM)   There are three methods of communicating an estrangement, which include synchronous, asynchronous, and non-synchronous methods.

Estrangement Duration (ED)   The duration of an estrangement, i.e., how long the current estrangement has lasted.

Estrangement Reason (ER)   The reason(s) for an estrangement.

The Estrangement Radius   The network of people in the client's life who are directly or indirectly affected by an estrangement, and can include the principal estranged parties, non-estranged nuclear or immediate family members, family friends or neighbours, extended family, mutual acquaintances, and others aware of the estrangement.

The Estrangement Toolbox   A set of strategies to assist a client with some of the challenges of the Estrangement Impact Triad, which includes clarifying and validating, resourcing, communication, repairing, parking, re-engaging, and purpose and meaning strategies.

Introduction

"I didn't come here to talk about this"

(My first client)

You never forget your first client session. Maybe it was the nerves, the desire to make a difference, or the fear of messing up, but my own experience never left me. Linda, which is not her real name, sought therapy as she was struggling with workplace bullying and felt she was being set up as a scapegoat for shortcomings within the organization she worked for. Her career meant everything to her, and she derived much purpose and self-esteem from it. Naturally, when she felt several colleagues were undermining her ability and threatening the stability of her career, this became a huge crisis for her. She discussed in great length the situation at work and why she had done nothing wrong, but I was struck by how she didn't discuss any other aspects of her life, aside from briefly mentioning a small number of friends. I wanted to inquire about the support she had through this difficult situation and specifically asked about her family, but as soon as I mentioned the word family, she turned her eyes away from me and uncomfortably said "I didn't come here to talk about this". I would never force a conversation with a client if they didn't feel comfortable doing so, even if I felt it was critical to understanding her reality, her needs, and how she shaped her identity around her career. However, over time, she began to provide some insight into her family life, sharing how she moved out when she was 17 and never returned home. She had some contact with a sibling but nothing from her parents, and she was uncomfortable even sharing this. My intuition told me the dynamic at work was mirroring something deeper; however, I would never find out as she just wasn't ready to explore this. Since those early sessions in my career, countless adults have come to my practice who had a limited or no relationship with their family for a variety of reasons. The two lessons I learned in those formative years were that not everyone is ready to acknowledge their family situation as estrangement, and not everyone is ready to address the deep pain that lies underneath their estrangement.

My interest in family dysfunction and estrangement began with the breakdown of relationships with close family members. These were people whom I loved deeply, but I struggled with their expectations and with how little regard they had

DOI: 10.4324/9781003362203-1

for how this was affecting me. I felt I had to pull back from them completely; however, the eventual estrangement became an unmanageable crisis that I could not deal with alone. That is not to say I didn't try to deal with it alone; conditioned not to depend on others and overcome with both shame and anger, and shame about being angry, I put on a brave face and acted as if I was fine to non-estranged family, friends, and colleagues, but I wasn't. Internally, I had bottled up so much emotion that life was a constant struggle to hide how I felt while publicly holding down my job and managing relationships and my health. After a year and a half of trying in vain to live with the punishing self-doubt, high levels of stress reactivity, and deep, unending sadness, I considered contacting a local psychotherapist. After weeks of research and a phone call to clarify their therapeutic approach, I made an appointment. To say I was a nervous wreck attending that first session was an understatement, but I quickly discovered there was no need to be, as thankfully the therapist was genuinely compassionate and understanding of what I was going through. She could see past my subjective feelings and difficult family history, which had shaped these feelings, and this facilitated more self-compassion.

Such was the positive impact of this support that I made the life-changing decision to return to college and re-educate as a therapist. At the time, I had a successful career as an IT professional, but the calling to help others in the same way I had been helped was powerful, and so for many years I worked during the day while studying psychotherapy in the evenings and weekends. In 2011, I began working with clients, and by no conscious choice of my own, family estrangement followed me in this capacity as well. In my early days, I focused on the perspective of adult sons and daughters who were estranged from their parents, siblings, or both. While I was aware there were many sides to family issues, it wasn't until several years later that parents estranged from their adult sons and daughters reached out to me for help. It quickly became clear that all estranged parties needed support, and I endeavored to find a neutral approach that respected the many perspectives and experiences of estrangement.

This book is not intended to be a definitive guide to estrangement or working with all estranged adults. It is just one way of working and is not a substitute for training in psychotherapeutic or psychological models, although I am conscious that not everyone reading this will come from a psychotherapy or psychology background. I would encourage all professionals to continue to explore other approaches, particularly those that address working with complex relational dynamics and their impact on psychological wellbeing, as research highlights the role mental health issues, emotional distress, and trauma can play with estrangement, either in response to an estrangement (Agllias, 2011a; Dattilio & Nichols, 2011) or as a catalyst for an estrangement (Carr et al., 2015). This book is also not a replacement for actual clinical experience in a recognized field of study, although I hope my own experiences are helpful to all. Separated into four parts, below are details on the contents of this book and how to utilize it.

Part 1: The Never-Ending Story

This section discusses the dense narratives that shape each experience, including the overt and covert signs that will need to be identified when a client does not explicitly name their situation as estrangement. It will then look at the layered psychological, relational, and other social challenges of estrangement, referred to as the *Estrangement Impact Triad*, and their codependent nature. Finally, I discuss the controversial topic of reconciliations and when they might be appropriate.

Part 2: The Support Dilemma

This section discusses the difficulties of finding the right type of support, whether from a professional or a peer. It explores the potential roadblocks to effectively supporting an estranged person and the ethical considerations, ensuring each professional is asking themselves important questions before engaging with this work. Finally, it discusses interventions and characteristics of helpful encounters with psychotherapists, and what a successful outcome for the client might look like.

Part 3: Navigating Estrangement

This section discusses the origins of my work, how I came to specialize in estrangement, and how I struggled to find a way to help my clients. It then walks the reader through the *Estrangement Inquiry Model*, which I developed as a way of drawing out details that were important to the client's estrangement, and how to use this as a guide in determining how best to help them. Finally, it introduces the idea of the *Estrangement Toolbox*, which contains the strategies and potential interventions a professional can make.

Part 4: Case Studies

This section offers a look at five case studies, bringing together the previous sections to explore each hypothetical client's backstory, eventual estrangement, and impact. These will be viewed through the lens of the *Estrangement Impact Triad* and how we might potentially use the *Estrangement Toolbox* to help in each case.

Conclusion: Widening the Estrangement Lens

This book concludes with a discussion on the stigma surrounding estrangement and how all professionals and estranged adults alike can collectively work together to destigmatize this phenomenon and promote a more open, safe, and nuanced discussion.

A Somber Reality

Since I am writing a book on family estrangement, I feel it necessary to share my own personal views to contextualize my work. I believe family is the foundation of our society and would never encourage or promote estrangement within families, as the wounds of family can quickly become the wounds of society, although the reverse is equally true. Having experienced estrangement first-hand I know how painful it can be, both for the parties directly affected as well as those caught in the crossfire. Such is the importance of recognizing the far-reaching implications of estrangement on others that I coined the term *Estrangement Radius* (see Figure 0.1) to describe the web of people directly and indirectly affected by a client's estrangement.

This radius distinguishes different and converging social circles potentially caught up in the estrangement dragnet and can include the principal estranged parties, non-estranged family members, extended family members, family friends and neighbors, mutual acquaintances, and others who are aware of the estrangement and who may not be known to the client. The more people contained within the radius, the more challenges there will be, both for the client and everyone else, and this might even propagate further estrangements across future generations as it becomes a 'normalized' response to family issues. I will expand on these in Part 1, when I explore the layered impact of estrangement.

Despite my own personal values, family estrangement is a reality that many will have to contend with. It happens, sometimes for valid reasons, and after hearing

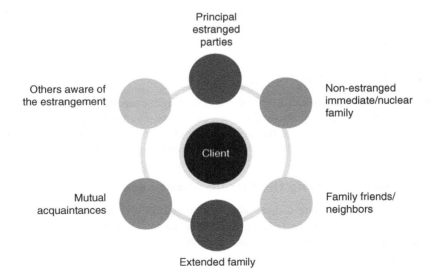

Figure 0.1 The Estrangement Radius

countless stories of damaging and abusive behaviours within some families, it is hard not to see the need to create distance. Sometimes it can be for tragic reasons, and issues such as addiction, sickness, and devastating losses can make it feel too painful for family to be around each other; and sometimes it can be for reasons not fully known, particularly in more passive estrangements where there is no overt conflict or clear history of problems and yet the family relationship appears to be devalued, often over a very short period. And irrespective of the reasoning, or lack thereof, reconciliations between estranged family members are not always desirable or even possible.

I have always felt those who are estranged, and when a reconciliation is unlikely to happen, have a right to be free of shame or guilt; have a right to compassion and understanding; and have the right to support from as many sources as possible. By providing this support, we might, in some way, reduce the stigma and potential impact of estrangement on future generations. This has been the focus of my work for several years now: to help individuals effectively reconcile with themselves and reconnect, not just with their pain but also with their intrinsic strengths, worth, and wisdom. After this, they can decide the next step and whether reconnecting with family is the right choice or whether it will lead to more suffering. The reality is that we might not be able to positively influence the estrangement specifically, especially if only one estranged family member requests support. However, there are still many ways in which we can help, and this book will show professionals how to do this.

Using this Book

I am always curious as to the path that brings people to the topic of estrangement; maybe it is personal experience, perhaps it has touched someone close to them, maybe it has been presented as an issue many times in their work, or maybe it is just curiosity. Nonetheless, here we are, and it is good to have you here. It is also not an accident that you found yourself reading this book; either you bought it, or someone bought it for you for a reason. Perhaps you are hoping to help estranged people in some way, or maybe someone is hoping you can help them.

Such is the complexity of this phenomenon that it can be hard to know exactly how to help. While there is a body of excellent academic literature on this topic and a variety of self-help books, when I began this work there appeared to be no clear approach to understanding estrangement dynamics and the type of support each client needs. So, I learned on the job, just listening to countless stories, seeking out recurring themes, and trying to understand what exactly my clients were struggling with.

The essence of therapy is validation, and it became clear that this validation was a key part of helping. Later, this would be validated by research exploring the therapeutic experiences of estranged adults (Blake et al., 2022a), but this was just one aspect of helping. While my clients felt less alone on their journey, it was still a dark and unknown path. Over time, I tried to get a better sense of the landscape they were travelling through, and it became clear that there were certain aspects of their story that seemed essential to their experiences and interactions with family. From this, the model presented in this book was conceived. I wanted to create something both practical and collaborative where myself and my clients could work together to deconstruct their estrangements and use this information to guide how we proceeded. As well as validating their experiences, this process extended to validating important decisions, reinforcing strengths, and addressing specific challenges.

However, irrespective of my personal goals for this book, I would ask each reader to take from it what they can and not hesitate to come back to it several times as the years go by. You may dip in and out, or you may read it cover to cover; it depends on how much you feel you need to know. Some aspects may not resonate with you personally, or you may find yourself questioning the information. This is a normal part of embracing this complexity, and while our clients need patience, we must equally practice this patience with ourselves. As I write this, I'm conscious that this book will be read by both professionals in their respective fields and those who are estranged and who may or may not work with estrangement. In response, I want to speak directly to these two groups to acknowledge their positions and how this book might help them.

Dear Professional

Firstly, I want to say thank you for taking an interest in this topic, irrespective of your background, which might include but is not exclusive to those involved in psychology, psychotherapy, counselling, and coaching of various kinds, including estrangement, life, leadership, relationship, health and wellness, and spiritual coaching, social work and care, mediation, litigation, religion, and healthcare. I also wish to extend my thanks to those who volunteer their time to run estrangement support groups globally, and I hope this book helps you in the way you need it to.

If there is one professional insight I would like to share and which was a consistent theme with most of my clients, it is how the experience of rejection was at the core of each story, whether it was one or more family members experiencing feelings of rejection as a result of an estrangement or if historical experiences of rejection caused people to become estranged. This was irrespective of whether the client was a son or daughter, mother or father, sibling, grandparent, or any other family role. Because of these powerful experiences of having their feelings, their values, their needs, their perspectives, and perhaps their very existence rejected, many estranged individuals carry with them a great sense of shame (Agllias, 2016; Coleman, 2008), isolation (Agllias, 2013; Pillemer, 2020), and loneliness (Pillemer, 2020). For this reason, as a professional in your respective field, your role in the estranged person's life and ability to help them cannot be overstated. In fact, if you are in a position of authority, with the trust that accompanies it, you may be the first person they have reached out to for help. It might also be the first time they have felt comfortable discussing their family situation, which is why I reiterate that patience is incredibly important, both with the client and with yourself. I appreciate that this may feel like a huge responsibility, but you don't need to have all the answers, you just need to care. In fact, various estrangement books and papers have emphasized the need for compassion in healing from estrangement as well as the role compassion plays in creating a positive therapeutic relationship (Blake et al., 2019, 2022b; Coleman, 2008). If an estranged person is sharing some aspect of their story with you, then there is something about you that makes them feel somewhat safe and understood. It should go without saying that whatever they share is privileged information and should be respected as such. We must also acknowledge the influence you have coupled with the client's vulnerability; if they view you as an expert, they may also cling to your every word, and thus you must be careful to ground expectations and be thoughtful and considerate in each response. While you don't need to be an expert in estrangement per se, having a nuanced understanding will give you an edge over the average person. This knowledge, coupled with a willingness to listen, to be open, and to care, will make a profound difference.

That said, research has highlighted that compassion alone is not enough, and having a collaborative framework based on respect is also necessary to create a positive outcome for the client (Blake et al., 2019). I developed the model described in this book as a way of interactively working with each client and guiding the conversation so that together, you might be able to make sense of their situation and determine the type of support they need. This will be a very confusing and chaotic time for the client (Scharp and McLaren, 2017); they may be desperate for answers but, most importantly, to receive some measure of understanding, and one should use this process to build on this understanding. At different points, you might question the necessity of some of the estrangement information gathered and its relevance to you, but this may be very relevant to the client, and our job is to find out if so and why. As already stated, this approach is not a replacement for how you work or a catch-all solution for estranged people, and the clients themselves might question the process; however, only when prompted to reflect will it become obvious and reveal new insight to them.

Dear Estranged Person

Firstly, whether you are here to better understand your own situation or to help someone in your life who is estranged, I hope this book provides some guidance. For those specifically estranged, I want to state clearly that you deserve all the support you can get, whether that is from a partner, a friend, a colleague, or anyone else you have reached out to. I appreciate how difficult it can be to ask someone close to you for help, especially if you feel you are being a burden, but you are not alone in your struggle.

I also appreciate how you might not have anyone close to you who can provide this support, but such is the desire for human connection and validation that you might find yourself sharing your situation with someone in the professional field. In an ideal world, this would be someone trained specifically to work with family issues and individuals in emotional distress, such as a psychotherapist or psychologist; however, you might have no choice but to open up to a doctor, a social worker, a teacher or lecturer, a counsellor, or anyone you feel you can trust. I wrote this book specifically to help these professionals help you. Reaching out for support takes great courage, as the stigma and fear of judgment are real (Agllias, 2011a, 2011b, 2013a; Scharp, Thomas, and Paxman, 2015; Scharp and McLaren, 2017; Sims & Rofail, 2014). You might have bought this book to heal, and understanding the process of working with estrangement might be helpful in seeing aspects of your story that are not yet visible to you. However, my preference is for you to do this work with someone else, as you do not have to do it alone. I appreciate that we are all different, and some are more introverted and less inclined to want to share their struggles. Estrangement is fundamentally a human issue; your connection to the most important human(s) in your life may have been ruptured or completely severed, and in my personal and professional experience, to heal from this, we need to forge healthier connections to other humans. This requires patience (there's that word again) on your part, as you might not be ready right now to talk, and this is completely ok. I would also ask that if you have had negative experiences in the past when you reached out for help, not to be disheartened. Unfortunately, not everyone can or will get the nuances that come with complex family histories, interactions, pressures, and expectations that lead to estrangement, but this does not mean you should give up hope of meeting someone who does.

As you read through this book, I would ask you not to worry if the information presented is too overwhelming to follow right now. Estrangements are like a dense maze, and we are slowly trying to chart a way out of this denseness so we can better navigate the terrain. This is not about getting every detail right, but about being open to what comes up and how it will help you find a way to move forward with your life.

Part 1

The Never-Ending Story

"Where do I start?"

(Many of my clients)

I've lost count of how many sessions began with a confused look, a baffled shrug of the shoulders, and the aforementioned question. Such is the seriousness of an estranged individual's situation, the chaotic nature of their family dynamics, and the complex ways these dynamics affect both the entire collective and the individuals therein, that it is understandable that some do not know where to start. The natural answer might seem to be "*we begin at the beginning*", but even that may be unclear as timelines become skewed by a countless number of experiences and the feelings and emotions underpinning them.

"When does it all end?"

(Many of my clients)

However, once my clients and I found a starting point, and after a period of reflection and analysis spanning weeks, months, and sometimes years where little had changed between family members, we were presented with the above philosophical question. Family estrangement and uncertainty go hand-in-hand (Agllias, 2011a, 2013; Carr et al., 2015; Scharp and McLaren, 2017), and I found many of my clients would ruminate over every aspect of family life, past, present, and future, in an attempt to make sense of something or anything. Like a broken record, they appeared to be stuck in a perpetual loop, as they eventually returned to the start without ever reconciling any aspect of the story. In practical terms, this would manifest in the therapy room as a data dump of information with little context: a disjointed narrative of names, events, dates, and feelings, occasionally injected with colorful language in the form of expletives. While it was clear we were getting a taste of the emotional impact, we were not getting to the essence of the situation. This was a place I was all too familiar with, as there was a time when I was equally stuck in my own estrangement narrative.

DOI: 10.4324/9781003362203-2

"Where do 'I' start?"

(Me)

As much as they were struggling for answers, I also struggled to see the bigger picture. But my desire to help, 100% rooted in my own experiences, prompted me to keep trying. Later, I would discover that this is not uncommon amongst some others who focus their work on family estrangement and who were equally drawn to this topic for reasons other than professional curiosity. Having been personally touched by this phenomenon, perhaps they felt compelled to help others in whatever way they could. However, I did not start out on a mission to specialize in this field; like every other psychotherapist, I just wanted to help, irrespective of the issues presented. These issues would vary, ranging from mental health struggles and general relationship challenges to work problems.

Slowly, a recurring theme of family breakdown was forming, and more and more adults presented to my practice who appeared to be caught up in an internal and external tug of war with family, where they would ambiguously need to create distance and yet, at the same time, yearn for connection. Sometimes this was the obvious source of distress for my clients, but not always. In fact, some clients regularly attended therapy for months and never mentioned family at all until, mid-conversation, they would drop in how they had no relationship with a parent, a sibling, or any other family member. Perhaps they did not see the significance of this; perhaps they became so accustomed to family issues that they were somewhat normalized; or perhaps they feared judgement and felt more comfortable playing down the role and importance of family. When they did begin to share their stories, what defined them was their deep and complex history with various family members, often spanning several generations. Because of my own estrangement history, I was already familiar with my version of the chaotic family narrative they were describing, such as accounts of senseless conflicts, confusing interactions, unreasonable expectations, and an inability to accept others for who they are. Due to the open-ended nature of estrangement, the chances of reconciliation with either estranged parties (Agllias, 2013) or with oneself may seem impossible to conceive, but this does not stop estranged people from desperately seeking answers or a clear next step. Although some may reluctantly learn to accept the situation or even see it as a positive step, for others, this desperation may turn to hopelessness as they feel powerless to influence their equally chaotic inner world. And importantly, this was irrespective of whom in the family the client was estranged from.

Family estrangement is effectively an umbrella term that accounts for a wide range of people who identify as not having an ideal or any relationship with some or all of their family members. Due to its broad nature, family estrangement is often categorized in different ways to identify and isolate specific cohorts and their experiences. One common category is based on the person or people someone is estranged from, referred to as the Estranged Parties or the EP, with the most common being parental estrangement, adult child estrangement, and sibling estrangement. The experiences of these three can be quite different; their needs may also be different, and thus some professionals, such as academics, psychologists, psychotherapists, and coaches, as well as peer group support providers, might choose to focus their efforts on helping just one perspective, e.g., supporting either parents or adult children. This could also serve to provide safety for a specific cohort who fear judgement and personal attacks from someone of an opposing cohort; e.g., in an online social media estrangement support platform, a person who identifies as being an estranged parent may have their perspective dismissed by a person who identifies as being an estranged adult son or daughter, and vice versa. While it is necessary to delve into how estrangement varies across different family types and perspectives, with my own work I did not want to restrict myself to just one cohort and miss the opportunity to learn from others and perhaps find ways to help them all. Over time, as I listened to the many diverse estrangement stories, it became clear that the majority of those I spoke with felt lost and yearned for some way of getting a handle on their lives. For us professionals to effectively help them do this, we first need to get a handle on the topic of estrangement in its many manifestations and how it can potentially affect clients.

Chapter 1

Context and Complexity

One presumption I made early in my career was that estrangement was when family members were simply not talking to each other and were not in any way involved in each other's lives. However, I was struck when more and more of my clients identified as being estranged but still appeared to be actively engaging with family in various ways. This might include attending family occasions, planning events, or even exchanging gifts during holiday periods; however, despite these interactions, there was something else happening between families that was less obvious and unspoken and yet could still be considered an estrangement. This begs the question: What exactly is family estrangement?

In the context of my own clients and how their estrangement would frequently change due to a range of complex factors, I began to view estrangement as an act of consciously putting distance between one or more family members, where the estrangement can sit anywhere between emotional and/or physical distance. The *emotional* type of estrangement is when there is physical contact with estranged family members but efforts are made, mostly communicatively, to share less personal information. Any time spent together may be the product of circumstances, such as an obligation to visit for family events, emergencies, or general responsibilities. The *physical* type is where efforts are made to completely limit contact and create as much geographical distance as possible. The estrangement literature shares some extreme examples of this, where people have changed their address and even their name to create a new identity (Scharp, 2014).

The very nature of family relationships and subsequent estrangements means they can take different forms and change over extended periods. This was emphasized by the work of Professor Kristina Scharp, whose research focused on the perspective of adult sons and daughters who are voluntarily estranged from one or both parents. Scharp concluded that estrangement is an on-going process and more nuanced than a singular relational state, i.e., it is not simply being "estranged" or "not estranged", as there may be no clear status of the relationship. Scharp coined the term the *Estrangement Continuum*, to highlight how this process sits on a spectrum and that there may be more or less distance between family members (Scharp, 2014). This would explain why estrangements can look so different and yet still be considered the same.

DOI: 10.4324/9781003362203-3

On one end of the estrangement continuum, there are those who are *less estranged* and might see each other regularly. This might have the feeling of an emotional estrangement where there is frequent or infrequent contact for reasons such as obligation, habit, tradition, or changing family circumstances. Alternatively, those who exist on the *more estranged* end of the continuum might never see or speak to their family, or keep in contact via phone or text only and reduce physical or face-to-face contact, thus feeling like a physical estrangement. When working with my own clients, once I have identified estrangement, I try to get a sense of where they lie on this continuum so we can name some of the specific challenges facing them. For example, if they are less estranged, there may be greater stress due to impending family visits, and help is needed to manage potentially difficult conversations. If they are more estranged, there may be more uncertainty around the future of the relationship, and support is needed for the grief they may be experiencing.

While the estrangement continuum was framed around one perspective, that of adult children and their efforts to create and maintain distance from parents (Scharp, 2014), having spent many hours listening to estranged parents, it was clear that all estranged parties exist in some way on this continuum. Alas, there is more to estrangement than just the dual perspectives of adult children and parents. While sibling estrangement is also featured in the literature (Blake et al., 2015, 2022a; Hank & Steinbach, 2022), aunts, uncles, cousins, grandparents, grandchildren, and every other person who is considered part of the family may be estranged but receive minimal attention in the research. We might also factor in friends of family or anyone connected to kin who may also be estranged. Aside from *emotional* and *physical* estrangement, there are other types. In fact, in the book *Family Estrangement: A Matter of Perspective*, author Professor Kylie Agllias has defined eight types, including *cyclical, absent, mutually-disengaged, inherited, secondary*, and *self-protective* estrangements (Agllias, 2016), which I will explore later (see Part 3: The Model/Step 2).

To understand estrangement more, I wanted to see if there was a clear definition in the literature, and adding to the complexity, I discovered that there is no singular definition but several that academics have created to frame their research objectives as well as to provide clarity to potential participants. Here are some of the definitions I found, although this is not an exhaustive list and others exist:

"The breakdown of a supportive relationship between family members"
(Blake et al., 2015, p. 7)

"An intentional, voluntary communicative effort to gain distance from a negative relationship commonly taken-for-granted as undissolvable"
(Scharp, 2014, p. 6)

"estrangement involves the absence of verbal communication between parents and children"
(Carr et al., 2015, p. 139)

"The condition of being physically and or emotionally distanced from one or more family members, either by choice or at request or decision of the other. It is generally enacted to reduce implicit or explicit conflict, anxiety or tension between the parties. It is characterised by a lack of trust and emotional intimacy, disparate values, and a belief that resolution is highly unlikely, unnecessary or impossible"

(Agllias, 2016, p. 4)

"Estrangement from a family member is characterised by lack of trust and emotional intimacy, and often includes ceased communication and contact"

(Linden & Sillence, 2021, p. 325)

"managing unresolved emotional problems with family members by substantially reducing contact or remaining in physical contact but maintaining emotional distance"

(Gilligan et al., 2015, p. 2)

"situations in which a family member has cut off contact from one or more of their relatives"

(Pillemer, 2020, p. 23)

"estrangement is an ongoing process in which one or both parties are actively communicating to adjust and renegotiate intimacy boundaries"

(Rittenour et al., 2018, p. 2)

The last and perhaps most detailed definition is contained within these four characteristics:

"1. A complete communication cut-off between relatives, which means absolutely no intentional direct communication between the estranged parties. Indirect communication may occur, for example, through other family members or lawyers.
2. The communication cut-off is maintained deliberately or intentionally by at least one person.
3. The estranged relatives know how to contact each other. Neither is considered missing.
4. At least one of the persons involved claims that something specific about the other person justifies the communication cut-off, like something the other person did, does or failed to do."

(Conti, 2015, p. 31)

What struck me was that while there were clear interconnections with some of the definitions, including how the majority emphasized the role communication plays (Carr et al., 2015; Conti, 2015; Gilligan et al., 2015; Linden & Sillence, 2021; Scharp, 2014), there was diversity in other aspects. For example, some acknowledge the behavioural causes, such as a breakdown in support (Blake et al., 2015) and conflict; some acknowledge the physiological and psychological causes of the estrangement, such as anxiety, tension, lack of trust, and intimacy (Agllias, 2016; Linden & Sillence, 2021); some emphasize the enduring nature of estrangements and how there is no visible resolution (Agllias, 2016); others speak from or acknowledge how an estrangement can be either chosen or not (Agllias, 2016; Conti, 2015; Scharp, 2014); and some define estrangement as an ending of the relationship (Pillemer, 2020), whereas others view it as on-going (Rittenour et al., 2018).

Despite how varied these concepts of estrangement are, each one is accurate within a specific context. This is because estrangement can be all of these and more, and as a result, this might prompt a professional to dismiss a client's situation as estrangement. Thankfully, there is more information via mainstream media, books in various forms, and personal blogs to educate the masses, but the fact remains that having more than one estrangement definition can make it difficult to establish if a client's present situation could be considered one.

Another source of conflict could derive from the belief that estrangement should always be viewed negatively. This is challenged in the paper "Troubling the Functional/Dysfunctional Family Binary Through the Articulation of Functional Family Estrangement", where the authors Allen and Moore explore the idea of functional families, characterized by "connection, communication, problem-solving, and shared time" (Allen & Moore, 2016, p. 288) and question the alignment of dysfunctional families and negative estrangements. Offering an alternative view to the distance between family members being a problem in need of fixing, Allen and Moore, researching individuals who self-identified as being estranged, proposed the idea of *functional estrangements*, where, for some, an estrangement was in fact the preferred option. From my own research into the experiences of estrangement, it was clear that despite how difficult an estrange-ment can be and irrespective of whether it was voluntary or involuntary, some felt it also represented an opportunity for personal growth (Melvin & Hickey, 2021). Similarly, the existing research on estrangement cites examples of an improvement in quality of life after an estrangement. This included a study from the estrangement support organisation Stand-Alone (www.stand-alone.co.uk), which found 80% of the participants felt there were positives to estrangement, such as reduced stress and greater independence (Blake et al., 2015). A Washington Post article entitled "Family estrangement is not necessarily a bad thing, for par-ents or children" (Hax, 2016) similarly cited examples supporting this, with one contributor wishing they had instigated their estrangement sooner. Another study highlighted the positive impact of estrangement on psychological well-being if the family relationship was previously viewed as unhealthy (Scharp, 2014). There seems to be some agreement within the research community that estrangement can be viewed as healthy in the context of an unhealthy family (Agllias, 2011a;

Scharp & Dorrance Hall, 2017; Scharp & McLaren, 2017), so taken together, estrangement "has the potential to be bright, dark, and somewhere fluctuating along those binary poles" (Scharp, 2014, p. 2).

Due to the complexity of human psychology and attachment, I don't feel there is a black-and-white, one size fits-all view of estrangement, and this was highlighted in another study that found estrangement can have both positive and negative effects on psychological wellbeing (Linden & Sillence, 2021). I also feel it is insulting to those living with it to insist on how they should feel about their situation. By dismissing the powerful bond to those who our clients love, the mind's vice-grip ability to cling to nostalgia and good times long past, the enduring sense of history and accompanying loyalty, and above all else, the unique process of grieving one or more people who are still alive (Agllias, 2011a, 2013a, 2016; Scharp, 2017), we only contribute to the shame that plagues many estranged people (Agllias, 2016, 2017; Coleman, 2008; Scharp & McLaren, 2017).

Uncommonly Common

At this point, it would be useful to explore how prevalent estrangement is and how many people might need support, and while the research figures vary, they do give us a strong indication. One prevalence study came from Stand-Alone in conjunction with the market research company Ipsos MORI in 2014, where they found one in five families were affected by estrangement in the UK (Ipsos MORI & Stand-Alone, 2014). The following year, a study of students in the US found that 43% of the 354 participants were estranged from one or more immediate or extended family members (Conti, 2015), and a more recent study from social scientist Karl Pillemer, PhD, found that 27% of individuals are estranged from a relative in the US (Pillemer, 2020). If we dig a little deeper into the prevalence research, we can see differences based on specific estranged parties. For example, a 2015 study involving 566 families found that approximately 11% of mothers are estranged from at least one child (Gilligan et al., 2015). A 2019 study of just over 3,800 adults from the Netherlands found 13% had no more than one contact with siblings in the past year (Kalmijn & Leopold, 2018). In a 2021 German study of just over 10,000 adults, 9% were found to have experienced estrangement from a mother and 20% from a father (Arránz Becker & Hank, 2021). Interestingly, while not an empirical study, googling the term *family estrangement* produces an increasing number of results, which include articles in the mainstream media, personal blogs, educational websites, and estrangement support pages on social media.

Another question is whether estrangement figures are on the rise. If so, could it be that there is a rise in awareness of what exactly family estrangement is, and thus more people are adopting this term for their situation? Maybe the figures are not on the rise, but changes in contemporary attitudes might mean more people are comfortable sharing their estrangement, and modern technology means they have more ways to communicate this. Interestingly, in an article for *The Atlantic* magazine entitled "A Shift in American Family Values Is Fueling Estrangement", psychologist and estrangement expert Dr. Joshua Coleman discusses this in the context of America and questions whether there has been a shift in values, deprioritizing family over the needs and rights of the individual (Coleman, 2021). I can't comment on the accuracy of this, although I do have my own concerns regarding the current interpretation of what individuality is and how it appears to me more as a push against co-dependence, such as feelings of insecurity and inadequacy, at the expense of healthy interdependence and authentic independence. However, I wish to acknowledge the role abusive behaviours play in fueling some estrangements and how the victims of this are not simply focusing on individuality. In fact, many genuinely desire a healthy and closer relationship with family but desperately need to create distance due to the toll the abuse has taken on them. If we now consider how many people are living with some form of estrangement and how this figure may be on the rise, this could suggest there is a growing demand for specific resources and support to help those struggling with this very complex phenomenon.

Chapter 2

Signs and Labels

Definitions aside, I have found that my own clients and workshop attendees tend to have their own interpretation of what estrangement is based on their own family situation, although I do occasionally need to correct them. For example, estrangement is not when family members lose contact with each other; this is something that happens when there is no closeness to begin with and members just get on with their own lives. It is also not the same as normal family disagreements, as these may be circumstantial and the result of a stressful issue that will be resolved in time. Also, it is not when family members are separated by state bodies as a result of fostering or imprisonment (Scharp & Hall, 2017).

What separates estrangement from these is the conscious effort from one or more sides to enforce it. Another study recognizes how estrangement is different from two other similar relational processes that distance family members: *alienation* and *marginalization* (Scharp & Hall, 2017). Alienation involves someone attempting to negatively influence a relationship between one or more family members and is often associated with *parental alienation*, where a parent uses a set of strategies to "damage and sever the relationship between the child and the child's other parent" (Verhaar et al., 2022, p. 1). Marginalization, on the other hand, is when someone is treated differently within the family because they do not conform to some established "norm", and are often perceived or labelled as the *black sheep* (Dorrance Hall, 2016). Comparisons to estrangement are understandable, as these two phenomena may ultimately lead to the distancing process of estrangement. It is important to note that while there are no legal ramifications with estrangement and marginalization, there are with alienation, and specifically parent-child alienation when the child is a minor, as this is decided by a court of law (Scharp & Hall, 2017).

However, there are those who simply don't know if they can be considered estranged, and below are certain identifiers a professional might look out for. There is a strong subjective element to these, so each professional should presume nothing and remain curious. These are just rough markers that might lead to a deeper conversation around the family situation and if they feel it is estrangement.

DOI: 10.4324/9781003362203-4

The Language of Estrangement

The client might use terms to describe family or their interactions, such as "dysfunctional", "toxic", "gas-lighting", "narcissistic" and/or "abusive"; this might also include words that allude to abuse or aggressive behaviors, such as "control", "walking on eggshells", "chaos", "madness", and "crazy"; and they might use a series of expletives to describe family members or explicitly describe a dynamic suggesting estrangement, such as "We don't talk to each other" or "We haven't spoken in years".

The client might also vehemently defend an attitude or stance against a family member(s). Tone of voice (such as raising or dropping the volume), body language (such as looking away, shoulders hunching over, or appearing agitated), and pace of speech (such as talking very fast or slow) may indicate a history of distance between family members or uncertainty about the future of the relationship. Alternatively, when the conversation moves to family and the client changes the topic, this may be a subtle indicator of problems and their difficulty with discussing them, but it is hard to know for certain, and in these cases, I would respect the client's boundaries while continuing to work on building safety and trust.

The Behaviors of Estrangement

A client might allude to certain behaviors that are specific to family and suggest estrangement. This might include avoiding spending time with family, perhaps to prevent confronting issues, or, alternatively, constantly calling family for reassurance or in an effort to avoid losing contact. This might extend to other aspects of life, such as recurring themes of miscommunication or misinterpretation with partners, children, friends, and colleagues, which mirror family issues, refusing to set boundaries, or constantly compromising their own needs for others, i.e., people pleasing.

The Feelings of Estrangement

A client might struggle to describe their family overtly or tend to focus more on their subjective feelings, such as anger, sadness, guilt, shame, depression, hopelessness, confusion, etc. They may also experience two opposing feelings at the same time, such as anger and sadness. These feelings may not feel safe to them as they may be sensitive to further social rejection and disapproval and may consciously hide them from others, so it may require looking for subtle signs of clients holding back information out of fear of expression.

The Patterns of Estrangement

A client might not even be aware of the term family estrangement and yet detail events and interactions within the family that suggest estrangement, such as patterns of conflict, regular periods of silence or no contact at all, perceived collusion amongst several family members, and/or recurring experiences of pressure and/or rejection. These may be contained in many stories of painful exchanges and accusations, either in person or through other mediums.

The Necessity of Labels

Perhaps another important consideration is whether the label family estrangement is useful to a client and their unique situation. At times, after discussing an estrangement with a client or even a professional with personal experience, I have heard some say that while they now understand what estrangement is, the label did not alter any aspect of their situation, and in truth, maybe it won't. Some families or their individual members have become accustomed to never having a good relationship, and while this might technically be considered estrangement as they are actively avoiding each other, they may just consider it normal within the context of their own history. The flip side of this is that many will find the term family estrangement very helpful in describing their situation, as it reduces the necessity to explain, in detail, the complex, sensitive, and upsetting nature of their relationship. It might also make accessing support easier, as the client can seek out others who identify with this term. Unfortunately, labels can also serve to stigmatize people, especially those who refuse to look past the label to see the individual and their experiences behind it. The label "estranged" may be a curse for some, as they walk through life carrying it and identifying with it.

Now that we have established what an estrangement might look like for clients, it would be remiss to dismiss the equally complex impact an estrangement can have. Ultimately, although helping the client determine the cause might be useful, we might be more effective in addressing some or all of the consequences.

Chapter 3

The Impact Triad

It can be difficult to accurately describe exactly what it is like to be estranged, but one analogy that resonated with my own clients is that of a huge boulder weighing down on their shoulders. A symbolic representation of the heavy burden they carry and the energy it consumes; however, how well a client carries this load can vary massively and frequently change based on several criteria.

Perhaps another way to view estrangement is like a turbulent journey, where travelers are adrift on a dark path influenced by the past relationship dynamic; the events leading up to the estrangement; the specifics of the estrangement itself, such as how it was implemented and how long it has lasted; the impact of the estrangement both on them and others in their life; the quality and quantity of support they receive; and the many other pressures they have to face along the way. This creates a triad of psychological, relational, and other social challenges (see Figure 3.1), which interact and determine how the client responds and copes with the estrangement. It is the combination of these that makes each estrangement unique and enduring. These three areas can be viewed both in isolation and in how they converge with each other to emphasize the cyclical and dependent nature of the many challenges estranged people face. This cycle will initially be framed around the client's present status, but it is equally important to understand the broader impact on others within the client's *estrangement radius* (see Figure 0.1 in the Introduction).

With that said, I want to emphasize something very important. A professional may feel compelled to let the client know of this impact on their family as a whole, and there are many reasons for this, including the belief that stating these might lead to a better relationship with family. However, they might also be simply stating the obvious, i.e., that which the client is already fully aware of. Ultimately, we are temporary visitors to their reality, but they may be prisoners of it, and while we have the luxury of moving on with our own lives and forgetting, they do not. Thus, while they might appreciate professionals acknowledging this, they might also perceive such comments as colluding with their estranged family members (Blake et al., 2022b).

This is not to say we should dismiss the larger impact on others, and there may be a time when this needs to be discussed, especially if the client is hoping to prompt some change with their *estrangement radius*. For example, if the client

DOI: 10.4324/9781003362203-5

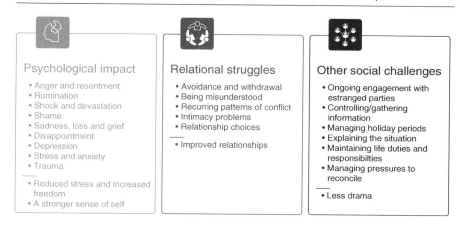

Psychological impact

- Anger and resentment
- Rumination
- Shock and devastation
- Shame
- Sadness, loss and grief
- Disappointment
- Depression
- Stress and anxiety
- Trauma

- Reduced stress and increased freedom
- A stronger sense of self

Relational struggles

- Avoidance and withdrawal
- Being misunderstood
- Recurring patterns of conflict
- Intimacy problems
- Relationship choices

- Improved relationships

Other social challenges

- Ongoing engagement with estranged parties
- Controlling/gathering information
- Managing holiday periods
- Explaining the situation
- Maintaining life duties and responsibilties
- Managing pressures to reconcile

- Less drama

Figure 3.1 The Estrangement Impact Triad

expresses a desire to cause damage via their estrangement and is intentionally min-imizing the effect on others, there may be a call to action required to emphasize this observation to them. However, this is only after the intent has been explored and we have built enough of a therapeutic relationship with them to start sharing their true thoughts and feelings.

Exploring the bigger impact serves to better understand what the client is deal-ing with and to highlight the various ways they might be struggling, perhaps in a way they themselves cannot recognize. Such is the overwhelming nature of some estrangements and their challenges that the client might be living in a blind state of survival and/or avoidance. Disconnected from how tough it really is for them, a professional is in a position to help them feel supported by someone who really understands their plight, or is at least trying very hard to understand it.

Embracing the role of working with estranged individuals will also involve embracing the fact that there is no universal way in which a person or persons will be affected by it. As mentioned, both in my own research and that of others, there is the potential for positives from being estranged, such as less stress and increased freedom (Blake et al., 2015; Melvin & Hickey, 2021). It could also be a complex contradiction of both good and bad feelings and positive and negative outcomes, or maybe the positives may not present themselves for several months or even years. This ambiguity might add to the confusion and distress felt amongst the estrange-ment community at large, whose experience may be more predominately negative than positive. Clients should take some comfort from the knowledge that this is a reality for others (Linden & Sillence, 2021), but to presume it is always negative may lead professionals to miss how the client actually feels.

We will now break down the different components of the *estrangement impact triad*, starting with the psychological challenges. Unlike the qualitative literature, which focuses on estrangement experiences from alternative perspectives, such as parents (Agllias, 2013, 2016; Gilligan et al., 2021) and adult children (Agllias, 2016, 2017; Gilligan et al., 2021; Scharp, Thomas, & Paxman, 2015), I do not distinguish between these family roles. While there will naturally be differences in the experience, there are also similarities, such as how feelings of isolation are common for both parents and adult children, resulting in either side not feeling comfortable sharing their story with others (Blake et al., 2022b), and thus I feel it important to promote a neutral view where all experiences are acknowledged and all estranged parties feel they can reach out for professional support.

Psychological Impact

The disruption or complete ending of a family relationship, whether voluntarily or involuntarily, is not simply a case of walking away with no repercussion. The unseen scars, punishing memories, oppressive beliefs, and other painful remnants are not sectioned off in a nice, safe boundary away from day-to-day life and can become a huge struggle to contain. An estrangement can have internal consequences; a division can be formed between wanting distance and yearning closeness, or a complete fragmentation of a person as they are devastated by what has happened and question the very essence of who they are, perhaps creating what could be considered a self-estrangement. Ultimately, how a person is impacted by estrangement is as unique as their DNA. Although research suggests there could be negative consequences for a person's wellbeing (Blake, 2017), there is no hard and fast rule on how a person will be affected, nor is there a right or wrong way to feel about the estrangement.

In my clinical practice, I have had clients who have been psychologically affected in countless different ways, and below are some of the most common. While I discuss this within the context of potential clients, these can also be experienced by any family member across the *estrangement radius*, and being conscious of the broader psychological impact might provide insight into historical family patterns of psychological issues as well as the potential impact on future generations.

Anger and Resentment

Anger has been frequently cited as common within the literature (Agllias, 2013, 2015, 2018; Blake et al., 2015; Melvin & Hickey, 2021; Scharp, 2017), and there are many reasons for this: it could be due to how the client was treated by the estranged parties, which can include years of bad behaviors pre-estrangement and how these behaviors are affecting others, such as the client's children. It could be because it appears family members have devalued their relationship with the client, especially if they feel they have made sacrifices in the past, or it could be due to perceived unfairness, such as unreasonable expectations that are not distributed equally across all family members, and which might then lead to resentment.

This anger may have festered for many years, and the client may have felt they could not express it out of fear of being met with a similar or even greater level of anger. This anger might be compounded if there is currently no way to communicate with the estranged parties or if they simply refuse to listen. It is hard to indefinitely contain such anger, and it may contaminate other areas of life, including their relationship with their partner.

As a client describes the reasons behind their feelings, the specifics might not seem to merit the level of anger, but it might be a small sample of their history, and it is necessary to see past what is said to what has yet to be said. Interestingly, the level of anger may be relative to the amount of contact there is with the estranged parties (Melvin & Hickey, 2021), so there may be less anger if the client is on the more estranged end of the *estrangement continuum* (Scharp, 2014).

Rumination

Ruminating has featured several times in the literature (Agllias, 2013; Blake et al., 2015; Sichel, 2004) and is common for estranged clients as they play and replay the situation over and over in their minds, hoping to find some answer. The need to ruminate may run deeper than just clarifying events or reasoning decisions and could be more like a battle for an identity. As the overall family story, traditionally shared across different generations, has diverged and the estranged parties now have a completely different perspective on their history, their shared identity may have also diverged (Suter et al., 2016), and the client may become confused as to who they are now. As the duration of an estrangement is unpredictable and possibly never-ending, many feel trapped in a maze of obsessive thinking and unable to focus and function effectively in some or all areas of their lives. See Part 2: The Toolbox/T2 for resourcing strategies to manage rumination.

Shock and Devastation

The shock and devastation that many experience are also frequently featured in the research (Agllias, 2013, 2015, 2018; Blake et al., 2019; Melvin & Hickey, 2021), and for a variety of reasons. This might include shock that they were cut out. The shock may be reflective of how normal estrangement is to estranged parties, in that creating distance from family is not something the client would ever consider, even in the worst possible scenarios. The shock could be how the relationship appears to mean nothing to the person or people who initiated it, and shock can quickly lead to devastation, especially if it has happened repeatedly. In fact, one participant in my own study (Melvin & Hickey, 2021) who, despite having had three previous cycles of estrangement from her sibling, still felt shock and devastation each time they estranged despite the historical precedent. This anecdotally suggests that no amount of prior experience or sense of impending estrangement (Agllias, 2017) can mitigate against the shock. Perhaps not surprisingly, choosing estrangement and actively planning how to initiate it can also lead to feelings of shock (Agllias, 2017). This may be due to the weight and finality of the decision, and these feelings seem to manifest more at the early stages of the estrangement (Agllias, 2017).

Shock, as well as other aspects of the *estrangement impact triad*, could also be a symptom of grief, especially in the initial phases of the loss (Engel, 1961).

The devastation could run deep, as the estrangement rocks the very core of their existence and security with family members. This could be exacerbated when the client is surrounded by those who appear to have a positive relationship with their own family. The devastation could be caused by a lack of regard for how the estrangement might affect others in the family, particularly if children are impacted. A client could feel devastated by the inability to reach and reason with the estranged parties as they appear to be locked into their own views and beliefs or are comfortable with the distance of estrangement. This might not be immediately obvious to the client until perhaps a social media post or conversation with others indicates the estranged parties seem to be fine. The devastation can be further compounded by secondary consequences, such as being excluded from a family event due to sides being taken.

Shame

As mentioned, shame is commonly cited for those who find themselves estranged (Agllias, 2016, 2017; Coleman, 2008; Scharp & McLaren, 2017), and there are many reasons why shame is experienced. It could be the result of being shamed by family members for not conforming to what is considered "normal", whether these are behavioral and/or cultural norms (Blake et al., 2015). These norms can include inherited rules and expectations around family roles, duties, and loyalties, and the client may feel conflicted about this inheritance, as while they feel shame for disappointing family, including estranged and non-estranged family, they may also not personally agree with the rules enforced. One specific rule could be related to the expression or suppression of emotion, and thus there could be shame linked to these specific emotions. I have found this to be particularly true with anger, which is a natural response when boundaries are being crossed but will be frowned upon in families with no concept of what boundaries are.

There may be shame in initiating an estrangement or not attempting to reconcile if the estrangement was involuntary (Agllias, 2017). Shame might also be linked to the estrangement reason, especially if a client feels this is connected to their poor decision-making. There could also be shame if the reasons are not known and the client is left to create a negatively biased reason.

Naturally, this shame will be worse if others have been affected in some way by the estrangement, and this will be particularly relevant to highly sensitive clients who are empathetic to the thoughts and feelings of others. This empathy might extend to the estranged parties, and this may be a source of inner conflict for the client. One example of this is if the client is estranged from a vulnerable person, such as an aging parent (Agllias, 2016). Shame may be compounded if the client's circle of friends or others in their network appear to have a good-quality relationship with their own family.

While I am consciously not distinguishing the estrangement perspectives and shame can be felt by all parties, I feel it is important to acknowledge that there seems to be a greater degree of shame for women than men (Agllias, 2013), although more research is needed on the gendered experience. It is hard to identify why exactly this is, although one study suggests it could be due to the greater responsibility women take in maintaining social connections with family and friends (Thomas et al., 2017).

Sadness, Loss, and Grief

Loss and grief are featured several times in the estrangement literature (Agllias, 2011a, 2011b, 2015; Agllias & Gray, 2013; Blake et al., 2022a), and in some cases, grief via estrangement might be considered *complicated grief* due to the unresolved nature of grieving for family members who are still alive. But the relationship may have been severely damaged or completely severed and "can dramatically interfere with function and quality of life" (Zisook & Shear, 2009, p. 67).

It is worth noting that even if there has been or there currently is a period of reunification, there may still be strong symptoms of grief, as there was a time, over weeks, months, and years, when the client did not know if there was any hope of an improvement in the relationship. This time might have been lost as the client existed in a whirlwind of sadness (Agllias, 2013, 2018; Scharp, 2017) and perhaps even despair (Gair, 2017) if the situation felt hopeless.

We must also factor in the loss of identity that might present itself now. For example, if the client reveals they are estranged from a son or daughter, or both, they are also losing the role of parent, i.e., a mother and father, which they have heavily identified with (Agllias, 2013; Schwartzman, 2006). Similarly, they may have derived a positive self-image from this role and the function it serves, and a client might doubt who they are now. This might spark a conversation around who they were before they became parents, exploring their loves, passions, and dreams.

Other losses might include financial support (Agllias, 2017). This can affect anyone who finds themselves unemployed and without the means to pay bills, but this will be particularly relevant if the client is a student and does not have access to other sources of money (Bland & Stevenson, 2018). Understanding the unique challenges students face is also very important, as this will influence the issues they need help with. For example, due to their age and vulnerability, there may be greater concern for their mental health and a need to focus on helping them in this aspect. They may also feel a heightened sense of isolation, particularly if they have no one in their life who understands what they are going through. While it might be realistic to expect financial support from a professional in this context, having knowledge of local government bodies that can help the client would be useful.

There is also the loss of social ties, which may come from the estrangement (Linden & Sillence, 2021). Connections to others who are part of the *estrangement radius*, such as extended family, friends of the family, or even neighbours, may be disrupted or lost due to the uncomfortableness of the relationship dynamic. Referred to as a *self-protective estrangement* (Agllias, 2016), these people may have no involvement or even interest in the estrangement, but the client may still have concerns around trust and sharing personal information and thus distance themselves from these as well.

Another dimension to this is the non-human losses the client may experience, such as a connection to one or more family pets. The pet(s) could have been part of the client's life for many years, and thus they formed a close bond. Due to the estrangement, they may not have access to each other any more, and this can be devastating on top of everything else.

This can also extend to inanimate losses, such as the loss of historical and sentimental objects of personal importance to the client. This could be photos, clothing, books, toys, or anything else that has meaning to them. Later, we will actively create a list of the estranged parties for each client and might not necessarily document pets or objects, but it is imperative we respect and acknowledge their significance as they add more layers to the client's losses.

Clients also have no way of publicly grieving, as there are no funerals or closures, and so they often grieve alone or silently. They are also expected to function as normal at home, at work, and in every other context. This grief can become disenfranchised when no one has died or there is no confirmation of death (Boss & Yeats, 2014), and as a result, society does not acknowledge it (Agllias, 2013, 2016).

A client may feel constant sadness and struggle to hold back their tears, which will make functioning hard as they may feel they cannot contain their pain. This might lead to secondary consequences, such as anxiety over feelings of sadness and fears of breaking down in public. Depression is also a symptom of grief (Zisook & Shear, 2009) and can manifest in different ways, such as a lack of interest in life, low energy, and chronic feelings of disconnection from others.

A common question I am asked is, when is it time to start grieving? The answer is in the question; the very fact someone is aware of their losses indicates they need the time and space to acknowledge these emotions and their true impact on their lives. In the context of death, one such impact of grief might be feelings of helplessness (Worden, 2009), but an estranged client might similarly feel this helplessness and lose any sense of purpose or meaning. For this reason, I have added some strategies to hopefully inspire the client to keep moving forward and use their estrangement and losses as a stepping stone to something productive and fulfilling (see Part 2: The Toolbox/T7).

Disappointment

Disappointment is cited several times (Agllias, 2013, 2015; Jerrome, 1994; Schwartzman, 2006; Sims & Rofail, 2014), and the client might be disappointed that estrangement was chosen as opposed to addressing the family issues directly. This disappointment could be rooted in ongoing experiences with family where they repeatedly appeared to put their own needs first, if they have let others down through broken promises or not demonstrated any concern for the wellbeing of family members. Disappointment can be crushing, and lead to the client becoming cynical as they anticipate more disappointments from others outside the family.

Depression

Often, a client might state they are struggling with their mental health as a result of family issues and the eventual estrangement (Agllias, 2015, 2016; Conti, 2015). Alas, mental health is a broad term to describe a cluster of symptoms that can fluctuate and that the client might struggle to verbalize properly. The mental health concerns may range from feelings of depression for extended periods to feelings of anxiety, or both, at different points in their lives.

Experiences of depression have been cited in several estrangement books (Coleman, 2008; Agllias, 2016) and papers (Blake et al., 2015; Linden & Sillence, 2021). Clients may report feeling depressed for various reasons, including hopelessness that the relationship with estranged parties will not improve and the loss of the relationship(s). Feelings of depression may not be limited to the estrangement itself but are the product of ongoing conflict within the family and an inability to resolve these issues so they can create a stable and loving home environment. There may also be patterns of depression within the family, passed down through the generations, with the findings of one study highlighting how the offspring of depressed mothers are three to six times more likely to develop depression (Gotlib et al., 2020).

The client might not explicitly mention depression but may disclose mental health concerns, and it might be these concerns that were more the impetus for the client to connect with a professional than the specific struggles with family. In fact, some may not attribute these struggles to issues between family members. For example, many of my own clients found their way to therapy via a referral from a GP after reporting mental health concerns, and it was only after a period of several sessions that the client revealed a negative relationship with their family.

Please note that any mental health condition(s) are understandably difficult and complex and in need of specific support. Unfortunately, this is outside of the scope of this book, although I will briefly discuss the reasons and impact of such conditions for clients within the case studies section (see Part 4).

Stress and Anxiety

Defined as "an imbalance between demands and an individual's available resources" (Churchill et al., 2021, p. 2), it is no wonder stress and anxiety are also regularly cited as common in the estrangement literature (Agllias, 2015, 2016, 2017; Conti, 2015; Melvin & Hickey, 2021; Scharp & McLaren, 2017; Scharp, Thomas, & Paxman, 2015). These could be a result of the experiences before the estrangement, such as abuse in different forms (Agllias, 2015, 2016; Conti, 2015; Scharp & McLaren, 2017; Scharp, Thomas, & Paxman, 2015), as well as conflicts over relationships, politics, sexuality, and finances (Conti, 2015). If there is still contact with the estranged parties, stress and anxiety may be a by-product of the vigilance surrounding this contact.

Agllias also shares how chronic stress and anxiety may lead to more serious health issues (Agllias, 2017), and this includes impacting cognitive function and specifically accessing stressful memories if the exposure to stress is over an extended period (Yaribeygi et al., 2017). While the period will be unique to each client, it might explain why some struggle to recall and explain in detail stressful events with family. Chronic stress can also lead to decreases in brain function and specifically impact mood, with research highlighting the physiological effects stress can cause in the brain, which sometimes, although not always, look similar to depression (Yaribeygi et al., 2017). See Part 3: The Toolbox/T2 for strategies for helping clients manage stress and anxiety.

Trauma

I feel it would be remiss not to highlight the role trauma plays in estrangement, as this is featured in some studies (Agllias, 2011a, 2013, 2017; Blake et al., 2015; Sichel, 2004). The reason for trauma could be the previously mentioned abusive behaviors and experiences of rejection in the family, but also the estrangement itself (Agllias, 2017). Interestingly, traumatic events have been found to be one of the causes of estrangement (Blake et al., 2015), and this could include a serious accident, a sudden and unexpected death, or the ending of a relationship. Alternatively, being involuntarily estranged could be traumatic and detrimental to the estranged person's wellbeing (Agllias, 2011a, 2013, Jerrome, 1994).

The trauma may not be rooted in the present but rather in childhood experiences of maltreatment, which can later lead to issues with trust, identity, and relating to others in adult life (Linden & Sillence, 2021). The trauma can manifest in different ways, including the previously mentioned sadness, rumination, and disbelief experienced directly after becoming aware of the estrangement (Agllias, 2011a, 2013; Sichel, 2004).

Reduced Stress and Increased Freedom

So far, I have highlighted the negative psychological impact, but it is important to highlight any potentially positive effects an estrangement might have on a client. My own research cited participants who spoke of feeling less stress and a greater sense of freedom and independence, particularly when it comes to life decisions, finances, and careers (Melvin & Hickey, 2021). This is echoed in another study (Blake et al., 2015) and could highlight the damaging family dynamic before estrangement. Similarly, another study found participants experienced freedom from "distressing experiences, reminders of the past, or feelings of being controlled" (Linden & Sillence, 2021, p. 331), particularly when estranged from a parent. The reference to reminders of the past might also suggest they now have distance from the impact of historical traumas.

A Stronger Sense of Self

Another finding was how estrangement gave participants the space to be themselves (Linden & Sillence, 2021), and some estranged people felt a strength that they did not have before (Melvin & Hickey, 2021). Again, this could be in response to no longer having to deal with pressures and expectations that compromise boundaries. The client might derive strength from putting their own needs first or standing up to controlling or abusive family members. See Part 3: The Toolbox/T1 for strategies for validating the impact an estrangement has had, whether positive, negative, and/ or both.

Relational Struggles

Even the best relationships face tough times, but add to this the residual impact of broken ties with family, and clients could find themselves in a perpetual world of misunderstandings and conflict. Recurring patterns of distrust, distractedness, distress, and other such traits can make sustaining a lasting and healthy relationship a huge struggle for all involved (Agllias, 2017). One severed attachment affects all attachments, and particularly a client's ability to be present with non-estranged family members, friends, colleagues, partners, and children alike. The hurt they feel can make it hard to be around others, especially those who have no comprehension of the figurative island they exist on. The task of crossing the expansive sea separating them can seem insurmountable, but a client believing they deserve love and understanding may be the greatest challenge.

Avoidance and Withdrawal

Due to the psychological impact, and in particular the overwhelming feelings of shame, anger, or grief, it could be hard for the client to stay connected and present with those in their life or even with themselves. They may feel the need to regularly pull away to work through whatever feelings they are dealing with; they may leave conversations or situations that might lead to family discussions or avoid any form of conflict as it may trigger further overwhelming emotions. My own clients have shared how being at large events was a sensory challenge, and they had to pull back to allow their mind and body to settle. These could be events, such as weddings and birthday parties, that are synonymous with family, and they leave early or cancel at the last minute as they feel it is too much for them. This could then lead to conflict with those who are impacted by these actions, and even worse if the reasons are not properly communicated to those affected and who wish for more engagement from the client.

Boundaries may also be an issue here, and clients may fluctuate from rigid to non-existent boundaries. This could be relative to how accepting the estranged parties were with each other's boundaries, but also others in the client's life, and so they may need to set these boundaries firmly in order to create some sense of control. However, if their boundaries are inflexible, it may appear as though they are being unreasonable. Alternatively, the client may withdraw to a different room when put in a position where they need to set some form of boundary, or they may compromise their boundaries when they feel under pressure but later regret it, further impacting their self-worth.

Being Misunderstood

Estrangement studies have highlighted how some feel misunderstood by those close to them (Blake et al., 2015; Melvin & Hickey, 2021) and have been accused of being selfish as well as having their own feelings dismissed (Blake et al., 2015). They may subsequently feel misunderstood even by those who are genuinely trying to understand, and this exacerbates feelings of isolation. Considering estranged people may struggle to trust others (Agllias, 2017) and have chosen to keep others at arms-length, this may compound the many struggles they are already dealing with.

Recurring Patterns of Conflict

There could be themes of conflict that began with the family of origin, were never resolved in a healthy way, and thus found their way into present relations. These conflicts could be around mismatches in expectations and roles, which are featured as a common reason for estrangement (Blake et al., 2015). Presumptions around schedules and availability, a lack of direct communication around these, and general issues around respect for boundaries, efforts made, money contributed, and personal feelings can also cause conflicts. These can recur repeatedly and lead to deeper rifts with those they love and who are supporting them.

The sources of stress leading to these conflicts can be dependent on biological vulnerability (Schneiderman et al., 2005), and thus, what stresses one person might not affect others. As mentioned, control might be important to the client and their partner, depending on their history, in managing stressors. Where some will be more concerned about personal space, others will be more focused on finances, timekeeping, pursuing goals, etc., and communicating these effectively is essential but also a huge struggle due to unhelpful patterns of miscommunication or non-communication. This can include if a client has adopted a more passive style of communication around family, which can be very frustrating for a partner or non-estranged family member who wishes to resolve any issues directly. Such conflicts can be with anyone, and if they mirror family dynamics, the client may recognize their overreactions and yet still struggle to prevent them.

Presumption will be an issue here, where the client, or their partner or friends, feel others should know their needs or what they are struggling with. I have found this particularly relevant when a partner seems oblivious to the client's struggles, even after multiple discussions. With no personal context, a partner may never fully comprehend the full extent of what the client is going through, and actively repairing rifts as a result of this will be part of the client's recovery process.

Intimacy Problems

Another aspect of this is avoiding intimacy with a partner, such as a husband or wife, boyfriend, or girlfriend, not because they do not love them but because of their vulnerable state. The psychological impact of an estrangement might mean the client does not feel safe and secure in themselves, and emotional and physical closeness is uncomfortable and perhaps even intrusive. Again, if not appropriately communicated, this could be personalized, leading to hurt feelings on both sides and more isolation. However, if their partner is also estranged from the same person or people, or even others from their own family of origin, they could equally be struggling in their own unique way. In an ideal world, those with subjective experience can be a great source of support for each other, but this is not always the case. The anger, shame, and/or grief they are experiencing may be so overwhelming that it may divide them as they remind each other of what has happened. They may be in completely different places, with some experiencing more anger than grief. Because of this, they may not be able to meet each other in the middle and thus support each other, and their emotions may influence their responses to further challenges. For example, a husband or wife may react with anger to an exchange from an estranged son or daughter, which upsets their partner, who feels only sadness for the situation they have found themselves in or fears further conflict will only widen the rift. To be clear, I believe there is no right or wrong way to feel, and validating both people's subjective experiences will be necessary to help them move past their hurt and hopefully reconnect from a healthier place.

Relationship Choices

The client may be drawn to certain people who echo the estranged parties. They may find themselves in unhealthy relationships with controlling, emotionally unavailable, and perhaps abusive partners or friends (Agllias, 2017), and such is their desire for a family that some might remain in the relationship and normalize the damaging behaviours.

This could be due to a lack of self-esteem (Agllias, 2017) and feeling they don't deserve a better relationship, which might be rooted back to childhood, their relationship with the estranged parties, and particularly their parents (Agllias, 2017). These could also be connected to feelings of shame, and the client could be confused as to how they came to be in these relationships and even more uncertain about how to get out of them. The lack of support from family may influence these choices, and combined with the challenges of the *estrangement impact triad*, the client might feel desperately alone and in need of human connection.

Improved Relationships

Again, not to just focus on the negatives, there are reports of when an estrangement has been beneficial to relationships (Blake et al., 2015; Melvin & Hickey, 2021). For example, one participant in my own study shared that they could now focus on the well-being of their children as well as personal growth, although this was after seeking professional support (Melvin & Hickey, 2021). Anecdotally, I have also heard several stories from clients of different perspectives sharing how relations with non-estranged family improved as a result of the distance from those who were a negative influence.

Other Social Challenges

When I reflect on the damaging and yet unspoken nature of estrangements, it often evokes the image of a silent bomb exploding, creating an impact radius that extends past the principal parties to others directly or indirectly affected by it. During the initial stages of an estrangement, the aforementioned *estrangement radius* might contain just immediate family as well as partners and children; however, as it continues, it may also extend to those not personally known to the client but who are aware of the situation. The wider the client's *estrangement radius*, the exponentially greater the social challenges they will face, and this includes more uncertainty regarding who knows of the situation, what they know, and how they will respond. There may then be a higher likelihood of pressure, judgment, or isolation, and subsequently more hurt and anger within the family as the estrangement is now public knowledge, thus reducing the chances or willingness to reconcile and making it harder to forget about the situation. This creates a bind, as everyone living with estrangement needs some form of support, but the more people aware of the situation, the greater the potential for negative reactions, which can compromise any sense of privacy and security.

There may be no escaping this, which is why I empathize with those in the public domain whose estrangement is widely known and who are forced to read painful and probably inaccurate stories about themselves and their families in the various media outlets. This is also why I discourage anyone from airing their grievances on public forums for others to see, comment on, and share. Alas, this can become a double-edged sword, as many who do this are making a cry for help, so it might be wise to suggest to clients that they stick to dedicated online and offline support platforms, which are hopefully closed to the general public and thus provide some privacy and confidentiality.

Ongoing Engagement with the Estranged Parties

Due to family ties and the type of estrangement, there is the potential for the client to regularly or irregularly have contact with estranged parties (Blake et al., 2015; Melvin & Hickey, 2020). Hallmark dates, pre-arranged annual meetups, urgent situations, such as an illness, and life tragedies, such as a death, all contribute to the need to spend time around family. A common example is a sickness in the family, which can be a chaotic time of heightened dependency and requires a level of involvement and coordination that might not otherwise happen. Ultimately, the context of each engagement determines the specific types of expectations, stressors, and strategies needed to manage them. See Part 3: The Toolbox/T6 for advice on helping clients manage re-engaging with family.

Controlling/Gathering Information

Depending on the family history, the client might want to protect their privacy from the estranged parties and will be cautious with whom they share information. This might be particularly relevant if they fear that personal information will be weaponized and used as leverage. This might also extend to withholding information from others unless explicitly asked (Agllias, 2017); however, this could just be a concerned family member who wishes to check on the wellbeing of the client or yearns to be involved in their lives in some way.

Protecting or seeking out information on the various social media platforms represents another layer of complexity within the *estrangement radius*, potentially exposing the client's private life as well as the private lives of the estranged parties. This might include seeing photos of events posted on social media and realizing there was a family gathering where the client was excluded, which under the circumstances will feel like a huge rejection. The superficial nature of posting images of events might create the appearance that the estranged parties are unscathed, living their lives happily, whereas the client is in a completely different place. Social media may also be used to relay information intentionally and covertly between family members, knowing it will antagonize the client, which might set them back further.

Social media may also present an opportunity for reconnection, irrespective of whether it is desired or not. Revealing an aspect of their lives that is celebratory may become a reason for the estranged parties to send a message, whatever the intention is behind it. Hearing second-hand information about serious life events can also be devastating. One trend I am personally uncomfortable with is the need to overshare the ins and outs of family difficulties in return for temporary validation. This level of transparency, while being very biased, can also widen the rift and add new stress as more people now know about the situation.

For the above reasons and more, many are reluctant to have an online presence or opt to have a simple profile with no image and possibly a false name. While some clients will not be too bothered by this, for others it might represent another loss, i.e., the loss of a normal life with normal interactions in the different ways available in contemporary society. This might seem insignificant to those who feel social media is overused and overrated, but when framed around the various other ways an estrangement can contaminate life, this might just add more salt to the wounds.

Managing Holiday Periods

Estrangements are understandably hard during times of celebration and may contribute to a sense of isolation or loneliness. Christmas, Thanksgiving, birthdays, and national holidays can be difficult, with 90% of estranged people finding Christmas particularly tough (Blake et al., 2015). For some, they might dread not seeing or hearing from the estranged parties, and for others, it is a time of great dread when there is no choice but to at least make an appearance for family gatherings. Beyond specific events and dates that can influence the decision to visit, there could be external pressures from non-estranged family with expectations to be present, whether that means just showing up or actively partaking.

The pressures could also be internal, such as feelings of guilt for not being there for someone or fear for the consequences of not visiting. There may also be an element of conditioning over a lifetime, where visits are done by default and without conscious planning, or it could be a combination of all of these. As mentioned, this could all be compounded when there are young children involved; no one wishes them to inherit an estrangement with grandparents, aunts, and uncles and lose out on a relationship with cousins, but this adds to the burden of deciding what to do and creates even more guilt and fear.

Another aspect of the social challenges is the lesson the COVID-19 pandemic taught us about how global events can change estrangement dynamics. For example, such pandemics, with large-scale social distancing and lockdowns, acted as the ultimate excuse to not spend time with the EP. Even the most difficult and unreasonable family member would struggle to argue with the need to maintain distance to avoid catching or spreading a virus. This also eased the conscience of those who did not enjoy lying to family, despite the need to protect themselves or others from negative attitudes and behaviors. In the event of another health pandemic, similar to COVID-19, a client may be greatly concerned for the EP's health (Blake et al., 2020), but have no lines of communication to check in with them. Alternatively, if the EP does not express any concern for the client's wellbeing, the client's sense of worth will be further damaged.

Explaining the Situation

Explaining an estrangement and the complex history that led to it can feel impossible, often leading to individuals and entire families feeling stigmatized by those unable to contextualize how and why someone could not have a relationship with their family. This is very much a struggle during the previously mentioned holiday periods (Blake et al., 2020). When attempting to explain the situation, it will be a struggle to know exactly what to say, who to say it to, and when to say it. The context of the conversation will be a determining factor, as what the client tells a boss or colleague will be different from what they tell a close friend. Helping clients clarify what they wish to share and how might become necessary at some point, and I will discuss this in Part 3: The Toolbox/T3.

Maintaining Life Duties and Responsibilities

An estrangement can have a detrimental effect on other areas of life, and this might include a client's ability to focus on their career (Melvin & Hickey, 2020). I have heard many stories from clients about being distracted as they ruminated about the family situation and eventually making mistakes at work. They may also find themselves distant at functions or during general family time, which can be another source of distress. Helping clients draw a line and focus on important aspects of their lives would be very beneficial, and I will discuss this under the parking strategies in Part 3: The Toolbox/T5.

Managing Pressures to Reconcile

Feeling pressurized to reconcile with the estranged parties is consistently featured in the literature (Agllias, 2013; Blake et al., 2022b; Jerrome, 1994; Scharp et al., 2015; Schwartzman, 2006). These pressures can come from non-estranged family, such as a sibling when the client is estranged from a parent (Melvin & Hickey, 2021), who are naturally upset with the breakdown in the relationship. However, their motivation may be due to being personally affected by the situation, particularly if they are caught in the middle. Those applying the pressure may feel obliged to take a side or feel more loyalty to one side of the estrangement versus another (Scharp, 2019). They may be expected to take a side and are being coerced to prompt for reconciliation or to involve the client or the estranged parties in events. These pressures can come from anyone close to the client and possibly even a professional, such as a psychotherapist or psychologist, who feels this is the best thing for the client, even though the client feels differently.

Less Drama

Perhaps resulting in the aforementioned reduced stress and increased freedom, estrangement may mean fewer interactions with family and less pressure to attend or involve themselves in events when they would rather not. This may free them from the guilt of saying no to an invitation or allow them to enjoy events knowing the estranged parties will not be there.

Holding Everything Together

To fully understand the triad of psychological, relational, and other social challenges and how they affect each client, it is not enough to view these independently but more as co-dependent and often uncooperative factors that interact, influence, and compound each other. The psychology of a person will inevitably and invariably shape their social and relational life, and vice versa, with each client living in a precarious house of cards that can fall with the slightest pressure. There are countless iterations of how the client's challenges can affect their life, but here are some examples.

A client's experiences of feeling shame may lead to social repercussions as the client engages less and less with their support network. This can lead to relationship problems, such as becoming more emotionally distant from their partner and then potentially compounding their shame as they become attuned to the effect this is having on their partner or others.

A client may feel shattered and depressed about the loss of family, but if they have the right support and feel connected to their kids, partner, or friends, they may find the strength to keep going and focus on other areas of life.

A client may feel calm and confident until extended family members invite them to a party, creating a scenario where they might cross paths with the estranged parties, and suddenly they become overwhelmed with anxiety and ruminate for weeks over every potential scenario they can imagine.

A client's partner may seem to really understand them and how they are feeling until the partner makes an innocent remark regarding family, and the client might wonder if they have been listened to at all. This might then trigger deep anger in the client as they become enraged with their partner. I'm reminded of the writings of trauma expert Bessel Van Der Kolk, author of the highly popular book *The Body Keeps the Score*, who emphasizes how "Faulty alarm systems lead to blow-ups or shutdowns in response to innocuous comments or facial expressions" (der Kolk, 2015, p. 62).

A client may attempt to reconnect with the estranged parties and be hopeful that their feelings have changed, but this can lead to disappointment when there is no response to a text message or when they are met with the same anger with which they last left off.

A client may have forgotten about their estrangement situation and allowed themselves to enjoy being with friends, but a simple reminder of good times long past may cause them to internally shut down and engage less with family.

Or a client may be making progress with their therapist and feel they have a handle on their emotions, only to have a setback for no discernible reason and become disheartened by the perceived regression.

Any of these scenarios might unearth a lingering sense of isolation and self-doubt (Melvin & Hickey, 2020), prompting the client to consider reconnecting with family, only to remember why they are estranged in the first place, and so the cycle continues. Another layer of complexity is how others will be affected by an estrangement. Much of my work is focused on the individual client, simply because other family members chose not to attend therapy. I only occasionally get to explore the views and feelings of others and garner more insight into their causes and impacts. As such, there could possibly be other factors outside of the client's awareness, such as the generational nature of many of the family issues that appear deeply entrenched in the past and brought forward to the present. Many of my clients felt there had been a pattern of issues pre-dating the current situation, and the silence that pervades estrangement means this history may remain hidden and quietly linger in the psychology of the family.

I hope a picture is formed of how complex each estrangement can be and the struggles each client might have to face. As professionals, I don't believe our job is to know all the answers but to embrace these complex situations, have an interest in the client's reality, and be open to the many ways we might be able to help them. One way of helping them from the beginning is to acknowledge how they each found their own unique way of managing their situation and effectively holding it together. This includes emphasizing their strengths, whether they are innate or developed through other areas of life, as well as the coping mechanisms they have adopted, perhaps as a result of their own research and the process of trial and error. The client's own negative bias might blind them from seeing their courage and resilience in the face of huge odds, but knowing in detail the many challenges they face, we are in a unique position to validate these and, over time, re-establish their sense of connection and confidence. Another challenge they might have to face is potentially reconciling with the EP, and I will discuss this next.

Chapter 4

Reflections on Reconciliations

Another divisive aspect of estrangement is the topic of reconciliation and whether a client should or could reconcile with the estranged parties. Reconciliation can be viewed as "the restoration of compatible and harmonious relations that have previously been destroyed or halted by a lack of understanding, intolerance and disrespect" (Agllias, 2016, p. 188), involving a "long-term process of reinstating trust, truth, justice and healing through forgiveness and reparation" (Agllias, 2016, p. 188). A reconciliation is a very delicate thing, and the decision to initiate one must be made carefully and with consideration of the effort and possible reactions. This might include understanding what a reconciliation might look like for the client and grounding their expectations. For a reconciliation to be genuine and successful, I have found it to be generally preceded by a shift in perception or priority, possibly after a major life event, which triggers a desire on one or both sides to have a different relationship. There are exceptions to this, with one study finding that serious health issues with an estranged mother did not lead to a reconciliation (Gilligan et al., 2021). Having mutual acceptance to actively work on relationship issues is a benefit, and depending on the reasons for the estrangement, there might need to be at least an acknowledgement and, at most, a legitimate apology. While not everyone insists on hearing "sorry", resentments can silently grow if the past is quickly brushed over in favor of a new and possibly unearned future.

With research suggesting 46% of estranged nuclear families have reconciled (Conti, 2015), it appears reconciliations are possible. I personally believe that reconciliations can happen in some families but not all, and these are predicated on several factors.

Firstly, it's a personal choice each individual must make for themselves. I don't believe anyone should be coerced or pressurized into reconciling "for their own good", and I have heard stories of reconciliation attempts failing as they were forced, one-sided, or driven by complex dependencies as opposed to a healthy balance of individuality and closeness.

Secondly, there must be a legitimate desire on both sides to make some degree of amends. It can't just be about one specific person; otherwise, it might revert to an exercise in, at best, avoidance or further tension, and at worst, accusations of gas-lighting and scapegoating. The intention is equally important, and if it is driven

DOI: 10.4324/9781003362203-6

by selfish reasons, then any history of distrust will only continue. The intent must be made clear, as it will drive legitimate, affirmative action in exploring the most appropriate next step as well as enabling more patience, which is very much a virtue when it comes to estrangements and reconciliations.

And thirdly, expectations of each other must reflect the altered dynamic that the estrangement has caused. For example, attempting to re-establish the original relationship set point after a period of distance and naively thinking years of conflicts and stress can simply be forgotten might lead to even more reasons to maintain the estrangement.

The process of reconciling may take months or even years, and it might mean altering the standards set for each other, having difficult conversations, not settling for superficial solutions, learning to let go of past indiscretions, making and honoring more commitments, and accepting that there is more to know about the client and the estranged parties, and now is the time to learn.

Not all reconciliations are the product of a deep yearning to reconnect and heal the wounds of the broken attachment. The passing of a life stage may prompt a revaluation of the relationship, of the legacy left behind, and of how individuals might be remembered. There might be a change in life status, such as having kids or a personal illness that evokes a desire to reconnect. For example, in times of sickness, attitudes might change, thus facilitating a new relationship. There may also be a strong seasonal element to this desire, such as the nostalgia of Christmas prompting a reconnection.

As mentioned, external influences may be a factor, and the thought of how a breakdown in relations can affect others may compel some to find ways of bringing the EP back together. For example, some non-estranged family members might insist on dismissing behaviors and maintaining some kind of relationship with the EP. They may also insist a client forgives and forgets; however, these overly simplistic views and expectations disregard the complexity of family struggles and the process of piecing together broken trust. In this case, a reconciliation may better serve the overall family, but at the cost of individuality. This cost will be acceptable to some, but not all. Many who find themselves estranged hope their friends will become their family of choice and fill the relational void they are left to carry, but this is not always possible. Family is not always replaceable; the love and affection of friends may not penetrate deep enough to reach the wounds, and their supportive words may not be powerful enough to nourish the spirit. If a reconciliation is fuelled by desperation, ignorance, pride, or pressure, there may be no onus on the client or the EP to address the reasons behind the estrangement. This might result in a tenuous truce between warring factions, which begs the question: can it be considered an actual reconciliation?

In my work, I have always worked with estranged individuals, as opposed to the entire family, who felt a reconciliation was either not desired or not an option. Perhaps this is due to the fact that I personally did not reconcile with my own EP and empathize with those who are stuck exploring every avenue to make sense of their situation and have reached a point where they just want to find a way to move on with their lives. I also understand the inner conflict of wanting to reconnect and yet knowing it might not be safe to do so, as well as establishing if, when, and how to initiate a reconciliation and dreading a negative response.

Despite the dysfunction that exists in some families, there can be a genuine desire to work through the issues and have some semblance of a close relationship. Even in antagonistic relationships, there can be love that has no healthy outlet for expression, and sometimes the stresses of existing in this world are too great to permit a safe level of interdependence. I wish more families were open to family therapy, as it can sometimes facilitate this, enabling new ways of communicating, understanding, and integrating individual perspectives and subjective experiences while maintaining cohesion within the collective family members. As I have said previously, many estranged families will never attend therapy, will never recognize their vulnerabilities, or will never face the secrets and lies protecting the façade of security. Some relationships are too far gone, too locked into their bias and their pain, to seek professional help. It is important to note that while exploring the family history in detail, I never insist to a client or anyone else that they should reconcile. I also believe it is completely unethical to stage some kind of surprise intervention, and I'm abhorred by reality TV's insistence on bringing estranged individuals together for entertainment masked as goodwill. I would rather empower individuals to believe they know the best thing to do and to trust their intuition, as many have done a great deal of tough emotional work, and it's important to not undo that. If no part of their history or present circumstance indicates the EP are in a different place, it is important to at least acknowledge that any vision of reconciliation may not match reality.

Despite my observations, this does not mean a bridge cannot be found outside of the therapy room. Love is a biological phenomenon, and it doesn't discriminate against those who treat us badly; it simply loves. This is why estrangement will forever be painful and why, in some cases, it is worth trying to see if the relationship can be mended. To truly understand each client and provide them with the tools to possibly repair the divide, it is important to first have awareness of what each side is seeing or not seeing and how these might be closing off each other's unique perspective of the issues within the relationship. As professionals, we can facilitate more depth of understanding for the client about the importance and impact of past interactions, but for the estranged parties, hearing each other, never mind listening, is maybe the hardest step. While there will be some who will be in denial, become defensive, minimize, exaggerate, and/or deflect, there will be others who might engage. It will be hard to know without the client first locating this bridge and hoping the EP is willing to cross it with them. Later, I will discuss how we can help clients potentially repair their relationship in Part 3: The Toolbox/T4.

Part 2

The Support Dilemma

Considering how prevalent family estrangement is, a great number of people are in need of support in various different ways. One effective source of support could be a husband or wife, boyfriend or girlfriend, or partner. Due to their intimate connection to the client, these could have some emotional understanding of the true impact of the estrangement and thus be a powerful source of compassion as well as practical support. In fact, a reported 73% of participants in one estrangement study found talking to a spouse or partner helpful (Blake et al., 2015). However, with no personal experience or biases on the side of the estranged parties, any efforts they make at supporting the client may fall flat or even make the situation worse. Another reality is that the client's partner may also be estranged from the same person(s) and caught up in their own hurt, and thus they may not be able to offer emotional support to each other. Then there is support from either non-estranged family members or those outside the family, such as friends, colleagues, and acquaintances. Their role in the client's life will determine the type of support they can or will provide, and if it is from non-estranged family, they might have important historical and first-hand interpersonal experience with the estranged parties. This will be a great source of validation for the client, especially if they had to deal with the family issues alone and have come to doubt their experiences. These people might also represent the client's only connection back to their family of origin; however, due to non-estranged family member's potential closeness to the estranged parties, their capacity to offer support might be stifled. This can become another source of upset for the client, as it may appear that sides are being taken when, in fact, this group might be simply choosing to remain neutral. Alas, the bonds of family are personal, and some will feel more loyalty or empathy for certain estranged parties over others, and the client may be left with only two options: suffer alone or seek out alternative help.

Option one, unfortunately, is a common one and perhaps the result of conditioning around vulnerability. Due to the closed-door nature of family relationships, some feel they are the only ones experiencing the issues presented and are too embarrassed to share (Agllias, 2013). It is telling that one study found only one in four estranged people seek clinical help (Dattilio & Nichols, 2011), and some might endure for years before they tell anyone and rely on their own resources to

DOI: 10.4324/9781003362203-7

maintain their painful inner world. They may be too afraid to ask for help, fearful of judgment or being a burden, or they might feel those close to them could never understand their situation. Such is the scale of impact that this might be too much for them to bear alone, but tragically, they might resist this and reach the point of complete breakdown before they can accept that they need help.

With option two, having someone to talk to can be a problem. If the client literally has no one to share their story with, they may find their way to different independent estrangement support groups, whether peer-led or run by therapists and held either in-person or online. There are also organizations that are dedicated to supporting estranged individuals, such as Stand-Alone (www.stand-alone.org.uk) and Together Estranged (www.togetherestranged.org). In fact, the effectiveness of one support group was highlighted in a study of a six-week facilitated group delivered by Stand-Alone, where attendees reported feeling less psychological distress, loneliness, and shame (Blake et al., 2022a). Naturally, experiences will vary, and while support groups in various forms can be an amazing source of validation and encouragement, not everyone will have the same experience. I have heard several stories of people being met with a negative reaction when they discussed their situation. Although this may or may not be a reflection of the group leaders or facilitators, it could speak to the divisive nature of estrangements and the many conflicting perspectives that can trigger defensive reactions within a group.

Regarding estrangement support groups and social media in general, as much as I appreciate the desire to maintain or form new connections, due to the remote nature of these engagements, safety and privacy will be difficult to find. It is also difficult to watch how family dynamics play out among strangers when views and experiences conflict. While I still encourage seeking out support groups and commend those who facilitate them, if the client is considering joining one, it is worthwhile suggesting to them that they take the time to observe how it is moderated, ensuring the facilitators are both skilled and knowledgeable, and how members interact and respond to each other, to get a better sense of the openness and mutual respect before sharing their story. Another struggle with engaging with support groups is that, despite their shared experiences, each person may be in a different place along their estrangement journey. For some, their estrangement may be very recent, and they have not had time to sit through some of the initial anger, grief, and/or anxiety. This is very understandable, and the group may offer hope by sharing how they eventually moved past these emotions. However, it may become a problem if the client starts to compare themselves with others who have had more time to discuss their situation and engage in different types of support, including therapy. These comparisons can create a new source of pressure, although a good group leader can acknowledge this and help members demonstrate compassion for where they are now.

For some, such support groups are not an option, and they may consider professional support. Depending on where the client is in their life, who they reach out to for support can vary. If the client is a student, they may reach out to a teacher or lecturer for help. One study of estranged students found that, of the 31% who did talk to a teacher or lecturer, 77% reported it was helpful (Blake & Bland, 2018). Similarly, in the same study, of the 36% of estranged students who spoke with student services, 90% found it helpful (Blake & Bland, 2018), highlighting how this group of professionals has a strong capacity to help. If someone is having health concerns, either connected to the family or completely unrelated, they may choose to talk to their local doctor due to the confidential and discrete nature of their profession, coupled with their perceived empathy. However, although one in four who reached out to a GP did not find it helpful (Blake et al., 2015), this is not always the case, and in the context of counselling and therapy, 54% found this helpful (Blake et al., 2015). Taken together, these findings highlight a need for guidance for those who professionally engage with estrangement in various contexts. There will be many challenges to this, and it is useful to explore these in detail in the next chapter.

Another consideration is the possibility that the client will have no access to any form of support and feel their world is completely isolated. This could be due to many factors, including the number of estranged parties involved and the loss of contact with several family members. Depending on a client's stage in life, they may have lost touch with friends who are focused on their own families and priorities. The client may have limited mobility and/or transportation, which makes physically accessing support hard or impossible; they may have ongoing and chronic health issues; or they may have limited finances and cannot afford professional support. I'm sure there are many other reasons why support will be tough to access, but as the topic of family estrangement grows in relevance and mainstream acceptance, hopefully national and global policymakers will recognize the necessity of providing more support for those struggling.

Chapter 5

Therapeutic Roadblocks

Throughout the many client sessions, group discussions, email exchanges, and general conversations I have had with estranged adults, there were accounts of negative experiences when engaging with different professionals for support. These experiences clearly stayed with them, as they questioned whether they could or should trust another professional again. Anecdotally, I have heard stories of professionals offering advice that did not match the client's personal situation or feelings or opinions on what to do next. In some cases, they felt the professional had more compassion for other family members but not the client, and they left the session feeling further isolated. This was echoed in two studies of the experiences of counselling for estranged people, where participants felt the professional did not understand complex family dynamics and how one becomes estranged (Blake et al., 2019, 2022b).

With one study highlighting how 78% of their participants had reached out to a therapist (Blake et al., 2015), it is clear there is an interest in engaging with professional support. Interestingly, a recent study identified how not understanding the client's needs was a reason some estranged individuals had a negative experience with therapists: "unhelpful encounters with therapy were those in which participants felt that their counsellor, psychotherapist or psychologist was disinterested in them, could not empathize with them or did not advocate for them in the way that they wanted and needed" (Blake et al., 2022b, p. 109).

There are several factors that may contribute to these negative outcomes, including personal bias towards an estrangement perspective, such as that of a parent or adult child, as well as a lack of training in the many factors that shape and influence an estrangement. Aside from the study of family systems or family therapy, there appears to be a small number of training programs designed for professionals who work with adults or families who are experiencing estrangement.

Subjective experience may be a factor here, where the therapists' own stories influence how open they are to their clients' experiences. While first-hand personal experience can be a huge benefit in establishing emotional context and building trust with the client, it may prove a problem if strong beliefs around loyalty, caring for family, respect for elders, and self-sacrifice compromise the therapeutic relationship. This may also lead to a bias towards specific estrangement outcomes,

DOI: 10.4324/9781003362203-8

such as insisting on reconciliation. A lack of awareness of the long-term psychological impact of damaging behaviours within the family or the consequences of failed interventions may also lead to ill-advised suggestions. Research emphasizes the need for training in understanding the causes and consequences and helping estranged individuals make their own decisions, "whether this was to initiate and maintain estrangement or seek reconciliation" (Blake et al., 2022b, p. 107). The client might not have any concept of what they want or need from a professional other than to just talk. I feel this is a natural response to the complexity of what they were dealing with and not knowing how to move forward, but over time, any goals and outcomes will reveal themselves with ongoing collaboration with each client.

Estrangement and Bias

Irrespective of any specific outcome the client might desire, our ability to help them will be determined by the *therapeutic alliance*, i.e., "a cooperative working relationship between client and therapist" ("Therapeutic Alliance", n.d.). In fact, studies have highlighted how the quality of this relationship is the best predictor of a positive clinical outcome, despite the approach taken to achieve these outcomes (Ardito & Rabellino, 2011). Renowned psychologist Carl Rogers had ground-breaking ideas on the necessary conditions to facilitate personal growth for the client (Rogers, 2004). A pioneer in person-centred therapy, this was a non-directive approach that put the relationship with the client as its primary focus and was characterized by an openness to the client's reality and experience, a tolerance for uncertainty, and compassion for each client's autonomy (Wilkins, 2015). Rogers established that there were six components or core conditions needed for therapy to be effective; these were 1) *a psychological agreement between the therapist and client* which establishes the working relationship, 2) *the client is incongruent*, i.e., they are not in a good place and need help, 3) *the therapist is congruent*, 4) *the therapist demonstrates unconditional positive regard for the client*, e.g. they are actively seeking out traits and characterizes which they respect in the client, 5) the client experiences *empathy from the therapist*, in that the therapist really understands their inner world, and 6) *the client feels and perceives acceptance and unconditional positive regard from the therapist* (Rogers, 2004). What makes Rogers' work and these core conditions so powerful is how they are not specific to a psychotherapeutic relationship but many different relationships (Wilkins, 2015), and this can extend to the different professionals working with estrangement. Agreeing with the client to work on some aspect of their estrangement, knowing how vulnerable they are, and the professional's own congruence, acceptance, and positive regard could be both opposite to what they experienced with family and exactly what they need to start to feel good about themselves again.

Each professional's ability to create this therapeutic alliance and put these six components into practice might be hampered by any personal and unconscious biases they might have. These may be rooted in religious, cultural, or broader societal values, or they may come from personal experiences, but it is important to at least acknowledge their existence. Any bias has the potential to invalidate the client's thoughts and emotions and interrupt the therapeutic process (Ardito & Rabellino, 2011). Another problem with these is that they may mimic biases within the family and those of others in the client's life and thus trigger many painful emotions. It might also widen the sense of isolation they might feel; if a professional is telling them they were wrong or reminding them of the weight of consequence, a weight they already struggle to carry, then whatever shame the client might carry could be made worse. The next question is, what do these biases look like? Below are five examples of biases from my clinical experience and how they might negatively affect working with estranged adults.

Reconciliation Bias

It is not uncommon to hear of pressures to reconcile from those in caring professions (Blake et al., 2022b), as they envision how healing this might be for the client, and as a result, may try to influence the client towards making amends with family. However, suggestions on how to reconnect can sometimes be odd. For example, one member of a support group once shared how a professional he attended suggested he write 100 letters (one letter per day for 100 days) to an estranged family member to let them know the client loves them. This is obviously an extreme case, but I hope I don't need to explain why this type of exercise is not only highly inappropriate but could have legal ramifications.

The motivation to push for reconciliation could be deeply personal; the professional may feel a strong compassionate connection to some family members but not all, perhaps due to the challenges and losses they have experienced with their own parents, siblings, sons, daughters, etc. If the client is themselves an adult son or daughter, the professional may feel pity for the parent, particularly if they are elderly, and may insist on putting aside the past to care for them. If there is much unsaid between estranged parties, the professional may insist the client must express these at all costs to make the situation better. By focusing on a specific estrangement outcome, i.e., families reconciling, a professional could be dismissing the core reasons why the estrangement happened and disregarding the traumatic impact of a failed reconciliation. As mentioned previously, they are also depriving the client of their autonomy and undermining their confidence if the client knows the distance of estrangement is best for their wellbeing.

Estrangement Bias

I have heard how some professionals were quick to label the client's family as toxic and insisted they should "just walk away", effectively moving further down the *estrangement continuum*. I have similarly seen this propagated on social media, particularly by those who felt they themselves had no choice but to move on from family and perhaps needed to defend this decision. By dismissing the powerful bond of family and the countless memories and experiences that may define them, the client's desire to estrange and not exploring the consequences of doing so undermines the client's autonomy, and they are not allowed to work through their own process. While I fully appreciate any concerns a professional might have for the wellbeing of their client, the reality of walking away may not feel like an option, and despite how difficult and damaging the relationship is, the client may still love them and not be ready to just remove the estranged parties from their lives. In practical terms, the client might just need space to make sense of everything and come to their own conclusion about whether estrangement is the best choice in their unique situation.

Perspective Bias

There may be some professionals who believe one side is always at fault or must take precedence over others. For example, some might believe an estrangement between a parent and adult son or daughter must always be the result of poor parenting, and while this is one valid reason (Agllias, 2016), there are a wide range of other factors that prevent a parent from fulfilling their role to their full capability, such as divorce and/or influences outside the family. This overly simplistic view reduces each person to a generic family role as opposed to a human being, minimizing their feelings and experiences.

Forgiveness Bias

Many estranged people are carrying a great deal of hurt, and after many years of neglect, abuse, and/or rejection, they may not be ready to forgive now, or perhaps never will be. A professional might not push for reconciliation, but they may insist on the client forgiving their family. While I feel we should never encourage a client to hold on to anger or resentment, particularly due to the potential impact this can have on mental health (Adler et al., 2020), even by suggesting to a client to forgive estranged family, the professional could be dismissing the client's need to come to that place naturally and when it feels right for them.

Attributional Bias

Finally, there will be professionals who insist that all estrangements happen for the same reasons. For example, while abuse in its different forms has been cited as a common reason for estrangement (Agllias, 2015, 2016; Blake et al., 2015; Conti, 2015; Scharp & McLaren, 2017; Scharp, Thomas, & Paxman, 2015), this does not mean all estrangements are the result of abuse. To attribute all estrangements to one reason, and particularly abuse, is a very damaging bias to have and will only serve to propagate the sense of shame and stigma that already pervades estranged adults. Similarly, if an estrangement is chosen, the professional might feel the person who initiated it is simply selfish and uncaring, when this could be very far from the truth.

I would like to point out that, despite any bias a professional might have, this does not negate their genuine desire to help. So, if a client is dissatisfied with the professional they are working with, instead of just walking away, they could actually tell them what they need and how the professional could help. This will not only promote a better collaborative relationship and trust in the professional, but it will also boost the client's self-worth as they have the courage to express their needs.

Professional Limitations

Psychotherapy is specifically about solving problems, but it also presents problematic situations and dilemmas (Ulrichová, 2014). Considering the vulnerable position estranged individuals are in, it stands to reason that all professionals should have an ethical framework from which to address these situations and dilemmas and protect their client's wellbeing as well as their own professional position. As an accredited psychotherapist in Ireland, I am bound by the code of ethics of my accrediting body, the Irish Association of Counsellors and Psychotherapists (*IACP*, n.d.), as are other licenced professionals, such as psychologists. While I understand not everyone reading this will be bound by an ethical code, there are some considerations I would ask all professionals to honestly reflect on. From my experiences, therapists and professionals at large will make mistakes (I certainly have), and this is part of life. But if the intention is to genuinely focus on each client's wellbeing as well as constantly learn from every session or client engagement, we increase our chances of improving our ability to help and leaving a positive and enduring impression on the client.

Aside from the aforementioned biases, there will be other professional roadblocks that prevent them from making this impression, such as limitations in their role and capacity to help. The context in which each professional is working and their relationship with the client will determine the types of limits in place, as well as how they work and what the client expects from them. For example, psychotherapists and psychologists in private practice may have more time to work with clients as opposed to those working in the public sector, who may have only a finite number of contact hours with service users. Below are more examples of the limitations a professional might have to contend with.

Availability and Time Restrictions

Each professional might have a limited timeframe with which to work with the client and thus might not be able to explore the family history in detail. For example, if they are a medical professional, they might have a large caseload and only have a small window to discuss the client's health, so they could not be expected to explore an estrangement in detail if it was disclosed by a client.

Psychotherapy and psychology clinics may have long waiting lists, which discourages clients (Blake et al., 2022b). Similarly, support groups can only dedicate a certain amount of time to each person. Some institutions may only provide a certain number of visits for clients, so while there may be no time constraints per session, the professional will still have a short period in which to delve into the estrangement. This might be very frustrating for the professional who genuinely desires to work more with specific clients or has concerns for their wellbeing. This is a reality of life, but just familiarizing themselves with the complexity of estrangement will be helpful in grasping a basic understanding of how clients might be struggling. There may be nothing they can offer but an empathetic ear, but sometimes that might be enough.

Environmental Considerations

There may be environmental considerations that affect working with estranged people. Privacy is an obvious factor, and if the professional does not have a dedicated space to work, isolated from the eyes and ears of others, then the client may not feel safe enough to talk. Any space available that provides visual privacy might still not be soundproof, and thus the client may still be aware of others in the immediate vicinity. Naturally, many professionals might have a waiting area that may make the client feel uncomfortable, and this is unavoidable, but making everyone feel welcome while practicing discretion and not emphasizing why they are there will be appreciated. If a professional's role involves home visits, such as a social worker, this location and proximity to the estranged family may limit how much a client shares. The professional might subtly acknowledge this, and if appropriate, suggesting a different time or setting to talk may be helpful to them.

Another dimension to online therapy or support groups is that, while they are accessible to all with a digital device, such as smart phones, laptops, or computers, the professional cannot influence the client's home environment to ensure it is private. This might become a bigger problem during group sessions, where a member might fear someone in another home will hear and potentially share their story.

General Accessibility

Due to the geographical location of a professional, the client may struggle to access them. If they are located far away or the client does not have adequate transportation, they may not be able to work with them regularly. Thankfully, the use of technology to deliver telepsychology services, including telephone and video conferencing tools, is commonplace now (Varker et al., 2019), perhaps even more so after the COVID-19 pandemic, which necessitated the need for more distanced services. This being said, remote sessions will have their own challenges, including technical issues such as network slowness as well as sound and camera problems. I have had sessions where there was a lag or delay in communication, which was frustrating for all parties. If working with clients where communication breakdown is at the heart of the issues, experiencing communication issues with a professional whom they are depending on might exasperate their distress. Another challenge will be creating a strong interpersonal connection with the client despite physical distance. Part of this will be creating a consistent experience, such as making sure they are on time, ensuring the background is always the same, and making it clear they are listening intently; e.g., if they take a sip of a drink just as the client is sharing something, they might perceive it as a lack of interest. If professionals wish to improve their ability to work with clients online, I would suggest the book *Theory and Practice of Online Therapy*, edited by Weinberg and Rolnick and published by Routledge, which offers great insights from different experts on delivering therapy across digital platforms (Weinberg & Rolnick, 2019).

Competency

A question all professionals should ask themselves is if their qualifications, skills, and experience lend themselves to working with the issues discussed within the *estrangement impact triad*, including mental health issues such as depression and anxiety as well as more complicated conditions. By not having a nuanced understanding of the causes and consequences of estrangement (Blake et al., 2022b), the professional may step outside the boundaries of their competencies by ill-advising a client and doing more harm than good. For example, I have no training or experience as a legal professional, so it would be inappropriate for me to comment on any potential legal issues between the client and their family, although I can express an understanding of how challenging these might be. Another example is if the estrangement is the result of abusive behaviors which may lead to the client suffering from complex trauma. If the professional has had no formal training in working with trauma, they may rush in to discuss distressing memories that trigger deep-rooted anxieties before adequately preparing the client and making sure they feel safe and ready to do so.

Some professionals, such as psychotherapists, might work within a specific modality that does not align with the client's needs or personal understanding of their situation. Acknowledging this and working with the client to collaboratively overcome such challenges could be very helpful in building a strong therapeutic relationship. With that said, continuing professional development is also important to acquire more knowledge and skills to help clients. Another dimension is maintaining their own wellbeing and having a consistent self-care protocol to manage the emotional demands of this work (Ulrichová, 2014) in order to avoid burnout.

Poor Boundaries

Unfortunately, not everyone has a clear concept of what boundaries look and feel like due to their subjective nature and whatever lessons they have been taught or not taught throughout their lives. I found this particularly true when it comes to discussing family issues and how many feel it is completely appropriate to offer unsolicited advice. If the client themselves is struggling with their own boundaries and is put in a position where these could be further compromised, this could hurt them more, as they had trusted the professional to intuitively respect them. An overly simplistic view of boundaries can also be a problem, and the professional may struggle to understand how these can fluctuate based on different variables and contexts. For example, the client might feel comfortable saying no to a colleague or friend where there are no overt or covert power hierarchies, whereas they may impulsively say yes to authoritarian figures, such as a boss, who may unconsciously represent an estranged family member who positioned themselves in a similar authoritarian position.

Boundary violations can include the professional oversharing aspects of their personal life with the client, effectively making the session more about them than the client. As we will learn later, a therapist offering something of themselves, whether it is a perspective, an opinion, or maybe even a relevant experience, can be very helpful (Blake et al., 2022b). However, if it forms an ongoing pattern, it can undermine the client's worth and perhaps even burden them with the professional's own issues. The professional may struggle to separate their personal experiences from those of the client, especially if there are strong similarities, and this can take away from the uniqueness of each client's story. Another dimension is when a professional is unable to push back against requests for personal information from a client. Being curious about the person helping them is natural, particularly if they are vulnerable and seeking something in the professional to connect with. We need to be cautious, as it can quickly overstep the mark if the client is trying to turn the professional relationship into something more akin to a friendship. This is a delicate situation to be in, and it will take time and experience to find the best response to it.

Transparency and Honesty

It may be essential to directly relay to each client their qualifications, skills, and experience. This will be important to ground the client's expectations and remove any ambiguity about the professional and the type of help they can provide. This will be particularly important if the client has placed great demands on the professional to change their situation or take their pain away; understanding the limitations of the professional can save time and keep the focus on what can be done together to better their situation. This transparency might include knowing how much of their own estrangement story, if they have one, to share. This type of sharing is a personal choice and hopefully will be driven by a desire to relay their familiarity with estrangement and the client's struggles.

This level of honesty should be reflected inwardly, as each professional needs to assess their own limitations, including those mentioned here as well as others I have not considered. For example, do they feel uncomfortable working with certain issues or scenarios, and if so, why? Do they feel they can stay with difficult conversations, with a great deal of pain and despair, or is it too much for them? The professional may not feel okay working with abuse in its different forms, and it is important to express compassion and support to the client while establishing that this is not their area of expertise. There is nothing wrong with acknowledging this as it honours their own humanity, but not at the expense of dismissing the client, so being sensitive to the client's struggles will be helpful and welcomed by them while maintaining a boundary and the professional's own wellbeing.

Accountability/Supervision

Another consideration is ensuring each professional has someone, either a senior or a peer, whom they trust to discuss difficult cases. This will be particularly important when assessing a professional's capacity to remain neutral and bring any resistance to clinical supervision when possible. Whilst I was not aware of anyone in Ireland working exclusively with family estrangement, there were times when I wished I had my own peer support network who were familiar with the depth and nuance of these issues, although I was very lucky to have a great clinical supervisor who I could share my struggles with and receive feedback from.

Lack of Compassion

With one study finding the therapist "cold or unresponsive" (Blake et al., 2022b, p. 105), there may be a range of reasons for this, but perhaps a lack of compassion could be one. This could be due to burnout, resulting in compassion fatigue, which is not uncommon amongst healthcare, community, and emergency workers who are regularly exposed to the traumatic experiences of those they are working with (Cocker & Joss, 2016). Powerful personal values and beliefs around family may conflict with the client's, and the professional may struggle to sympathize with them.

Awareness of Age, Religious, Cultural, Political, or Gender-Related Issues

There could be broader societal issues that the professional might not understand that contribute to the estrangement situation and the client's struggles. Examples of these are if the client is marginalized within a family due to conflicting beliefs and disapproval over life and relationship choices, religious practices, gender and sexual orientation, age and life status, neurodiversity, or any other factors. By not understanding these differences, a professional may miss where estrangement sits in an increasingly complex and diverse society and how conflicts affect what is considered normal. For example, most of the existing estrangement research comes from Western Europe (Blake et al., 2022b), where Christian family values are strong but can vary. Pitch this against those of other religious beliefs, such as Muslim or Buddhist, where family bonds might be considered tighter and estrangement is even more frowned upon. Under these circumstances, a client who is estranged from family, irrespective of whether the estrangement was chosen or not, is opposing not just their family but those within their religious community as well. Another example is that if the client is a member of the LGBT community, they may be more vulnerable to poor mental and physical health in their youth

(Katz-Wise et al., 2016), and they may now experience estrangement within their family due to conflicts over their gender and/or their sexual or romantic desires and needs, and the client's wellbeing could further spiral downwards. A professional who is not in touch with such contemporary issues may dismiss them due to their own traditional views, and they may further stigmatize the client instead of offering the acceptance for which they might yearn (Katz-Wise et al., 2016).

Client Resistance

While clients have reached out to a professional for help, this does not mean they will be fully open and engaged when it comes to working together. To understand why the client might resist a professional's help, it is useful to frame this against the *estrangement impact triad*, as these factors have the potential to deeply affect a client's ability to engage with support in a meaningful way. Below are some of the challenges a professional might face, but each one should be met with compassion and tolerance, as underneath these may sit a distressing and painful experience with the estranged parties.

Lack of Trust

It is understandable that the client will have issues with trust if they have been mistreated by family or for any of the other reasons why families become estranged. They may automatically disbelieve anyone, particularly a professional who is not known to them. The client may be slow to divulge private aspects of themselves out of fear of judgment or blame; they may fear their private situation will be discussed publicly; or they might not trust the therapeutic process and the professional's ability to help them. The client might have concerns about the *Estrangement Inquiry Model* process described in this book, such as what emotions might come up as it touches the very essence of their pain. While this may not happen, it is important not to pressurize a client to follow this and to allow them to stop if they feel too overwhelmed. Another reality is that the client will not have answers to all the questions, but that's ok, as the reflective process is more important than a specific outcome.

It is important to note that family relations and their impact are not always obvious, particularly if the client has their own biases, and they might not connect with how their experiences with family led to their distrust (Ulrichová, 2014). For this reason, there may be a period where they scrutinize the professional before trust is established (Ulrichová, 2014).

Lack of Hope

Perhaps as a consequence of the previously mentioned psychological impact of isolation and depression, especially if endured over a period of months and perhaps years, the client may have reached a point of hopelessness, questioning the point of attending therapy or if change is possible. This will be particularly powerful if they feel they have tried everything to improve the relationship with their estranged family or if previous therapy has not worked for them.

Communication Struggles

The client may struggle to articulate their situation and/or their feelings, perhaps due to the complex family history and/or the overwhelming and fluctuating emotions they are experiencing. They may discuss aspects of their history that do not appear to be relevant and repeat the same story multiple times. This reflects the personal importance of these stories and their need to have them validated. We must consider the potential impact of trauma on the client, as accessing language in a traumatized state will be tough (der Kolk, 2015). Relaying this back to the client may remove any pressure on them to explain everything in detail while normalizing their communication struggles. Communication strategies will be discussed in Part 3: The Toolbox/T3.

Bottling-Up

Due to negative experiences around expressing difficult emotions, the client may have learned that it is better to suppress them and keep them bottled up inside. They might mask their feelings with an insincere smile, creating the pretense that they are fine, which could be connected to their fears of being a burden to others. This can naturally lead to all manner of psychological and physical health concerns, but it also results in the client being incongruent and not sharing their true feelings.

Too Soon

Later, I will discuss how the duration of an estrangement impacts the experience, but if it is still relatively recent, despite having a desire to talk, the client might feel it is simply too soon. They may not have realized this until presented with someone who is genuinely prepared to listen, and they may become overwhelmed with emotions. There is no defined timeline for when a client is ready, as each client's situation is unique, and our role is to respect this and let the client know we are ready when they are.

Impatience

The client may be desperate for change and thus feel like it is not happening fast enough. This might be linked with anxiety or anything else listed in the *estrangement impact triad*, but it might also be connected to pressures the client is feeling if others are affected by the situation or if others expect the client to be doing better than they are. They may be feeling time pressures as well, in that if they don't feel better soon, the estrangement may get worse, or if they are in their later years, they may feel time is running out for them.

Financial Struggles

The client might not have the financial resources to attend regular sessions or can only attend once. This might be connected to the loss of financial support as a result of their estrangement (Agllias, 2017), but also to their employment status, health problems, debt, and other responsibilities. This could be particularly relevant for students who struggle to prove their estrangement status and thus cannot receive statutory funding for their education (Bland & Blake, 2019).

Support Saboteurs

Another consideration I have seen are negative influences in the client's life that might undermine their efforts to seek or regularly engage with support. This could be anyone they are close to and might be due to their discomfort with their own vulnerability, resentment, and/or traditional views around asking for help. They might not understand the scale of the estrangement issues and their impact, and minimize the client's need for help. This will particularly be the case when the client has spent years bottling up emotions and the people in their lives are oblivious to what is really happening.

Chapter 6

Exploring what Works

Once a professional steps away from the structure of formal education and faces the many people who need their help, they must find their own way of working that reflects the client's needs as well as their own experiences, garnered both within their specific training and outside of it. When I began working as a therapist, I was naturally taught the various models of therapy and techniques associated with each. In the early days of clinical work, I gravitated towards Cognitive Behavioral Therapy (CBT), a practical approach designed to focus on how a client's thoughts, emotions, and behaviors were contributing to their distress (Fenn & Byrne, 2013). Later, as other therapists might attest, I absorbed other approaches that I had studied, including somatic work, which places primary emphasis on what is happening within the client's body in the present moment as difficult issues in their lives are explored. However, the specific challenges of working with estranged adults remained.

Thankfully, ongoing efforts have been made to study the effectiveness of therapy and, more specifically, the experiences of therapy for estranged people (Blake et al., 2015, 2019, 2022b). These provide us with essential insight into what helped and led to positive outcomes for the participants, and below are some of the findings of these studies, coupled with my own thoughts.

Relationship, Relationship, Relationship

While I discuss different strategies that might help the client, ultimately there is no solution that will fix everything quickly. What we do have to offer is a unique and badly needed connection where the client can be themselves, open up safely, and find their own answers, and this is where any professional can enter stage left and make a real impact. Research indicates the previously mentioned *therapeutic alliance* is almost universally accepted as a strong factor for positive psychotherapy outcomes (Arnow & Steidtmann, 2014). As we found, trust is another victim of estrangement, and developing a therapeutic alliance is a step towards rebuilding it (Agllias, 2017). It appears humility and professional self-doubt are also important characteristics to demonstrate and cultivate (Mahon et al., 2023).

DOI: 10.4324/9781003362203-9

Warmth

Another relationship quality sometimes missing between estranged families and one highlighted in the research as helpful is warmth (Blake et al., 2022b; Moors & Zech, 2017), but how does one relay warmth? It might be a simple smile to let the client know they are welcome, or it could be open physical or verbal language to relay to the client that they are accepted. Warmth could be demonstrated through empathy, which is particularly important for those who have "chaotic social relations" (Wampold, 2015, p. 271), which is a fair description for some estrangements. One way to demonstrate empathy could be by expressing an understanding of what the client is saying by using the professional's own language to describe it, which will highlight genuine efforts to listen and interpret the client's story. I find sharing anecdotes or personal stories with similar themes can also help demonstrate understanding. These anecdotes will not always resonate with the client, but it shows a genuine effort to connect, and by disagreeing, it still demonstrates to the client that we are working together and hopefully builds their confidence.

Validation

I have heard countless stories from estranged adults where their experiences with family have been dismissed and minimized, and unfortunately, studies feature stories where participants had similar experiences with professionals (Blake et al., 2015, 2019). In particular, the below quote from a 2015 estrangement study stayed with me: "I found a brilliant private therapist, who actually believed me when I reported child abuse, at long last, aged 37" (Blake et al., 2015, p. 28). While I acknowledge that this is an extreme example and childhood abuse is not at the heart of all estrangements, to think such an experience would not be acknowledged highlights why the second quality of validation is so important (Blake et al., 2022b). These invalidating reactions may replicate the family dynamics that led to the rifts and reopen deep wounds. To make matters worse, this could be the first time the client has chosen to share their story, and thus, they could be highly sensitive and vulnerable to judgment. As a result of this, they may feel permanently misunderstood and distrust anyone who is not personally known to them.

Perhaps the most powerful intervention we can make is to accept what our clients are saying as their truth and fully recognize the deep impact the estrangement has had on them. This includes validating:

- Their various interactions with family, as they may come to distrust themselves.
- Their feelings, which may have been too much for them to bear alone up until now.
- The choices they have made, either in the past or going forward, regarding family or other areas of life.

- The losses they have incurred are not just due to the estrangement but also other relationships, which may feel compounded by the estrangement.
- Their human needs, such as love, safety, belonging, etc., may have been pushed aside in favor of the needs of others within the family.
- Their strengths, which they are blind to as no one else has ever acknowledged them.
- Or their very existence, as they may feel they are invisible or even worthless.

The process of validating may be never-ending as they have come to doubt every aspect of themselves, but over time they might start to rebuild trust in themselves and their ability to control their lives. Such is the importance of validation that it has a dedicated section in the *Estrangement Toolbox* (see Part 3: The Toolbox/T1).

Safety

The third quality found to be helpful is that of safety (Blake et al., 2022b), but due to the clients' experience, this can come as a challenge, particularly if the client is carrying trauma and naturally feels threatened. There are ways to create safety, which I discuss in Part 3: The Toolbox/T2.1, but it takes time to develop these and it cannot be rushed.

Collaboration

Another helpful aspect is how the professional works with the client to develop a collaborative approach where both sides share a common purpose. With research into the effectiveness of psychotherapy highlighting the importance of "agreement on the goals of the treatment, agreement on the tasks, and the development of a personal bond made up of reciprocal positive feelings" (Ardito & Rabellino, 2011, p. 2), having a collaborative approach where the client is involved in the planning of their own recovery could go a long way in not only building trust but also keeping them engaged and proactive. The same study also found that when a therapist verbally emphasizes a high level of involvement with the client, the alliance is subsequently rated higher (Ardito & Danellino, 2011). This is at the heart of my work: to find a way in which we could work together to map out the client's situation and hopefully make sense of it.

Part of this ongoing collaboration is to remove any presumption regarding how a client is affected by their estrangement. For example, as I am regularly exposed to the negative effects of estrangement, on occasion I would presume a client was similarly devastated and distraught, only to find out they were relieved by the distance. This could possibly be considered a negative bias, but fortunately, it can be repaired quickly by acknowledging with the client where the presumption comes from and validating their reality, including the experiences with family that led to a multitude of emotions, which might include relief.

Autonomy

It was also reported that therapists supporting the client to make their own decisions about family relations was helpful (Blake et al., 2019). This will acknowledge the client's expertise in their own family and their capacity to make the right decisions based on this expertise.

Deeper Exploration

Other helpful encounters involved the therapist addressing the causes and consequences (Blake et al., 2022b), or what I think of as the 'why' and the 'how', i.e., why did it happen and how it has or is currently impacting the client. Looking at causes might involve many accounts of exchanges that might seem insignificant but, in the context of the family history, could be part of a bigger and more damaging pattern. Similarly, exploring the consequences across different layers, like those defined in the *estrangement impact triad*, is helpful in validating the client's world and the challenges they are facing. This includes understanding the *estrangement radius* (see Figure 0.1 in the Introduction) and how an estrangement can have "a negative impact on the individual's relationships with friends, colleagues, and other family members" (Blake et al., 2019, p. 2).

Another aspect of exploration is discovering how exactly to help, especially in the early sessions. This might be tough if the client is unsure of what they hope to achieve in therapy or if their expectations are unrealistic. For example, if a client's desired outcome comes with consequences, such as requesting a professional contact estranged parties to initiate a reconciliation, even though these family members have made it clear they are not interested, this could take a further toll on the familial relationship going forward and might conflict with the professionals' own values around boundaries and autonomy.

Some clients might have a vague concept of being healed but are unsure of what this looks like, and others might be more practically minded and have a list of certain items to address. Exploring what they want or need could come organically through the process of conversing with them, or the outcome might change over the course of the estrangement. Below are some of the potential desired outcomes to keep in mind; although the list is not exhaustive and ideally these will come from the client, it is useful to be aware of them:

- To feel validated in their perspectives and decisions.
- To feel more secure and connected to others in their lives.
- To establish a stronger support network.
- To feel a sense of control over their overwhelming emotions.
- To feel resourced and empowered to manage the challenges they are facing.
- To prepare for a specific event, scenario, or conversation with estranged parties.
- To re-develop a better relationship with one or more estranged parties.

- To accept the situation so they can move forward with their lives.
- To connect with their grief and the losses they have incurred.

Patience

Another characteristic that is essential but might not come easily is patience (Blake et al., 2022b). For example, having the patience to wait and work at the client's own pace before jumping in and answering questions, to hear the same story repeatedly, or to trust the client's judgement and ability to heal, especially when they face setbacks.

Appropriate Sharing

It seems another characteristic of unhelpful encounters was when a counsellor, psychotherapist, or psychologist shared very little and simply nodded or repeated back what the participant had said (Blake et al., 2022b). This suggests that offering opinions and thoughts would be beneficial for the client. While boundaries are often a concern for professionals to ensure the client/therapist dynamic is upheld, sharing their views authentically (Ulrichová, 2014) will go a long way towards building trust as well as providing insight for the client that they may not have previously considered. Sharing thoughts and opinions does not mean the professional needs to share personal experiences, and doing so should be carefully considered. Knowing how much to share and when will be an ongoing process, but each professional needs to be clear of their intent when sharing, i.e., is it to help the client or for personal validation?

Skills Development

Another helpful marker is having practical tools that the client can learn and develop to improve their relationships with themselves and others (Blake et al., 2022b; Ulrichová, 2014). This can vary across different fields of study, including psychology, psychotherapy, coaching, mindfulness, etc., and will enhance both their self-awareness and their ability to express this awareness to others and potentially build or repair bridges.

Psychoeducation

While not featured in the research, another helpful intervention I have found is sharing concepts around topics such as trauma, attachment styles, mental health, physical exercise, and anything else that broadens their understanding. I also regularly suggest books and other materials to absorb in their private time, as this will help them to focus and continue the therapeutic process outside of the sessions, as well as create more talking points for the next session.

Other Considerations

Finally, below are some other considerations I have faced or have been asked about by other therapists.

Should we discuss the perspectives of other family members? Often, we are only presented with one side of the story and feel our work would be enhanced by other versions. While occasionally a client might offer up the perspectives of estranged parties, reflecting on the opposing side might broaden the conversation or induce guilt or shame. It will be hard to know this, and while I would not dismiss this conversation, it would be wise to approach it with compassion.

How much depth should we go into? For example, how far back into the client's or family's history do we go? This will be dependent on how much time the professional has, as well as their training and ability to help the client work through difficult emotions from historical events and, in particular, experiences of abuse.

Should the client attend a therapy session with one or more estranged parties? This is a divisive one if the estranged party is well known to the therapist, as there might be fears of collusion and creating an ambush situation, which could be very upsetting. However, I feel even bad communication is better than no communication, and I generally encourage the client to trust their intuition on how to proceed with this scenario.

So far, we have looked at estrangement through different lenses to get a picture of the look and feel of this diverse phenomenon. Now it's time to explore a more practical focus, examining the different interventions available to us and how to put these together to form a bespoke therapeutic approach for each client.

Part 3

Navigating Estrangement

I appreciate that I am repeating myself when I state this, but I have long held the belief that each estranged person is the true expert when it comes to not just knowing their family but also knowing how we can help them. Naturally, they can lose touch with their own wisdom over the course of time due to the importance of family in society at large, the dense history shared between family members, and the enduring impact of each estrangement. To help my clients effectively become unstuck, I needed to find a way to quickly get to the essence of the situation, but at the time, I wasn't aware of any training exclusively for family estrangement, aside from a few self-help books that were insightful but ultimately didn't offer what my clients needed.

I wondered if I could improve the conversation between us by broadening both mine and their understanding of the estrangement and then getting a more accurate sense of what they were dealing with and how we could work together. To do this, I thought back to my research on the experiences of family estrangement and specifically the paper I wrote entitled "The Changing Impact and Challenges of Familial Estrangement" (Melvin & Hickey, 2021). To provide clarity to the academic review board, I created a participant overview chart that acted as a quick reference visual aid and is condensed in Figure III.1. An obvious aspect of the overview chart was identifying which family member the participant was estranged from, but there were other aspects I felt were necessary to highlight. One such aspect I found interesting was how the experience of a voluntary estrangement was different from an involuntary estrangement, and so this was added separately to the overview chart, referred to as the *estrangement nature*. Another important finding was the difference between a direct estrangement, i.e., where estranged parties overtly told each other of the situation or estrangement, and an indirect estrangement, i.e., where the estrangement has not been communicated. This is referred to as the *estrangement approach* and was also added to the overview. The initial draft included the participant ID number, the estrangement nature, i.e., 'voluntary' or 'involuntary', the estrangement approach, i.e., 'direct' or 'indirect', and the family member or members from whom each participant was estranged.

Over time, I felt this paradigm needed to be expanded given that it had the potential to act as an educational and therapeutic tool to gather necessary information

DOI: 10.4324/9781003362203-10

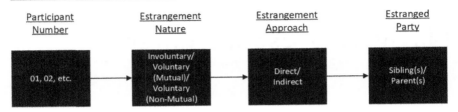

Figure III.1 Research Participant Overview

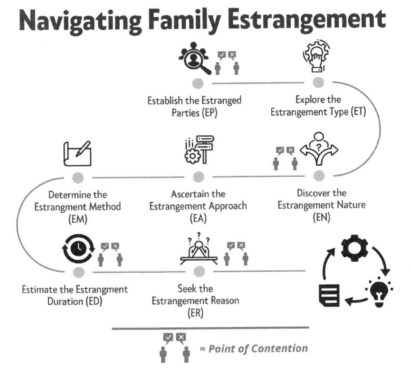

Figure III.2 The Estrangement Inquiry Model

and draw out each client's estrangement landscape. Eventually, the estranged family members or parties were prioritized and acted as the initial data point. The estrangement type was then included, followed by the estrangement method, the duration of the estrangement, and finally, the cause or reason for the estrangement, which is often difficult to accurately determine. The revised seven-step mapping process (see Figure III.2) emerged from these revisions.

Table III.1 Estrangement Map Template

Client Name: [Name]

	[Estrangement Type(s)]	[Estrangement Nature]	[Estrangement Approach]	[Estrangement Method]	[Estrangement Duration]	[Estrangement Reason(s)]	Notes for EP#
[Family Member #1]	[Estrangement Type(s)]	[Estrangement Nature]	[Estrangement Approach]	[Estrangement Method]	[Estrangement Duration]	[Estrangement Reason(s)]	Notes for EP#1
[Family Member #2]	[Estrangement Type(s)]	[Estrangement Nature]	[Estrangement Approach]	[Estrangement Method]	[Estrangement Duration]	[Estrangement Reason(s)]	Notes for EP#2
[Family Member #3]	[Estrangement Type(s)]	[Estrangement Nature]	[Estrangement Approach]	[Estrangement Method]	[Estrangement Duration]	[Estrangement Reason(s)]	Notes for EP#3
[Family Member #...]	[Estrangement Type(s)]	[Estrangement Nature]	[Estrangement Approach]	[Estrangement Method]	[Estrangement Duration]	[Estrangement Reason(s)]	Notes for EP#...

General Notes/Observations
Add details of specific struggles the client might have, other considerations outside of the estrangement dynamic and any potential approach/interventions

The eventual goal of using this approach is to create an *estrangement map* (see Table III.1). This is effectively a table of eight columns with a row for each estranged person. Each column represents an answer derived from the seven steps in the model, with the eighth column reserved for any professional notes and observations. The estrangement types, nature, communicative approach and method, estrangement duration (s), and finally the reasoning are all included. It must be noted that this will obviously be one sided, as it will come solely from the client's perspective. Unless the client shares the views of the EP, which might be biased, this is all we can work with unless estranged parties partake in the sessions. As this process is new to the client, they may not have all the answers either; this is fine as the goal is to explore their situation and views thereof to see what comes up. As such, I reiterate the need for openness and curiosity from professionals.

Another consideration when walking through this process is being cognizant of areas of potential conflict or contention for the client, both with their family of origin and those amongst the estrangement community. Due to the diverse and divisive nature of estrangements, at some point the client might be met with strongly opposing views and experiences on one or more of the seven considerations covered in the model. For example, if the client reveals who they are estranged from on an online support forum, such as a son or daughter, an estranged person from the opposing side, such as a parent, may respond negatively to any sharing. Similarly, if the client reveals they chose their estrangement, irrespective of their reasoning, they may get a negative response from someone who did not choose their estrangement.

I will now break down each step in the model. I would ask each professional to take the time to familiarize themselves with each step and its importance to the overall working process. If, at some point, they decide to try this model with a client, they might return to this section as a reference or if something resonates with them. Later, they might integrate other studies with this model to broaden its application to their work, and they might frame their understanding around their own family, which is perfectly ok if it does not negatively affect interpreting a client's details later. I believe each individual and their estrangement must be viewed on their own merits and based on the information provided, but this does not mean we cannot lean on personal experiences to offer a hypothetical understanding. This might land with the client or it might not; what matters most is that they are genuinely relaying to the client that they are trying to connect with their experience and are not minimizing any aspect of it.

Chapter 7

The Model

Before I go on, I want to be clear on one thing: the purpose of this model is not to dredge up the past or keep the client locked into analysis paralysis. The purpose of this approach is to improve the quality of conversation between the client and professional; to get a focused sense of the bigger picture of the client's reality; to aid their own reflective process through data gathering and the insight it provides; and perhaps most importantly, to discover how we can effectively help the client. There may be a hesitancy to this approach at first, as the client may not have reflected on these specific questions before or cannot see the merit, but professional curiosity might evoke curiosity in them. Timing is important, and while they might encourage the client to try this, if it appears they prefer the comfort of familiarity, despite how distressing it might be, then we can't force this. A client might request to come back to this approach later, when they do feel ready, or after a period of reflection.

This process looks at the current status of the estrangement, being aware that it might change at some point in time and for a variety of reasons. So bear this in mind, because this approach can be used iteratively after a period of weeks, months, or years and/or if circumstances have changed, and each review might highlight a change in needs or priorities and inform the direction of the sessions going forward. It is important to note that it is also not the goal to create a perfect depiction of the family but rather to introduce the client to ideas and a reflective process to elaborate and expand their understanding. Some answers to each step may come quickly, whereas others come from deeper moments of pause and reflection. Which is why nothing should be rushed, allowing plenty of time for each step or question to be explored, even if they are met with blank faces or do not appear to have a definitive answer.

Step 1: Establish the Estranged Parties (EP)

Potential Outcomes

1. Gather a disparate list of all the estranged parties involved, including primary, secondary, and consequential estranged family members.

DOI: 10.4324/9781003362203-11

2. Obtain an understanding of the family structure and history.
3. Get a sense of the scale of the impact of the estrangement as well as the losses incurred by the client.
4. Enquire about who within the family the client is not estranged from and if these non-estranged family members are a source of support.

Background

As estrangement is fundamentally a relationship phenomenon, it is necessary to begin by looking at the family relations affected by it. By doing this, we can create a separation between each individual involved and avoid generalities. As previously mentioned, the acronym EP refers to one or more estranged parties the client is estranged from. Alternatively, others might use EF to denote estranged family; however, for the purposes of this book, I will use EP going forward.

Families come in different forms, such as nuclear families, i.e., traditional two-parent families; single-parent families; extended families, i.e., connections shaped by marriage or by blood, that fall outside the nuclear family; blended or step-family, i.e., connections shaped by death and separation or divorce and subsequent new relationships, including re-marriage; and grand-parent families, where grandparents are the primary caregivers. As such, almost anyone considered part of the family will be directly and indirectly impacted by the estrangement, such as grandchildren, nieces and nephews, cousins, aunts, and uncles, etc. The more parties affected, the harder the situation will be. For example, there might be more uncomfortable conversations about the situation, fear of judgement, and/or doubt around how to manage upcoming family events; there might be more potential for pressure from non-estranged family members to reconcile with the EP; and there will be more losses incurred, amplifying feelings of isolation and grief. This step might highlight the support a client has and which family members they are not estranged from. This will be particularly relevant if, in their later years, they face potential health problems or the death of a partner, thus becoming widowed (Gilligan et al., 2021).

Perhaps most importantly, this step identifies the client's own role or position within the family, which is essential to understanding their experience. There are several ways to categorize estrangement, but one common way is from the estrangement perspective, i.e., parental estrangement, adult child estrangement, sibling estrangement, etc. This distinction will influence their experiences, as, for example, with research indicating there is greater shame for women than men (Agllias, 2017), perhaps this will be more so if the client or their EP is a mother, daughter, and/or sister.

Inquiry

One initial question is: are any of the EP estranged from each other? This might give insight into the intergenerational nature of the family issues, i.e., patterns of estrangement across different relationships and over different periods of time. I have found that this step in the model might highlight any common denominators amongst the EP, i.e., those whom the client feels may have contributed more to the issues than others.

This might also be particularly evident if the client expresses a desire to reconnect with a certain EP but fears the reaction of one or more primary EPs. We will discuss the different types and natures of estrangement in the coming steps, but Step One may begin by highlighting how not all estrangements are the same and how each EP should be viewed individually as well as collectively.

If an EP is a young child this will be particularly painful, with increased feelings of guilt and shame. The idea that a child will in any way be affected by the problems of adults, over which they have no say or influence, can deeply hurt those who feel responsible for or have contributed in any way to these problems.

Point of Contention

As mentioned, it is important to use the information presented during this process to get a sense of the diverse challenges the client may be experiencing now or in the future, in particular among their extended social circles.

In Step One, as the client reveals their list of the EP, thus offering their own subjective perspective and position in the family, if they were to do so in some other setting, this reveal might be met with strong disagreements and potential judgement from those who represent an opposing perspective or whose experience is different from the clients. For example, if a client is a daughter estranged from a parent, such as their mother, and they then share this with someone who has a close relationship with their own mother, the power of their attachment to this parent may result in a response that is less than compassionate and is more aligned with disbelief, disappointment, and maybe even disgust. This inability to see past the subjective is critical as it may mimic family dynamics, where the client's feelings or needs may be dismissed in favor of the EP, and these experiences may further the client's feelings of rejection. Similarly, if the client discloses she is a daughter and their EP is a mother in an estrangement support group, a collection of those mothers estranged from their daughters may instinctively react defensively or even offensively if they feel threatened by having their own experiences minimized.

This *subjective blur* can prevent individuals, both with their own experiences of estrangement and with no experience at all, from viewing another person's estrangement based on its own merits and circumstances and can fuel the societal stigma surrounding estrangement. As they reach this point in the model, a professional might check with the client to see if they have had any negative experiences since they shared this. Validating these experiences is another step towards developing trust, as the client will genuinely believe they are accepted by the professional.

Step 2: Explore the Estrangement Type (ET)

Outcomes

1. Determine the specific estrangement type for each person listed in Step One.
2. Determine if the EP is still part of their life and in what capacity.
3. Determine if the estrangement type has ever changed and why.

Background

As mentioned earlier, it is a common misconception that estrangement is just when family members are not talking to each other. In fact, this was how I personally conceptualized estrangement until I interviewed a research participant who identified as being estranged but yet spoke to them regularly. This emphasized to me the complexity of family interactions and why or how an individual might maintain contact while also maintaining distance. Soon after, I discovered the work of Professor Agllias, who has done extensive work exploring the perspectives of parents and adult sons and daughters and who has identified eight types of estrangement (Agllias, 2016). It is important to understand how each type relates to each of the EPs and how the type can change over time. The Estrangement Type (ET) will also provide some initial insight into how a person became estranged from each EP.

Physical Estrangement

This is when there is no or very limited face-to-face contact. i.e., there is a geographical distance separating them. There are several reasons why this might be chosen: it might follow a large argument when there is no desire to be around the EP; it might be part of a slow distancing process where the EP does not show up at the house or attend events; it might be chosen because it is felt that the EP either already knows the issues and feels no compulsion to confront them; or if the client or the EP do not feel comfortable discussing them. Safety is a key consideration when this type of distance is put in place, and I have heard some different examples of how a physical estrangement is maintained, including moving to another country without informing the EP.

Emotional Estrangement

This type of estrangement occurs when there is regular or irregular contact with the EP, but there are no meaningful conversations or the EP chooses not to share any personal information with each other. Generally, the core issues are not discussed, and exchanges might be initially superficial and polite but denigrate over the course of any visit. This can be very stressful, especially if communication becomes passive-aggressive, so there may be anxiety for the client about the next potential visit. Some estrangements begin at this point and eventually transition to physical estrangement after some time, again for a variety of reasons, such as initial fears around consequences from the EP as well as the potential impact of more distance on those caught up in the *estrangement radius*.

Cyclical Estrangement

This is when there has been an ongoing cycle of estrangements and reconnections over an extended period. With research highlighting how it is not uncommon to cycle in and out of estrangement up to five times or more (Blake et al., 2015), it is useful to put a name to this while also discovering which iteration the client is currently in.

Absent Estrangement

This is commonly the result of a divorce or separation of a marriage and the residual impact this might have on different family members and time spent together. For example, due to a parent subsequently moving out and a child's access to this parent being limited.

Mutually-Disengaged Estrangement

This is when each EP accepts the estrangement situation and no efforts are made to reconnect. This may come after a period of intense conflict, where it is felt that it is best not to engage in any form of communication with each other. This mutuality may not be the initial response, and there may be efforts made to make amends or maintain some or all contact. Over time, as the estrangement endures, efforts are not reciprocated, and the relationship effectively disappears, they may come to accept the situation as is. Professor Lynn Fay, who for several years has run online support groups for estranged parents, refers to this as *counter-estranging*, in response to parents' unsuccessful efforts to reconnect with their adult children.

Inherited Estrangement

This is estrangement through an association with another EP as opposed to something personal with the client. Examples of this could be grandparents who become estranged from their grandchildren due to a divorce (Gair, 2017) or cousins who become estranged from their cousins because their respective parents are estranged. With inherited estrangements, the relationship dynamic or distance is effectively passed from one generation to the next, and in some cases, the EP barely know each other as there was never any contact or time spent together to build a relationship.

Secondary Estrangements

This is a consequential estrangement where the EP becomes estranged due to their closeness with the primary EP. Different from an inherited estrangement in that this is chosen, examples include a daughter eventually becoming estranged from a father after primarily estranging from a mother, as it is felt the father is supporting his wife. Thus, this type may be the result of loyalties or the EP being forced to take a side. An example of this is siblings becoming secondarily estranged after one becomes primarily estranged from a parent.

Self-Protecting Estrangement

This type is driven by the need to estrange from others who are perceived to be close to the EP and thus to protect oneself, whether it is protecting privacy or personal safety. The primary EP may be friends with those who fall under this estrangement type, and thus, there are concerns around what they might relay back. These EP may be innocent and even unaware of the estrangement, but due to any damaging behaviors from the EP, such as weaponizing the client's personal information, this may be felt necessary.

Inquiry

At this point, after sharing the eight different types of estrangement, a professional might ask the client to write down the current type for each EP. The client might be unsure at first of the type or confused by the various types. This is completely fine, but I would encourage them to reflect on it in their own time. There is also a strong chance the type of estrangement will vary between different EPs. This could be due to differences in issues between individuals or circumstances as to why they became estranged.

There may be one type that resonates with them more than others, but there may also be several types, and this is fine as well. It is important to note that the type might change frequently over an extended period for a variety of reasons: it could be due to emotional factors, such as guilt; relationship factors, such as a change in the family dynamic or behaviors; or social factors, such as a family event or family crisis. This change reflects the enduring nature of family relationships and the long-term need for support and resources to manage them. It might also highlight periods of reconnection with family and then subsequent estrangements, and it might be worthwhile exploring these periods and what happened.

Step 3: Discover the Estrangement Nature (EN)

Outcomes

1. Determine if estrangement was chosen or not for each person listed in Step One.
2. Determine how the client feels about the EN.

Background

One thing highlighted during my own research was how the experience and impact of estrangement can be different for those who chose it versus those who didn't, with those who were involuntarily estranged describing feelings of devastation, whereas those who were voluntarily estranged describing feelings of relief (Melvin & Hickey, 2021). While there is no rule for how a person will respond, it is clear that this information is important to elaborate on the three Estrangement Natures (EN) and how they relate to their unique situation. The nature offered will be perspective-dependent, in that it focuses on the client and not the other EP, and as such, the EN could be different between them.

Voluntary/Non-Mutual

This is effectively a single-sided estrangement in that the client chose and is maintaining the distance, but the EP is not. This non-mutuality refers to the EP regularly or sporadically reaching out to the client to maintain some contact, irrespective of the intent for this contact, which may be another source of stress for the client. While unable to know the true intent behind contacts from the EP, a professional may have to defer to the client's interpretation.

While some might feel the aforementioned relief (Melvin & Hickey, 2021), due to the weight of the decision, others may experience powerful pressure and doubt, and thus, they may need validation of their decision with a strong emphasis on the reasoning.

Voluntary/Mutual

This is similar to the previously mentioned "Mutually Disengaged" estrangement type in that both sides of an estrangement are maintaining the distance. This nature may be the result of years of distance between the EP, and an acceptance from one or both sides that the relationship will not change. While the nature may begin as voluntary/non-mutual, the EP may eventually cease making contact. Due to the breakdown of communication, it may not be known if the nature is voluntary/mutual until it is apparent during important life events when the EP does not reach out. Despite accepting the situation, there may still be a great deal of anger, anxiety, and grief as nothing has been resolved between the EP and the core issues still linger in the heart and mind of the client.

Involuntary

Considered a one-sided estrangement in that the client did not choose it. With this, there will be a greater chance of shock if the client realizes they have been cut out; depending on the Estrangement Approach (see next step), they may not have known for some time. They may be particularly shocked if there is no apparent history of estrangement in the family history and/or if the relationship is so important to them that they themselves would never have considered it. They may also feel devastated by how the relationship with the EP was devalued to this extent and embarrassed if the client fears others in the family knew of the estrangement but they did not. There is a sense of powerlessness that can come from an involuntary estrangement, where the client might feel they have no ability to positively influence the relationship. This powerlessness may play out in other areas of life, where the clients try to control anything they can, including studying voraciously to understand any aspect of psychology and relationships in order to make sense of their estrangement. The client's need to control might also extend to working with a professional and rejecting their help in an effort to manage any perceived power dynamics. This will take patience and understanding to persevere with the client in helping them lower their defences to allow their vulnerability in.

Inquiry

The nature of the estrangement may have already been mentioned in conversation or alluded to with statements like "they don't talk to me anymore" or "they cut me out", but it might be worthwhile explicitly asking if the estrangement was by choice or not. Simply acknowledging this dynamic may help validate their experience and how difficult it must be for them. However, the EN might also be hard to establish if there have been recurring patterns of distance at different points in time by different family members, making it hard to establish if it was voluntarily chosen by the client or EP. Having the conversation about the nature of their estrangement may unlock the door to a deeper exploration of the impact as well as whether improving the relationship is viable or desirable. I would also like to highlight how loss and grief will be experienced irrespective of the nature (Agllias, 2017); even those who chose their estrangement are not exempt and can experience the same grief as those who did not.

Point of Contention

As mentioned, the EN depends heavily on the client's perspective, which might differ greatly from the EP. For example, one of the EPs might say they were cut out of the client's life, but the client might say they had no choice but to estrange, and thus both will consider this involuntary for themselves. In other examples, the EP may have been pressurized to take a side and initiate an estrangement out of fear of other losses. This difference in perspectives and the inability to recognize the other side might be the core of the family issues and eventual estrangement and could negatively affect the chances of a reconciliation, assuming one or both sides wish this.

Step 4: Ascertain the Estrangement Approach (EA)

Outcomes

1. Determine if the estrangement has been communicated to each person listed in Step One.
2. Determine broader communication patterns within the family.
3. Determine how the family has responded to the estrangement situation.

Background

Another important dimension is the Estrangement Approach (EA), i.e., the manner in which this has or has not been communicated between the client and each EP. This information will offer some insights into patterns of avoidance within the family, rules around expression, and how safety is prioritized over openness and addressing key issues. The following are two approaches.

Direct

This is when the EP is informed overtly of the estrangement and perhaps, although not always, the reasoning behind it. This approach could increase the chance of confrontation and a stressful conversation, and due to the triggering nature and past experiences of negative interactions, directness might be avoided at all costs, so the client or the EP might desire to directly discuss family problems, but this might be deflected or shut down completely by others. Also, due to the stress and history of negative behaviors, it might be difficult to relay the reasoning confidently and cohesively as the clients or the EP struggle to communicate in a direct manner. This EA may not necessarily provide certainty, as the reason, while relayed clearly, may make no sense to the client or the EP.

Indirect

This is when the EP is not directly informed of the estrangement, and this can be done through blocking on social media, not responding to phone calls or text messages, or hanging up the phone when they realize who is contacting them (Gilligan et al., 2021). As a result, the EP is left to guess where they stand as well as how long this might go on for. If the estrangement has not been directly communicated to the EP, there may be more uncertainty around the reasoning for the estrangement and the future of the relationship.

Inquiry

The client may need their estrangement approach validated, although the conversation might be more about how they wish they had approached it as opposed to what happened, with the goal of learning from the experience.

Step 5: Determine the Estrangement Method (EM)

Outcomes

1. Determine how the estrangement has been communicated for each person listed in Step One.
2. Determine if there was a lot left unsaid, or too much said.

Background

While the previous step explored *whether* the family communicates, this step explores *how* the family communicates. The Estrangement Method (EM) used to communicate will offer some more insight into the family dynamic, why there is so much uncertainty, and if there is an opportunity for further discussions with the EP. For example, if communication was via email, there is a chance of misinterpretation, but it might also mean this is the preferred medium and should be used for future exchanges. The methods can be broken down into three categories.

Synchronous Methods

These methods involve two-way communications in real time and can include traditional conversations, such as in-person conversations or phone calls, as well as digital mediums. With these methods there may be an instant reaction, which may not be desirable for some. Alas, while all these are considered live interactions, a phone call may feel more remote as there is no face-to-face contact. However, while digital mediums involve being in different geographical locations, there is still the chance for face-to-face interactions, such as on Zoom or Skype, and a simple look from the EP can be triggering and thus not necessarily safe. Again, as with the direct approach, the estrangement situation might not be obvious if the communication style is passive or passive-aggressive and can be left open to interpretation or misinterpretation.

Asynchronous Methods

These methods involve one-way delayed communications and can include electronic mail, text or video messages, or handwritten letters. Other examples include not replying to messages, not returning calls, or excluding them from an event. Due to the offline nature of these EM, they may appear safer and give both the sender and receiver time to think about their responses. That is not to say everyone will make a concerted effort to think their response through, and they might be so triggered by a message that they respond quickly and defensively and may later come to regret this. One issue with these methods is that the exchanges are now documented forever. While this is beneficial in one respect in that it gives the receiver time to read and space to absorb what was said, a letter might be used against the sender and worsen the overall situation.

Aside from the above, other methods that could be considered asynchronous include using a third party. Being told of an estrangement from others, either in the family or outside, can lead to feelings of embarrassment as others knew about this before them, but might also trigger feelings of anger as they may feel this method is disrespectful.

Non-Synchronous Methods

These methods involve no communication and may be the result of a long-term process of not interacting with family at all and communication eventually dissolving. This method could also be the result of inherited estrangements from extended family, where the opportunity to communicate was never there in the first place or was frowned upon by other family members who are similarly estranged from these EP.

Inquiry

There may be in-depth and ongoing discussions about exchanges between the client and EP, but there is more to learn underneath the words, i.e., what exactly are people saying and why? While the terms "synchronous", "asynchronous", or "non-synchronous" might not be explicitly used, asking the client how the estrangement and the issues were relayed for each person will indicate preferences for communication, i.e., email versus text versus letter.

Asking them about the chosen method also helps to get a sense of the client's instincts, i.e., why they feel this method was chosen, and were there others involved in the decisions? The manner chosen may make communication hard to understand or even unreachable if there are issues with technology, and the client may wish to explore other EM to get more clarity from the EP.

Step 6: Estimate the Current Estrangement Duration (ED)

Outcomes

1. Determine how recent the latest estrangement is.
2. Estimate how long the estrangement has lasted.
3. Establish past cycles of estrangement.

Background

The dimension of time was not one I initially reflected on greatly when it came to estrangement. While my time as a therapist has taught me that time does not heal all wounds, I did eventually discover how time was a factor when living with estrangement. Time might determine how comfortable a person feels talking about the situation. One research participant shared how two years ago she would not have been able to talk about her situation (Melvin & Hickey, 2021), and this may have been due to the raw emotion and deep uncertainty she felt over the losses she experienced. It quickly dawned on me to always factor in the Estrangement Duration (ED) when exploring my client's reality, but naturally, how it relates to each person will vary.

The client might want to talk about the situation a lot, perhaps repetitively for many weeks and months. There is no universal point when someone is ready to open up, but when they are ready and begin to talk, they may not come to any satisfactory conclusion. If the estrangement has gone on for an extended period, the client might be desperate to delve into the specifics of the family history and interactions and might dismiss any efforts made to connect with their emotions. There is no right or wrong here; this is just where the client is, but knowing they are being heard will be very helpful. Time might dictate the chances or even desire for reconciliation, particularly if it was quite recent, and thus, the client may fear compromising this or feel they are being disloyal by discussing the issues publicly. It might depend on how long they have endured the triad of psychological, relational, and other social challenges. Similarly, more time spent with no support might mean more anxiety due to the uncertainty and lack of hope for a resolution. This might also influence how comfortable they are discussing their situation, and more time may also mean more reflection on the family history and the reasons behind an estrangement, and I feel it is important to honour any insights the client may have garnered.

Time might lead to more tension between the EP (Gilligan et al., 2021), especially if the core issues have not been discussed. Time will indicate if there has ever been a relationship at all and if estrangement is the norm for the client and their EP. Another dimension to this is that there may have been no demarcation point, so the time might be unknown. This might be another source of distress as the client struggles to quantify how long this has gone on for or perhaps overestimate the time, which is a trait for those who experience post-traumatic stress disorder (PTSD) and develop a distorted sense of time (Vicario & Felmingham, 2018).

Interestingly, the duration of an estrangement varies depending on who the EP is. For example, an estrangement from the father can last 7.9 years, 7.7 years for brothers, 7.4 years for sisters, 5.5 years for mothers, 5.2 years for sons, and 3.8 years for daughters (Blake et al., 2015). Again, I acknowledge the lack of representation for other family roles, such as grandparents. What stands out for me is how the experience of estrangement from males is longer than that of females. As a man, I can only hypothesize that stubbornness and pride may mask a vulnerability that prevents reconciliation, but that is purely my own theory and not based on any research.

Inquiry

The obvious starting question will be "How long have you been estranged from [insert EP name]?". The client might not know this instantly and will need time to reflect; if they can recall it quickly, it might reflect the recentness of the estrangement or its impact on the client. When enquiring about the time for each EP, asking how they have been over this period or what they have done with their lives over this time might be helpful. I have found that many of my clients report feelings of being stuck internally, where they struggle to find a way forward in life. Despite how they feel, they may have made actionable changes, such as changing careers, returning to or completing college, meeting their partner, starting a family, or moving into a home. They may have also faced many challenges over this period, such as sicknesses, deaths, and failures, all without the support of the EP. In fact, due to the distance that estrangement brings, the EP may have no awareness that these events have occurred, and with the passing of time, there may be no desire to share. Inquiring if the client feels too much time has passed for a reconnection to be possible might be appropriate to validate the client's feelings on this.

Point of Contention

Another reality to consider is how the various EPs may potentially disagree strongly about when the estrangement started. This could present an issue if there is a chance to reconnect with the EP and discuss the issues. When the topic of dates and times comes up, it could present itself as just another "thing" to disagree on and a further recreation of conflicts and power struggles. With the client or the EP refusing to back down, this might become a source of frustration and sadness as 1) time becomes another roadblock to a better relationship, and 2) the disagreements over time might highlight a lack of concern for how long this has actually gone on for, particularly if it has not affected the EP as much as the client.

Step 7: Seek the Estrangement Reason (ER)

Outcomes

1. Determine the reason for the estrangement for each person listed in Step One, if one exists.
2. Explore the broader impact.
3. Discuss any lessons learned and how these can be integrated into their lives going forward.

Background

With research highlighting the need to address the causes of the estrangement (Blake et al., 2022), this might be the most important step; however, this might also be quite hard depending on several factors:

- The number of EPs, as per Step One. If there are a large number of EPs, the reasons may be lost in the sea of people affected. As a result of years of ongoing estrangements, some family members will be caught up in the riptide, and the client may find there is less and less engagement from others with little identifiable reason other than they are connected to EP.
- If the type of estrangement type is physical, as per Step Two, there may be no contact at all and no opportunity to establish the reason.

- If the estrangement nature is involuntary, as per Step Three. If the client did not choose the estrangement, there is a chance they do not know the reason or may not understand the reasoning. If the nature is voluntary, then there is a greater chance the client will know as they chose it, but this does not necessarily ease any uncertainty or doubt.
- If the estrangement approach is indirect, as per Step Four, the client may not have been explicitly told the reason.
- If the estrangement method is non-synchronous, as per Step Five, again the client may not have been explicitly told the reason.
- How long the estrangement duration has been, as per Step Six. If the estrangement is recent, the client might not have been told the reason; alternatively, if the estrangement has gone on for a long time, there may be important family information unknown to the client, and what they do know may only scratch the surface.

Every aspect of an estrangement has the potential to be both complicated and divisive, but perhaps none more so than the *Estrangement Reason* (ER), as the perspective of each family member can differ. For example, the reason an adult child describes will differ from that of their parents, although research suggests parents are more likely to attribute the estrangement to external factors (Linden & Sillence, 2021). Another study found that "Parents reported that their primary reason for becoming estranged stemmed from their children's objectionable relationships or sense of entitlement, whereas adult children most frequently attributed their estrangement to their parents' toxic behavior or feeling unsupported and unaccepted" (Carr et al., 2015, p. 1). Similarly, siblings will cite different and opposing reasons.

To get a broader understanding of the estrangement, it is useful to delve into the research to establish the common reasons others have cited. Although I have consciously chosen not to separate the experiences of estrangement, some studies choose to isolate adult children from parents and from siblings. I feel it is important to see how conflicting the reasons put forward might be to get a sense of the divisiveness of this phenomenon. This will also be particularly relevant if a client wishes to explore the idea of reconnecting with the EP and how each side might perceive the problems.

For no specific reason, I will start with the adult son's and daughter's perspective, then parents, and finally siblings. I would also like to acknowledge the other roles among family members impacted but not featured in the literature. Hopefully, in time, this will be addressed in future studies.

Perspective: Adult Sons and Daughters

Abuse in its different forms is found to be a common reason, with both emotional abuse (Agllias, 2016; Blake et al., 2015) and physical and sexual abuse cited (Agllias, 2016; Carr et al., 2015; Linden & Sillence, 2021; Scharp et al., 2015).

With emotional abuse, one paper found the percentage was highest for mothers (77%) as opposed to fathers (59%) (Blake et al., 2015).

A mismatch of expectations about family roles and relationships is another common reason (Blake et al., 2015) and appears to be more common with mothers at 65% than with fathers at 55%. This could manifest as a role reversal, where they are forced to adopt the responsibilities and duties of one or both parents, including tending to their own needs as well as those of their siblings. This is something I have experienced with my own clients, who are deeply frustrated by their parents unreasonableness and the pressures placed on them.

A clash of personalities and values is next cited, and again, it seems higher with mothers at 53% and fathers at 44% (Blake et al., 2015). This is not a huge surprise, especially if there are several strong-minded family members who feel very passionately about one or more issues and are unprepared to compromise. They could have vastly different outlooks on life and values (Gilligan et al., 2015; Pillemer, 2020) based on their upbringing and the generational gap that shaped these values.

Poor parenting and neglect were also cited as reasons (Agllias, 2016; Blake et al., 2015; Carr et al., 2015; Linden & Sillence, 2021; Scharp et al., 2015), and neglect specifically differs from other forms of abuse in that it is the "omission of caretaking behavior" (Mennen et al., 2010, p. 2).

Issues surrounding mental health and traumatic family events are grouped together in one study (Blake et al., 2015), with 47% for mothers and 36% for fathers, respectively, and several of my clients attributed their parents behavior to undiagnosed mental health issues. There are problems with this, as the client may not be qualified to make this assessment, and if it is true, the mental health issues often remain undiagnosed and thus untreated. As the parent has no support, the client might feel they have no choice but to distance themselves, particularly if the parent does not acknowledge or take responsibility for their health. Traumatic family events can range from a tragic death to a relationship breakdown, but they could be anything that rocks the family's stability.

Finally, while divorce is a common reason cited for parents (Linden & Sillence, 2021; Pillemer, 2020), it is cited less so for adult sons and daughters. This could highlight how a divorce can be experienced differently between family roles and, thus, not always felt to be the root cause. Alas, the division a marital breakdown brings might also create a division in loyalty between adult children and parents, leading to estrangement, and practically, as one parent may have to move out of the family home, they may have less opportunity to offer insight into the family dynamics and express their perspectives.

Perspective: Mothers/Fathers

A common reason cited by parents is a mismatch in expectations about family roles (Gilligan et al., 2021) and relationships, with 33% for daughters and 30% for sons (Blake et al., 2015). This highlights how generational gaps and societal changes over periods spanning decades can lead to rifts in families. With the parents I have worked with, many felt their adult sons and daughters expected them to provide constant support, such as financial aid, when they were more than capable of looking after themselves, or they were expected to always be available and to drop any plans at the last minute.

Relationship choices are another reason, with marriage issues between the adult child's partner having a negative impact on the relationship with the parent (Dorrance Hall, 2016; Gilligan et al., 2015). Similarly, if a mother disapproves of their partner of choice, this could lead to an estrangement (Gilligan et al., 2021). Another factor was how parents felt their adult children prioritized other relationships, such as with a partner or spouse and with the other parent. (Agllias, 2015; Carr et al., 2015; Schoppe-Sullivan et al., 2023).

As mentioned, issues relating to divorce were commonly cited, with 50% for daughters and 37% for sons (Blake et al., 2015), and interestingly, in his research into estrangement, Pillemer found divorce weakened the bond with a father more than a mother (Pillemer, 2020). Another study, which featured 1,035 mothers estranged from their sons and/or daughters found the majority of the participants (79.1%) felt family members turned their adult children against them, and in particular, the biological father, the EP's own children, or a spouse (Schoppe-Sullivan et al., 2023).

Traumatic events were listed by parents as a common reason, with 39% for estrangement from daughters and 28% for sons (Blake et al., 2015). Examples include a tragic death, with one study finding that mothers could become estranged from their adult children after the death of a father, although this is dependent on previous tensions and strains in the relationship (Gilligan et al., 2021).

Mental health problems were also cited by parents (Blake et al., 2015), with 62.4% of mothers in one study feeling their child's mental health was a reason (Schoppe-Sullivan et al., 2023). This also includes issues of addiction and alcohol abuse, including behaving abusively under the influence (Gilligan et al., 2021). Emotional abuse has also been cited as a common reason by parents (Blake et al., 2015).

Perspective: Brothers and Sisters

As with the other perspectives, a mismatch in expectations about family roles and relationships was cited as the most common reason, with 57% for sisters and 48% for brothers (Blake et al., 2015). Coordination of care for an elderly parent can impact the sibling relationship, especially if one sibling is providing more frequent care than other siblings (Blake et al., 2022b; Khodyakov & Carr, 2009).

A clash of personality or values is also cited here (Blake et al., 2015), and an example of this could be conflicting values around responsibility and support for an elderly or sick parent. It could be any aspect of a personality, including a general attitude and a lack of respect for boundaries. Emotional abuse between siblings is also mentioned (Blake et al., 2015, 2022), highlighting how frequently this might occur within families.

One aspect I have found is how one or more parents played a powerful role in propagating sibling estrangement, particularly through favoritism. This is where one or more siblings are prioritized over others for a variety of reasons, some of which may not be explicitly named. My own clients have often felt that one sibling was designated as the golden child, and their achievements were celebrated over others. Perhaps the golden child masks an insecurity within the family, whereas other siblings don't quite meet the expectations. Scapegoating may play a part in this, as other siblings are painted as the black sheep. Sibling order may lead to favoritism, but I have found it is not exclusive to any specific position, i.e., the favorite could be the youngest, eldest, or middle child. Other factors could be superficial, such as a sibling's appearance.

Traumatic events, including events involving family, are commonly cited (Blake et al., 2015). The death of a parent may lead to a rift between siblings, including regarding differences in how they grieve and if there are issues with inheritance (Blake et al., 2022b) and power of attorney (Khodyakov & Carr, 2009).

Perspectives: All

Perspectives aside, drug abuse has been cited generally as another factor (Conti, 2015), and understandably, any problem with addiction is tragic and will place a huge emotional toll on a family. Having the support of local services might help with this, but these might not be available or there may be no willingness to use them, which will add to the strain and perhaps prompt family members to distance themselves as it is too much to bear.

The experience of emotional abuse is consistent across all, but this begs the question: Why? This type of abuse can be tough to name clearly, as the abusive behaviors might be more covert and subtle as opposed to the more overt physical abuse. It is also harder to challenge these types of behaviors, as they can be denied or deflected. The client may have never shared their experiences of abuse before and be fearful of the consequences of doing so, such as further divisions in the family. However, irrespective of the type of abuse, the impact is no less powerful, and a voluntary EN would be understandable in these cases to ease any distress and heal (Agllias, 2016).

Reasons within Reasons

There is so much more to each isolated reason and so much dense history, which will take time to explore. The reasons a client cites might not be the actual reasons or reflect the full picture. They may be something they were told, such as ideas that society or those in their peer network tell them are the problem, or ideas that stem from generations long past, influenced by inherited traumas.

Another difficult aspect is how the client will have a combination of both good and bad memories and experiences with the EP. Even in the most difficult and damaging relationships, there are times of fun and even love, which obscure the lines of how a client might view and feel about the EP, as they can recognize both their good and bad traits. They might also feel guilt for focusing on the negative aspects of the relationship when there were strong and genuinely positive aspects, and validating how nuanced this is will go a long way to helping the client feel safe and understood.

Inquiry

Simply asking, "Are you estranged?" might kick off this step, but it might be akin to entering a rabbit hole and staying there for quite some time. While a client might automatically share the events, both recent and historical, that led to the estrangement, the deeper reasoning may not be clear. The reasons might be obvious with the primary estranged parties but less so with others, such as inherited estrangements from extended family. Also, if there has been a great deal of time since the estrangement began, the reason might have been forgotten and lost. In fact, maybe at this stage and after so much time has passed, the reason might not matter to the client.

If the client believes they are carrying trauma as a result of family relationships, perhaps another way to frame the question is "What happened to you?". This might emphasize that there is nothing fundamentally wrong with them, but rather that they (and their estrangement) are the product of incredibly difficult experiences over which they had no control. We don't pick our family, and thus, if there have been damaging and even abusive behaviors within the family, these may be part of patterns that go back many generations. Exploring the deeper meaning and impact behind the reasons will be part of this process, including how these experiences have shaped who and how they are.

The client might become agitated when exploring the reasons in more depth, especially if they have already shared aspects of their story. I vividly remember a client who once said to me angrily, "I already told you; are you not listening?" after they shared a vague story of a family event where there was a disagreement, and I wanted to clarify the build up to this confrontation. I still feel the question is important to get as much context as possible, and it might reveal an aspect the client might not have considered.

There may be times when there is a need to look behind their words and seek other clues to their reasoning, such as those discussed in Part 1: Signs and Labels. These might suggest a history of recurring conflict or even abuse that has been triggered by this conversation. This was particularly evident with the previously mentioned angry client, as it was clear he was re-experiencing the events he was describing, and this presented an opportunity to work with and validate the powerful emotions he was feeling. But to do this, we must contain our own defensive reactions and not personalize the client's attitude.

Unfortunately, the reasons for an estrangement may be lost on some professionals who struggle to understand their scale or significance, resulting in presumption, minimizing, and/or projection. For example, if a specific exchange with the EP is shared as the reason, the true intent behind these exchanges may seem benign, but it will be hard to know this without being open to the larger context. Alas, the specific reasons cited may only scratch the surface of what has happened between families over a period of months, years, and possibly decades, and we must be cognizant of what we don't know or what the client isn't telling us. Even if the reasons are clearly unknown in that the client may not be sure, the opposing side will more than likely have their own reason, and we must be cognizant of this as well, as this will be a source of conflict between the EP.

Point of Contention

The reasoning before each estrangement is both very sensitive and also very subjective, in that it might be based on personal feelings and beliefs as opposed to provable facts or professional insight. This subjectivity may be influenced by many factors outside the family relationship but also by the client's awareness. For example, the previously mentioned reasons for mental health issues may not be clinically diagnosed and are simply a layperson's opinion as opposed to a diagnosis. Plus, the root cause of the mental health issues is an important factor, i.e., did these issues cause the estrangement or were they a consequence of other issues in the family?

Sharing the reasons with others within the estrangement community may lead to highly emotional responses if they resonate with them personally. For example, I have seen parents share how their adult children's mental health issues made it difficult to maintain a relationship with them, and they were subsequently attacked by one or more adult children who have struggled with their own mental health as a result of relations within their own family. Similarly, it will be tough for either side of an estrangement to hear of abuse being carried out by others in the same role, and even more so if they are accused of being perpetrators by a stranger online, projecting their own experience.

The previously mentioned *subjective blur*, which prevents people from seeing how their own relationships and experiences with family can differ vastly from others, can fuel all the points of contention, but particularly the reason and can contribute to feelings of doubt and uncertainty experienced by the client or the EP. As professionals, we have a unique opportunity to really understand the reasoning in as much depth as possible, but this will be an ongoing and iterative process, and the client will need as much time as possible.

Notes/Observations

Throughout the inquiry process and further conversations, the professional can add general notes and observations for each EP. This might also include details related to each estrangement, such as past interactions or attempts at reconciliation; expanded details on the reasons for each estrangement; and/or the specific and current challenges related to each person. Another focus will be the *estrangement impact triad* and documenting any insights into the psychological impact, such as the affect the estrangement can have on the clients' thoughts, emotions, feelings, physical sensations, and behaviors; the relational struggles, such as the type of support available; and other social challenges, such as the affect the estrangement can have in various social settings. These notes can be as detailed as necessary, but as per local data privacy rules, I would suggest caution in documenting anything identifiable and ensuring all notes are securely stored.

Chapter 8

The Toolbox

As the title says, the goal of this book is to help professionals and individuals on their estrangement journey. The analogy of a journey is a poignant one in that each person is walking on very uncertain terrain with no clearly defined map or destination, and this is why the client has reached out for guidance in navigating this journey. However, aside from a vague concept of needing help, the client themselves might not know exactly what they need or want. They might just want to talk so they can feel understood and connected to another human being; they might be looking to work through a specific decision they are struggling with; they might be seeking practical advice on managing a specific situation; or they might be seeking a deeper meaning and purpose to their life as a result of the estrangement.

As mentioned, the supportive role will be specific and limited to each professional's training; if they are not trained in psychology or psychotherapy, or if their experience working with distressed adults is limited, it is not wise to bring a client to a place outside of the professional's skillset. Understanding estrangement and how it might be affecting the client and then framing this around their specific role and training is advised. The initial step might be to follow the model and create an *estrangement map* with the client, or maybe there is enough information via conversation to know where the client presently is. From this, we can view their experiences through the lens of the *estrangement impact triad*. Sometimes just listening compassionately is all that is needed, but there are a variety of interventions and strategies in the proverbial toolbox that we can suggest to clients. The following is just one toolbox, the product of my own clinical experiences and curated over years of working with estranged people from different backgrounds. I would hope that over time each professional might develop their own and become attuned to knowing when and how to help the estranged people who seek them out. This is not about being perfect, and there will be an element of trial and error in exploring how clients respond to suggestions. My own approach and general philosophy have always been "gently, gently", and I feel it works as it is often counter to how family has treated the client. I acknowledge that anything we do has to match the client's unique situation, the process for working, and our professional intuition in the moment. Once they feel they have a solid understanding of the client's situation and struggles, they might address what comes up in that moment as opposed

DOI: 10.4324/9781003362203-12

to following any sequence. The main thing is to remain open to what is revealed, as this may enable the client to access their own truth and wisdom as they move forward with their lives.

At this point, some might be asking if any professional can fulfil all of this, and perhaps not, but I believe it is worth trying. We don't need to have all the answers, all the tools, or all the strategies; we just need to have enough presence and compassion for the client to know that, in this time of crisis in their lives, there is someone who is here for them.

Below is a breakdown of the toolbox based on seven different categories, labelled T1 to T7. I would ask each professional to take the time to familiarize themselves with these and how they might work for different clients.

T1: Clarifying and Validating Strategies

I have repeatedly shared the importance of validation when working with estranged people, and not just because it is cited in research (Blake et al., 2022b), but on a human level, validation is something I feel we all yearn for. Depending on the professional's role and the limitations of time, validating might be all they can do, but do not underestimate the positive impact this can have. This might spark a sense of trust in the client, normalize their experiences, and reduce the shame they might be carrying. They may subsequently take more risks, share more of their situation with others, and hopefully garner more support. Validation might start early, as the professional acknowledges the courage it took to proactively reach out for help and show up, but we will also need to clarify many aspects of the client's situation to ensure we are accurate in our perception and understanding of their reality. This includes clarifying if they are estranged or feel they might be. As we continue this, clarifying and validating will open the door to possible strategies in the toolbox to suggest to the client. However, I reiterate that this is not about constantly trying to fix things but rather about listening, building a collaborative relationship, and having a range of options that might align with the client's struggles and personal goals. There are countless areas of the client's experience that we can clarify and validate, and I have listed five below that I commonly focus on with my own clients.

T1.1: Goals and Outcomes

To efficiently use our and the client's time, we might agree to a set number of sessions and a timeframe within which to re-evaluate the overall process. It will also be worthwhile to discuss the client's goals and ideal outcomes. This might involve clarifying if there is anything they wish to work on, as well as what change looks like to them. Although a client should make this decision, depending on their understanding of estrangement, the professional might suggest different goals to work towards.

This might include focusing on an upcoming and potentially stressful event, either involving the EP (see T6) or not, an impending conversation (see T3), attempting to repair the relationship (see T4), making a difficult and unavoidable decision (see T1.3), explaining the situation to a friend and strengthening their support network (T3.2), validating their story (see T1.2), or exploring the losses they have endured (see T1.4). The client may express a desire to work on their mental health, and while this is not within the scope of this book and is dependent on the training of each professional, we can still clarify how they might go about this and what approaches they feel might help.

However, their goals might have nothing to do with family, although they may need help parking the situation (see T4), and their goals could give them a sense of purpose and meaning (see T7). It is important to deep-dive into each goal and try to understand why it is important to them. This might include asking them what has held them back from setting or sticking to goals in the past, such as a fear of failure or if they were exposed to too much criticism and blame and have lost confidence in themselves. There may also be the risk that their goals appear too big, and suggesting they break them down into smaller, manageable steps might help. Referencing and reinforcing any strengths and coping mechanisms they have shared (see T1.5) will also help to overcome any doubts and fears they might have.

T1.2: Estrangement Story/Map

One important intervention will be validating the many layers of the client's personal story, the many experiences across the span of their lives, not exclusively with family but with others that are significant to them. Either in conjunction with the previously created *estrangement map* or in general conversation, validating this story might involve focusing on certain aspects, such as the parties involved and their role in the estrangement; the specifics of what happened between them and the client; and how it affected the client as well as others in the family. Some clients might focus on specific events and moments, both in isolation and in relation to other events, and they might need to have these moments validated to help them make sense of and maintain a clear contextual perception of life before the estrangement.

Validating their emotions is also important, as they may have been invalidated by family members. In fact, the client might have similarly invalidated how they feel, labelling these feelings as wrong or dangerous. This will be particularly true of anger, as the rules around against whom and when anger is permitted may have worked strongly against the client; repressed anger can leave lasting damage to the client's self-esteem and self-confidence, but allowing these powerful emotions to just be in the present may help the client accept them as true and relative to what has happened to them.

In the context of the client's *estrangement map,* here are some insights that can be clarified and/or validated.

Starting with Who

As the client shares the EP in step one, we can begin to clarify where they fit into the hierarchy, i.e., their family position. This will be obvious if they state the EP is a parent, adult child, or sibling, but it might not be if the list of EP is exhaustive and crosses multiple generations. Clarifying who else they are estranged from may also be necessary, as they may just focus on the main parties, but after some deeper reflection on the family history, they may open up about the other relationships affected. Clarifying how the estrangements listed have affected other relationships, such as those with non-estranged family, is also necessary, as there might be tension between these and pressures to reconcile, make peace, or remain silent, which might not feel right for the client.

Naming the Distance

As the client shares the estrangement type (ET) in Step Two we can start to get a sense of the different family dynamics at play and how each estrangement can vary quite differently across each EP. We might start by validating their uncertainty if the client is not sure what type matches their situation. If they feel one is more appropriate, we can validate the necessity of this type over others.

If the ET is *physical*, the client might feel the situation is final, and we might explore validating their grief (see T1.3), although this can apply to any type. To maintain the physical distance, the client might need help explaining the situation to others, thus requiring communication strategies (see T3).

If the ET is *emotional*, there may still be regular contact, and thus, the client might be stressed over an impending visit or event, so now might be the time to introduce them to resourcing strategies (see T2) or re-engaging strategies (see T6) to prepare for this. Discussing these may happen organically, or the client may present this as a specific issue. They may express a desire to relay something back to family, and thus, communication strategies (see T3) might be necessary.

If the ET is *cyclical*, we might clarify who initiated the reconnection(s) and why, and also validate how the relationship with the EP was during these periods before the current estrangement. This might help if the client wishes to repair the relationship (see T4) or explain the situation to others (T3.2).

If the ET is *absent*, we might validate not only the circumstances of this absence but also the losses the client might have experienced as a result.

If the ET is *mutually-disengaged*, we might clarify if it was always mutual or validate what triggered the transition from potentially mutual to mutual.

If the ET is *inherited*, we might clarify the circumstances of why this estrangement was indirectly passed on and validate how this affected the client and others.

If the ET is *secondary*, we might clarify the circumstances and validate how the client feels about this extended loss.

If the ET is *self-protecting*, we might validate any fears the client might have around their privacy being compromised by these EP and the experiences that led to these fears.

Power Dynamics

As the client shares the nature of the estrangement in Step Three we can clarify if it was chosen or not and how this is influenced by the ET and the EP. By establishing if they are a son or daughter, or mother or father, we can get a sense of whether they are using an estrangement to possibly maintain some control over the family dynamics. For example, if the nature is *voluntary/non-mutual*, we might clarify if there is more doubt as the burden of choice is on them, or is there more freedom and safety from taking action? If the nature is *voluntary/mutual*, we might clarify at what point it became mutual and what emotions triggered this, such as anger, grief, hopelessness, and acceptance. Or was it a combination of several emotions? If the nature is *involuntary*, we can validate how the client may feel powerless and devalued. We might also clarify the social ramifications, such as if other family members are aware and if this might lead to embarrassment, as they may have known before the client did.

Patterns of Avoidance

As the client shares the estrangement approach in Step Four and the estrangement method in Step Five we can clarify if and how the family communicates, and this might highlight patterns of avoiding confrontation. We can also validate how this has affected the client's experience. If the EA is *indirect*, this will bring with it uncertainty and the need to clarify exactly what indirect looks like and if this is worse than a more *direct* approach.

Time and Wounds

As the client shares the duration of the estrangement in Step Six we can clarify and validate the element of time and the lifespan of the family issues. Time might be an indicator that they need help to park the situation more effectively (see T5). There may be a greater sense of loss with the realization of time, or we might validate how the client may feel frozen in time, or they may have lost all sense of time. We might validate how well they kept their lives together and had the resilience to keep moving forward (see T1.5). We might also validate how time has impacted other aspects of life, such as their relationship with their partner, children, or friends.

The Lost Why

Finally, as the client shares the estrangement reason in Step Seven we can validate how difficult this is for them to discuss, and we might stress that there is no rush in discussing the reasons. We might also suggest focusing on resourcing strategies such as conscious breathing (see T2.2) and grounding (see T2.3) to help them feel a little safer.

Eventually, we might need to clarify the reasons in more detail and the events leading up to them. We might validate how they responded to these events and clarify what the client would do differently. Of particular importance is validating the true impact of the reasons, particularly if they are abusive behaviors. If they are unsure of the reason, we might suggest a journaling exercise (see T2.5) for the client to reflect in their own time, but we can also validate how some will know the reason but fear sharing it.

Client Reflection

Perhaps the most important intervention is enabling each client to find their own answers. Although the client has reached out for an expert opinion, the client is the true expert in their own family, and professionals can encourage them to trust themselves. If an *estrangement map* has been drawn out, instead of jumping into suggestions and strategies, asking the client to focus on what comes up cognitively, emotionally, visually, etc. as they reflect on it might be more helpful. This does not need to be done immediately and can act as homework ahead of another session. In an ideal world, this exercise might at least emphasize the need for compassion for oneself after all they have had to endure, and as well as validating the insight this has provided. I have also found it useful to ask my clients to write down what they will do next with this insight to reinforce its importance and keep it for future reference if needed.

T1.3: Decision-Making

An estrangement brings with it a set of ongoing challenges, with each one requiring an important decision or set of decisions. Because of the delicate nature of the family relationship, there will naturally be great worries and fears around these decisions. These fears can be crippling, especially if the consequences are high, and respecting their weight and seriousness for the client is critical to the therapeutic relationship. Underneath each fear sit experiences of rejection, loss, getting into trouble, and facing the anger of others. Taking the time to acknowledge and validate their respective worries and fears can help the client work through their own process and know how to respond or not respond. This might also help them reclaim any self-trust and start taking assertive action.

There are countless decisions to be made, such as: do I put more distance between family members or less; do I reconnect with family; do I visit family; do I attend a family wedding; or do I tell my friends of the estrangement and how much? There are no easy answers to these, and even when surrounded by great counsel, there may still be no clarity, which is why the best decisions can come from the client more than others. With that said, that does not mean we don't play devil's advocate with their decision-making process, especially if it is completely grounded in fear and not rational thinking. Validating how difficult these decisions are will be helpful, but equally, clarifying each decision in detail might help them find their own answers. Below are some ways a professional might do this.

Pressing the Pause Button

Due to the profound grief the client might be experiencing and their desperate need to attach themselves to the EP, they may feel a great deal of urgency around each decision and be compelled to act quickly as opposed to when and how it is appropriate. Suggesting to a client that there is no rush and they can take a step back to pause and reflect may be not only necessary but also appreciated, as this calm approach may be exactly what they need. The parking strategies section (see T5) will offer ways to postpone a decision, but allowing them to literally stop the clock may take an immense amount of pressure off them as well as help them connect with the impact more. This might also teach them to catch and break patterns of impulsively reacting to situations.

Decision Deep Dive

When the client is ready, and particularly after a period of pause, I find it useful to delve into the problem with the client before coming to a decision. To do this, there are certain pieces of information we might clarify with the client.

1. *What is the decision and the context?* The specifics of the decision and why it is necessary are a good place to start. This includes establishing what past events and current circumstances are driving the decision or the need to make one.
2. *When does the decision actually need to be made?* As mentioned, a decision may be time-sensitive, specifically if it is bound to an impending event, and clarifying this timeframe will explain why it is so urgent. They might also feel that once they make this decision, due to these time constraints, they can't change their minds. Aside from the aforementioned decision pausing, which might not be appropriate to the current predicament, resourcing them with ways to find some calmness, such as the breathing exercise in T2.2, might aid the decision-making process. It might also be worthwhile to suggest they wait until the last minute, as this might provide more time for them to gather more necessary details and make a more informed decision.
3. *Why is it on them to make the decision?* When there is a decision to be made, particularly one that involves estranged family members, I often wonder why this is left to my clients to make, i.e., why are they the bearers of responsibility? This need to decide may be influenced by obligation, loyalty, or a fear of repercussion, and asking the client to reflect on this might help to solidify the decision or question, if one needs to be made at all.
4. *What do they want to do?* This might seem like an obvious question, but allowing the client to share exactly what they want as opposed to what others in the family want will give them a chance to share their true feelings and also observe patterns of people pleasing. These feelings can range from a genuine desire to outright dread and can be powerfully disruptive for the client. Asking the client why they feel this way can act as an entry point for discussions of past or recent

re-engagements and what lessons were learned from them. Exploring the short, medium, and long-term repercussions might also help them re-evaluate a decision, especially if the impact will not be felt immediately.

5. *What will happen if they don't make a decision?* This will be more of a hypothetical conversation, but again, it will be worthwhile in allowing the client to have their fears, doubts, and hopes heard. If these are mostly fear-based, playing devil's advocate to challenge their validity might help, but they may also be grounded in reality, which we must respect. We might also acknowledge that their doubts may be related to how invested they are in the relationship and why the decision(s) are so important to them.

Pros and Cons

Another way to explore a decision is to isolate what could be considered the positives and negatives of each. This might seem basic, but asking clients to write a list of pros and cons may open up their thought process and help them weigh up their options more. From this, they may naturally gravitate towards one option over another, and most importantly, the decision will have come from them. Below is an example of the pros and cons list, based around a common scenario, i.e., deciding whether to contact an estranged family member over the Christmas period.

When doing this exercise, I encourage asking the client to reflect on past mistakes and lessons learned, so in the above scenario this would mean asking if they have previously attempted to connect with the EP and the outcome. Exploring what the client desires is also part of the process, as it will determine what can be considered a pro or a con. For example, if they wish to have estranged family members back in their lives, getting a positive response will be a pro, but if they want to maintain the estrangement, no response might be preferable.

Table 8.1 Decision Pros and Cons

Pros	Cons
They might get a positive response	They might get a negative response
If they get a negative response, it might validate their position and help to focus on other priorities	If they get a negative response, it might set them back emotionally, particularly over Christmas
They may take comfort from knowing they tried and ease their conscience	If they get no response, it might contribute to any anxiety and uncertainty regarding the future
It might open the door to further communication in the future	It might close the door to further communication in the future
It might appease others who insist on a reconciliation or just wish to have family together one more time	It might increase the expectations from others to reconcile

Embodying Outcomes

Another approach might be to suggest to the client that they take the time to visualize the outcome of a decision and let their imagination guide them as opposed to just cognition. This might help if they are struggling to think through the decision or are overwhelmed with options. When doing this, we want them to get a deep sense of the outcomes and embody them in terms of how they might make them feel, both emotionally and physically. If the visualized outcome evokes a neutral or even positive response, such as a feeling of connection or happiness, the emotions might guide them here. However, if it evokes a negative response, such as anxiety, then similarly the emotions might indicate they should not take action.

Like all the exercises in this book, these are just suggestions; the client should lead, and if they are not comfortable with them, then we must respect this. Even if they do consent, we must be careful with what might come up, as we do not want to distress the client more. If the professional feels the client is carrying trauma, this exercise might not be appropriate as their inner world and imagination may already be chaotic.

Lean on their Team

At different points in our lives, we will need the advice of others, and I have met many people who have genuine wisdom and the capacity to offer balanced and thoughtful suggestions. Unfortunately, not every client will experience this, and understandably, they may choose not to share their decision with others. Many will avoid discussing decisions with others in case they don't hear what they want or need to hear, or get an opinion that potentially goes against their own wellbeing.

What separates good advice providers from bad ones is how they seek out as much information as possible. They listen, they reflect, they look for more context, and then they offer something that is grounded in some version of the truth. They may come to the same conclusions as the client, or they may come up with suggestions the client never thought of. They may also come up with suggestions with which the client does not agree but have enough information to explain how they came to this conclusion in a manner that is non-threatening to the client. The client may then come to appreciate and integrate this perspective into their own decision-making process. This can begin with the client observing others to see how they relate and speak to others, how reflective they are, and the accuracy of their responses. Eventually, they may take a risk, look past their fears, and view this scenario as an opportunity for connection and growth.

T1.4: Loss and Grief

As I emphasized in Part 1: The Impact Triad, an estrangement from family is very much a loss, albeit a very complex one, as the client is grieving the living and not the dead. If a professional struggles to comprehend the losses the client is going through, they might reflect on the concept of loss as a whole and what it might be like to lose an important relationship. With that understanding, we can validate the very fact that they are estranged and that they do not have, and may never have, the relationship with family they wish they had. We can validate the specific relationships they have lost, whether it is a parent(s), sibling(s), son(s), daughter(s), grandparent(s), etc., i.e., the losses we discussed in Step One of the *Estrangement Inquiry Model*. If there is more than one person, we might clarify who each person is and their significance to the client, as not all losses are the same and we need to validate the depth and scale of these losses. Even if the client is estranged from just one person, the pain that comes from losing the relationship with a parent or adult child through estrangement cannot be overstated, and having this pain heard and validated is a step towards helping them heal.

There are many layers to grief, and the loss of family may compound past losses, such as bereavements of other family members or friends, or the ending of a relationship. This may not be obvious, but over time the client may reveal more losses, which will provide even more context to the depth of their grief and why they are struggling so much.

While our job is not to diagnose the type of grief a client is experiencing, unless specifically trained in bereavement and grief therapy, we can still validate the "emotional, cognitive, functional and behavioral responses" (Zisook & Shear, 2009, p. 67), which might range from "barely noticeable alterations to profound anguish and dysfunction" (Zisook & Shear, 2009, p. 67), and this might include the items listed under the *estrangement impact triad*. Where there may be no obvious signs, the grief may still be there, and we should not dismiss this completely, but instead view it as part of each client's unique process. Validating these responses might help the client recognize their grief and prioritize their health, particularly if they are experiencing mental health problems and need the assistance of a medical professional.

There are other social dimensions to these losses that can be validated, such as how the client has no funeral or public forum to grieve the losses of estrangement and garner the emotional and practical support they badly need and deserve. Because of this, the client must grieve silently behind closed doors, and many will have no idea about their pain. This is a great tragedy and one that is rarely seen but will be felt by others who are close to the client.

There is no right or wrong way to grieve, and it cannot be rushed or bypassed, although the client may struggle to express their grief. Suggesting resourcing strategies, such as journaling (see T2.5) or creativity (see T2.6), may help them explore this, but I am more inclined to focus on just being compassionately present for the client as they go through their own grieving process and at their own pace.

T1.5: Strengths and Coping Mechanisms

I admire all my clients for their resilience in the face of the suffering they have endured and always inquire how they have survived up to now. Although they often come to therapy feeling helpless, they are far from it, and sometimes they need an external and broader perspective to realize they are stronger than perhaps their family allowed them to believe. It is never hard for me to find strengths in anyone I meet; it has become a habit to focus on the aspects of individuals that they either devalue or simply can't see and that distinguish them from others, particularly when faced with ongoing family struggles. Some of these strengths are natural gifts that have not been nurtured and encouraged enough, and others are coping mechanisms shaped from necessity and vulnerability, i.e., survival and adaptation, perhaps as a result of their own research and process of trial and error. The fact that some of these are rooted in survival or are not recognized by family members or anyone else may block clients from seeing how talented and resourceful they really are. By validating these strengths and coping mechanisms, we are not only building evidence of competency but also seeking kindness and compassion in the client, replacing any guilt or shame.

At different points throughout the process of listening to clients, there are certain things a professional might hone in on. The details of the client's family history and the difficult experiences they have had to endure are obvious examples, but there is more to what they are sharing, and directly asking them, "How did you cope with all of this?" might evoke a new response. When I have done this in the past, some clients were disarmed by the question, perhaps because they didn't feel like they were coping well at all, and yet they are still here and doing their best. Others looked bewildered, like they weren't sure how they coped, but I would not accept a vague or blank answer and always looked for as much detail as possible to reinforce facts.

To be clear, focusing on these two areas is not the same as having a positive bias and constantly seeking the good in their family situation. I have found that attempting to spin their estrangement in any way as a good thing can be a source of frustration for the client, as it may be incongruent with how they feel. It is also important to note that there may be a dark side to these, as often they are forged in the fire of a chaotic home life, and we must be respectful of these circumstances. The next thought might be: What exactly are these strengths and coping mechanisms, and how exactly did they help?

Strengths

Below are some examples of strengths to validate, but there will easily be more to find with each client.

GENEROSITY

The client might be generous with their time, money, belongings, and space, and this is an honorable trait that can also instil a sense of purpose in the client. Helping others may have acted as a healthy distraction, but it also helped them stay connected and appreciated by others in their lives. However, this generous nature may have been their way of feeling valued, and they may find themselves habitually giving away too much of themselves and struggling to stop due to their deep need to put others first.

GRATITUDE

I have found that some of my clients are grateful for what they have in life, despite the family situation and the distress this has brought them. While this is not true of all estranged adults, those who are grateful ask for very little and appreciate any support they receive. This may be counter to how they are perceived by their estranged family, who may have decided they are ungrateful and selfish.

THOUGHTFULNESS

Whether they are thinking of others or thinking through situations, often clients will demonstrate concern for others in a way that creates a measure of safety while also relaying compassion. In a healthy relationship, whether it is with a partner, a child, a friend, or others, being considerate of their fears and needs would be greatly valued and bring them closer together. However, this may have developed as a pre-emptive effort to control the home environment and how the client is perceived.

PLANNING

Perhaps an extension of thoughtfulness, but consciously planning each decision in detail will serve them in many capacities, including managing their own inner world and actively finding ways of reducing stress. The flip side of this is that those who excessively plan may do so out of fear of catastrophe, and so they may take planning to the extreme.

LISTENING

The ability to truly tune in and hear what a person is saying is another great skill, and those being listened to will feel valued and, in turn, may reciprocate. Alas, the client may have had no choice but to listen, particularly if they were constantly criticized for not listening, and may suppress their natural urge to express themselves. This kind of self-censorship is very damaging and must be challenged in a safe way.

PROBLEM-SOLVING

I have found that many of my clients, perhaps out of necessity, have a good capacity to work through a variety of challenges in practical ways. This might be born from a need to exert some measure of control and make everything "right". This ability to stay solution-focused is priceless in many environments, but this can be a double-edged sword, as they may try to solve the family problems that led to the estrangement and simply can't because 1) they are not in a position of influence to affect change in the family, 2) they are too emotionally connected and thus too vulnerable to be able to fix the issues, and 3) these may not be their problems to fix, but rather they may have been caught up in a pattern of taking on other family member's responsibilities.

CRISIS MANAGEMENT

While a client's inner world may feel overwhelming, years of containing it might mean they are less inclined to lose their heads in an actual crisis. They may also have a more grounded sense of perspective and scale and instinctively know when a situation is big or small. While others might lose their heads over any challenge, estranged clients may just default to listening and problem-solving.

CREATIVITY

Creativity is one of the best ways for individual expression and can take different forms, such as art, music, literature, or science. It may have protected them from difficult times and/or acted as an outlet for their struggles. These gifts may have been devalued or unrecognized, and yet they may have helped them through the worst times, so acknowledging them is essential. See T2.6 for ways to promote creativity with a client.

Coping Mechanisms

Coping mechanisms are equally complicated and may in fact be maladaptive in that they don't necessarily serve the clients in the long term, but here are some examples.

WORRY

This may appear less than helpful, but worry facilitates a faux sense of control, and the client may feel that by worrying, they are doing something practical. Worrying is not the same as planning or problem-solving, although it may feel like it is. This will be a powerful coping mechanism and difficult to drop, as the client may be convinced that not worrying will increase the chances of the source of worry happening.

BREATHWORK AND YOGA

I am isolating these two as they are very popular amongst many of my own clients and both have bodies of research that highlight their effectiveness, which I will discuss in T2.2 and T2.5. We are in an interesting time when western society is fully embracing eastern practices, such as yoga, as a path to health and self-exploration, which may have traditionally been viewed with scepticism.

EXERCISE

Another common way to cope is exercise, which has many benefits, including stress management. Many of my own clients are dedicated to running or other sports or athletic hobbies, and these not only act as a healthy distraction but may give them purpose as well as social support from others involved, such as coaches and teammates.

HUMOUR

A sense of humour might be considered a personality trait and, thus, perhaps a strength, but it is also a way of coping with difficult situations and emotions. There may be an element of avoidance, but that could be said of all coping mechanisms, and adopting these may help the client to lower their shield and embrace their own vulnerability.

READING

Many of the estranged people I speak to are voracious readers and allow themselves to get lost in books and other forms of content. They may also be driven by a desire to understand themselves or those they are estranged from and absorb as much material on psychology and relationships as possible.

PEACEKEEPING

I'm including this as it is a common way to avoid confrontation and maintain some stability. The role of the peacekeeper and the peacekeeping behaviors that come with it may have been adopted in the family home to deflect blame and placate emotionally overwhelmed family members, and this may have then transferred to other contexts and relationships, such as at work with colleagues and bosses.

T2: Resourcing Strategies

As mentioned, one study found that a therapist's ability to help a client feel relaxed and safe was critical to a positive outcome (Blake et al., 2022b). So before delving into the estrangement details, introducing a client to strategies to manage the overwhelming psychological impact, referred to as resourcing, will be very beneficial. Even more powerful is teaching these to the client so they can lean on them when necessary and in their own time. This will be important if the client has experienced trauma as a result of abuse or neglect within the family, and resourcing will extend to working with the somatic, i.e., within the body, responses that come with this, i.e., instinctive survival responses such as fight, flight, and freeze (Ogden & Fisher, 2015). When resourcing, we are not always explicitly addressing the family situation but more the residual impact, although we can revert back to resourcing if we are discussing family and the client becomes distressed by the conversation. In fact, we might use these resources regularly throughout our time with each client. The different resourcing exercises will take time to develop as they might be completely new to the client, so a professional should not be afraid to repeat lessons and practices many times over to give the client a chance to absorb them. Even if the client appears to have some previous resourcing experience and training, such is the strong emotional bond of family that these exercises might not be available to them in this context, so we must presume nothing and continue to focus on helping the client.

Resourcing might involve the use of somatic exercises, such as breathing, grounding, and movement; cognitive exercises to challenge unhelpful thinking, such as CBT and mindfulness; creative exercises for expression, such as art therapy; and other therapeutic tools. There are countless resources, and I would encourage all professionals to draw on their training as much as possible. Each professional will have a formal education in their field, along with continuing professional development and invaluable real-world experience, which frames their understanding of their clients and contributes to deciding the most appropriate intervention for them. While the professional might not have specific training in estrangement, they may have comprehensive knowledge of the various modalities of psychology and psychotherapy, family and couples therapy, parenting and attachment styles, various approaches to communication, social care policy, cultural diversity, healthcare, and trauma recovery. At different points during the process of working with the client, a professional might educate the client on the theories, concepts, and techniques from these fields or other approaches or modalities they have studied and feel the client would benefit from. Such education has the power to empower them with an understanding of themselves, which could help to normalize their reactions, broaden their world view and perceptions of themselves and their family, and add more depth and nuance to their estrangement story. This will also provide them with the language and terminology needed to relay these to others, be it estranged family, those in the client's support network, or others they feel they need to share their story with. I will now elaborate on seven specific resourcing strategies below.

T2.1: Safety

Helping the client feel safe will be critical to their healing, particularly if they have experienced abuse, neglect, or rejection. They may be suffering trauma as a result and, thus, have become primed and ready for the next adversarial moment, even when surrounded by those who love and support them. Due to the powerful bonds of family and the potential to cross paths with the EP, the client may never feel fully safe, and their nervous system may subsequently be triggered by any stimuli, irrespective of how trivial they might be to others. It could be a look from a stranger, a casual remark, a specific scenario, a program on TV, or it may just be an old memory that causes the client to disappear into themselves as a protective measure. It should come as no surprise that, as professionals, helping our clients feel safe is essential for them to be comfortable enough to open up and share, but the client may not have consistently felt safe for many years, so this will take time and patience to develop. Below are some ideas on how we can help our clients feel safe, both in their work with professionals and in their private lives.

Structure and Safety

Building safety begins the moment the client walks in or joins an online call, and session one is always critical. The client could be anxious, as they might have built up this impending moment for a long time, playing and replaying what they will say and how the professional might respond. They might feel uncomfortable and unsafe, and they might fear judgment or blame, so now is the time to use what I consider to be the most important tool available: communication. We begin by communicating to them directly that they are welcome and that this is a judgment-free and pressure-free space. Explaining clearly to the client how the professional works, as well as credentials, experience, and policy around cancellations, and agreeing to review the working relationship after a number of sessions will address any doubts they might have and make them feel a little more comfortable. At this stage, creating an environment that helps the client feel at ease will also be very helpful, and there is safety in discreetness, so a quiet introduction if there are others around and not announcing the client's name publicly might be appreciated.

In terms of interacting with the client, I have found that being genuine and direct with my words and attitude helps my clients know who I am, where we both stand, and that it is ok for them to do the same. This level of honesty from the professional might facilitate a level of honesty and reflection with the client that they could not permit for themselves before. I previously mentioned how appropriate sharing might help the client feel safe, and I occasionally reveal some small aspect of my own story to provide context to the client. While professional boundaries must be considered, by giving something of myself not only did they appreciate it, but it also established how familiar I was with estrangement and their predicament, which quickly helped them feel safe in this context. However, there are other contexts in which a professional works, and one of these could be online estrangement support groups, where safety is paramount to their effectiveness. In cases like this, I find it best to set a clear group policy around ensuring each member respects both their own privacy and everyone else's by removing the pressure to share anything if they are not comfortable doing so. Another challenge is if one or more people in the group choose to remain anonymous by not displaying their name and leaving their camera off. Again, setting a group policy that applies to everyone will go a long way towards quickly clarifying what is acceptable and what is not. Naturally, some will not be happy if they are sharing and have revealed their identity, whereas others have done neither, but having a transparent group discussion where everyone has time to express their grievances about this may help everyone feel heard and respected, which may build group trust and eventual safety.

Recognizing Triggers

While the client might have a general sense of unease, there may be specific stimuli that trigger it, and taking the time to identify and name these triggers may prompt the client to temporarily avoid them, particularly during tough times. Triggers could be specific TV shows and themes addressed on these shows, including characters discussing how hurt they are or blaming others for their hurt, but it might even be moments of tenderness in a family that upset the client. Triggers could be songs, books, art – anything that evokes feelings of vulnerability. Recognizing this is the first step, but actively discussing the client's present-day triggers and how they can practically reduce exposure will help them consciously bring some sense of safety into their lives. While this is not a long-term strategy and the client will not be able to do this indefinitely, consciously reducing exposure to sources of stress is an act of self-care, particularly during times of setback.

Creating a Zone of Safety

I often encourage clients to seek out and cultivate spaces where they can feel secure and calm, particularly as *environmental mastery* is considered a component of psychological wellbeing (Ryff & Singer, 1996). This could involve selecting a room in their house where they can close the door, but it might be a public place such as a park where they have plenty of open space and perhaps are surrounded by nature, which is known to have a positive effect on mental health (Bratman et al., 2019; Jimenez et al., 2021). It might also be a busy spot where they can disappear or people watch to forget their own situation for a short time.

If their safe zone is at home, it might be helpful to suggest to them that they populate it with different items that feel good, such as their favorite pictures, clothing, and materials like comfortable blankets; their favorite music, which might include nature sounds and meditation videos; their favorite smells, which remind them of better times and places; anything that creates a full sensory experience where they feel present and calm.

Curating their Circle

Positive relationships with others is considered an important aspect of psychological wellbeing (Ryff & Singer, 1996), so encouraging a client to build their own tribe or inner circle will go a long way towards making them feel safe. With that in mind, carefully choosing to spend time with these people while also consciously limiting or completely avoiding exposure to certain people who could upset the client might be needed.

The process of curating their circle might involve setting clear boundaries around conversations and topics, although the right people will be sensitive to this anyway. The circle acts as a source of fun as well as support, and the client might need to be reminded of this and not let the intensity of their estrangement prevent them from laughing and enjoying this time. Curating does not mean pushing everyone else out of their lives but rather recognizing and accepting each person's capacity to help and amending expectations accordingly. For example, if the client has an anxious friend who is predisposed to worry, they will not be able to reassure the client if they cannot do it for themselves. Knowing this, the client might choose not to share their own fears with them, as this person might only fuel them. Blaming people for this is unfair, as these people are not choosing to be anxious any more than the client is. However, seeking out safety from people who are secure in themselves is a step towards autonomy and disrupting patterns of dependency where the client is repeatedly reaching out to the wrong people for support despite them not being able to provide it.

T2.2: Conscious Breathing

As mentioned, estrangement can be a stressful time for a variety of reasons (Rittenour et al., 2018), but most notably due to the tight bonds and dependencies within the family, which means there appears to be no way to address the source of this stress. Such stress can create a cocktail of symptoms, including chronic tension, fatigue, and high emotional sensitivity. Helping the client find ways to manage this stress can improve the quality of their lives and help them more effectively manage the different challenges they face. There are a variety of ways to take control of stress, but one popular approach that has gained mainstream recognition is conscious and controlled breathing exercises. In fact, recent research highlights that five minutes of conscious Breathwork can produce more physiological benefits than mindfulness meditation (Balban et al., 2023). There are a bevy of advocates of different breathing approaches, from the *Wim Hof Method* (www.wimhofmethod.com), to the *Buteyko Method* (www.buteykoclinic.com), *Yogic Pranayama* breathing, and many more.

There seem to be quite a few benefits to breathing approaches and, in particular, techniques that involve deepening each inhale and exhale by contracting the diaphragm and expanding the belly, and these include improved oxygenation (Ma et al., 2017), which helps to improve blood circulation and reduce levels of the stress hormones cortisol and adrenaline in the body. Slow breathing seems to have a positive effect on the symptoms of anxiety, depression, anger, and confusion (Zaccaro et al., 2018), which is very important when framed around the psychological impact of the *estrangement impact triad*. With this in mind, if clients are anxious and unable to think straight, showing them how to practice slow, deep breathing techniques might help them to consciously regulate their internal state (Zaccaro et al., 2018) and subsequently slow down their mind.

I would encourage everyone to take the time to study one or more breathing practices to help their clients, but for the purposes of this book, I will describe a simple exercise I was taught several years ago by a Tai Chi instructor. The main points of this approach are:

1. I start by asking the client to sit upright in a neutral position, with their back relaxed but their spine straight so their head and hips are aligned.
2. Wearing loose-fitting clothes is also helpful, particularly around the waist, to make sure there is no constriction to breathing.
3. Encouraging the client to consciously pay attention to any tension they are holding in their body and gently letting this go is a good place to start, as it will help the client become more aware of their body and present emotional and physical state.
4. Then ask the client to notice their breathing, not to change anything but just to observe the rhythm and pace of each breath, including if they are holding their breath.
5. Ask them to start consciously focusing on the in-breath (inhale), breathing through the nose, and slowly breathing into the belly, specifically just below the belly button. The image of viewing the belly as a balloon filled with air is accurate and might help the client visualize what they are doing. Taking in more air will help oxygenate different parts of the body and brain, which will have an overall positive effect on their wellbeing. Asking them to focus on the sensation of the cool air coming through their nose will bring more awareness to their practice.
6. The out-breath (exhale) should then be longer than the in-breath to promote activation of the parasympathetic system, also known as the *rest and digest* state, as it can decrease heart rate and increase a sense of calmness for the client. The outbreath can be out of the mouth or nose, and asking them to focus on the heat of this breath leaving their body will further their awareness of their body. As they are prompted to notice what happens in their body as they oxygenate, asking them to name how they feel will cause them to reflect even more.
7. The important thing with this exercise is that there is no rush, and each breath should be slow and relaxed. This is not a race, and rushing is counter to what we are doing here.
8. In fact, one study suggests slowing everything down so the client is taking ten breaths per minute (Zaccaro et al., 2018), but I would initially just focus on helping them find a gentle pace.

I would encourage each professional reading this to take the time to regularly do this, bringing more awareness to the client's body and tracking any changes they personally experience, as it will reinforce its effectiveness. Alas, like any technique or approach, this is only effective if practiced diligently, so it is useful to encourage the client to do this for ten minutes daily; do not be afraid to show them how it is done multiple times until they feel more comfortable doing it alone.

T2.3: Grounding

In an anxious state, the client may feel disoriented and easily flustered. There might be a general unease that they struggle to verbalize, but they may also feel disconnected from both their body and their environment. This might not be a problem until they start to discuss their experiences with family, as they may start to re-experience the distressing emotions from these memories that overwhelm them. This might be a good time to resource them and introduce the client to the idea of grounding, which is basically using the body as an anchor so they can stay connected to their present surroundings and the safety of now. Grounding will be useful in different scenarios for the client, including if attempting to repair the relationship (see T4) or re-engaging with the EP (see T6).

Here is an example of a body scan exercise to ground the client in their body and the space they exist in. The client can close their eyes or leave them open, whatever makes them feel comfortable.

1. Start by asking the client to notice their environment before guiding them through the next steps:
   a. Notice the walls and their distance from the client.
   b. They might reach out to the nearest wall and touch it to get a better sense of the distance.
   c. Notice any pictures on the walls and observe the details of each picture, including the shapes and textures.
   d. Notice the seat they are sitting in and how it feels. They can also feel the support the seat is giving them.
   e. Notice the air in the room or any smells.
2. Now we ask the client to observe, but not change, what is happening inside:
   a. Notice any tension in the body, from their forehead to their toes.
   b. Notice their body temperature – whether it is hot, cold, or warm.
   c. Notice their breathing – if it is shallow or if they are holding.
   d. Notice any other sensations, such as tingling in their finger tips or toes or subtle involuntary movements.
   e. Anything that they observe, encourage them to accept it all.
3. Now ask them to notice their feet and how they are connected to the floor. In particular, the four contact points on each foot.
4. Notice the bones in their feet and the tendons and muscles connecting them.
5. Notice the feeling of the floor, carpet, and shoes against their feet.
6. With a deeper awareness, we then ask that they allow themselves to be grounded in the present moment and connected to the floor.
7. After a period of minutes, if their eyes are closed, ask them to keep their eyes closed but to slowly bring their attention back into the room.
8. Then ask them to gently open their eyes, slowly at first to let some light in, then a little more until their eyes eventually open fully, and finally, ask them to observe the room and reflect and verbalize on how they feel now.

T2.4: Movement

With evidence highlighting the benefits of physical activity, such as protecting against stress-induced events as well as reducing mental health issues such as depression and anxiety disorders (Churchill et al., 2021), it stands to reason that some form of exercise can be encouraged as a stress management resource. The specific activity types cited in the above study include aerobic exercise, such as cardiovascular training like running, swimming, or cycling, and/or anaerobic exercise, such as weightlifting. This will suit many clients but not all, especially if they have no prior history of partaking in sports or exercise in general. In fact, certain exercises, such as running, might not be possible if a client has existing health issues, physical injuries, or disabilities. This does not mean the client just becomes sedentary, and it is worthwhile exploring and encouraging them to try different forms of movement.

There are other less intensive forms of exercise that would help to prevent mental illness, such as walking (An & Chuo, 2022) with walking in nature being linked to good emotional health (Zhu et al., 2020). There are countless other forms of movement that will aid a client's wellbeing, such as yoga, tai chi, and dance. To motivate them to embrace this, the conversation might start with what the client loved to do in the past, including when they were young. This might tap into the fun and freedom of movement, with no concern for anything other than having fun. Asking them to recall good times when they engaged in play and how it made them feel might help them recapture this in the present. Movement practice will act as a distraction, but it might lead to new goals around health and fitness and eventually become a personal project (see T5.5). Another aspect of this is discussing impossible standards they may set that are preventing them from acting and how to reappraise these standards.

T2.5: Journaling

Journaling is a written exercise where a client consciously spends time each day to document their inner world. Journaling can be a helpful aide when a client feels alone with their thoughts and feelings, and we now have research suggesting there is some benefit to journaling for managing mental illness, although further studies are needed to support this (Sohal et al., 2022). Journaling is a low-cost and worthwhile resource, and it might also promote more self-reflection and improve autonomy, particularly if a client uses the insight garnered to become less governed by the norms of everyday life (Ryff & Singer, 1996).

I personally enjoy the practical element of journaling in that a client is doing something, i.e., writing, as opposed to just ruminating in their minds. There are several other benefits to journaling, including helping clients find the right words to match their thoughts and feelings, processing and integrating new ideas and learnings, and breaking obsessional and unhealthy patterns of thinking. There is no wrong way to journal, but I encourage clients to regularly check-in and document aspects and changes in their *estrangement impact triad* and the events that trigger them, including memories from the past or even when the trigger is not obvious. Journaling could act as a necessary crutch during very difficult times, where the client can put it all down on paper and then park the situation (see T5) for another time in order to focus on more pressing issues. I find it useful to date each entry, as the client may return to it later to reflect on any changes in personal progress or remind themselves of how they previously responded to an issue. Some clients will not know where to start, so here are some suggestions:

- If they feel comfortable doing so, they can keep their journal on their person and jot down whatever comes to mind at different points throughout the day.
- The journal represents their own private space, which belongs to them, and they can write anything they feel is relevant.
- They can also journal plans and goals, as well as obstacles to reaching them, as well as upcoming events that they are looking forward to or are dreading.
- They might document exchanges and events with the EP to keep a historical record.
- I would encourage them to not censor themselves, to use as much creative and colorful language as needed, and to include hand drawings or imagery if they want to add more dimensions.
- They might read out certain journal entries in their sessions with the professional to have these validated (see T1) or just use the journal notes as topics of discussion.

There are some other considerations to make the client aware of, including security and making sure their journal is not accessible by anyone, as a journal entry could discuss any relationship and not just with the EP. For example, if read by a loving and supportive partner who is triggering the client, they may use the journal to vent and work through specific scenarios or frustrations with no intention of ever sharing this, and the partner may naturally become offended or hurt by what they read. An even worse-case scenario is if the type of estrangement is *emotional*, and thus, there is contact with the EP. This might include living with them, and the EP gaining access to this journal could be a disaster for the client. The solution to this is for them to have a routine regarding when and where they journal and a dedicated storage space. For extra safety, the client might not reference actual names in the journal. Thankfully, my own poor handwriting prevented anyone from understanding my prose, but having a journal read, even accidentally, can be perceived as a huge breach in trust and set the client back in their recovery, so while we do not want to deter them from journaling, we just want to reduce any potential negative side effects.

T2.6: Creativity

As there appears to be a link between positive mental health and creativity (Zhao et al., 2022), finding ways to help clients express their thoughts and feelings, their memories, and their talent and gifts through innovative and unique means could be very beneficial. This will be particularly true if words are not enough and clients struggle to find a way to relay their situation with their family or do not feel safe enough to return to past times. It is helpful if a client's career is linked with creativity, whether they are an artist, designer, inventor, or scientist (Khalil et al., 2019), and they may have already instinctually applied this to their estrangement, which professionals can validate. However, not everyone will have a natural inclination to creativity, or perhaps this side of them has been discouraged and suppressed, and thus helping them discover or reconnect with this could be a powerful resource for them.

One way to do this is by tapping into their imagination to find alternative solutions to the challenges of estrangement while also developing and nurturing their strengths and coping mechanisms. Specifically for their estrangement, here are two simple creative exercises that might help expand their awareness.

Suggest to the client that they draw out a timeline of the family's events. Focusing on dates might create a better sense of time as well as patterns of conflict, tragedy, and estrangement. This exercise might also remind the client of forgotten events and their importance to the overall history. Like the *estrangement map,* doing something cerebral and crafting something tangible to review might give them a fresh perspective and insight to share with the professionals they are working with. This exercise takes time, and I encourage my clients not to rush and include as much detail as needed. They might go more abstract and expand on the above exercise to include colors and images to express how they feel about those events in the timeline.

Similarly, suggest to them to draw out a family tree, going back as many generations as needed to highlight every person in the family and where they are positioned from each other and the client. This exercise might give them a sense of the relational patterns as well as losses, divisions, and hopefully sources of connection, support, and love within the family. Again, they can bring as much personal expression to this as they wish, including drawing faces with emotions to represent how the clients experienced them, such as anger or sadness.

Creativity may extend to finding ways of communicating with the EP (see T3) or working through difficult decisions (see T1.3). Creativity can also manifest in different ways and does not need to be connected to family, but it does require an openness to and curiosity about the world. While I rarely insist on anything from my clients, to drive this creativity I regularly ask them to start a project (see T5.5). When beginning any endeavor, it is natural to focus on the outcome or output and desire success, but the process is more important than the finished product. For example, the journey to writing this book presented many personal challenges, and while I dearly hope it helps those who need it, the act of researching the content and putting down my thoughts has been the greatest gift for me.

T3: Communication Strategies

Communication plays a key role both in creating estrangements and in living with them. If the client cannot effectively communicate with non-estranged family or with those within their support network, they will be left to manage the specific challenges within their unique *estrangement impact triad* completely alone. Due to the social nature of family relations and the sensitive nature of interactions between estranged family members, there may be several communication challenges a client might face. This could include finding ways to control private information being shared but also gathering new information when communication has completely broken down. It will also involve finding ways to explain their situation and balancing over-sharing and under-sharing.

Considerations

When reflecting on any scenario where the client is in a position where they must share something of their estrangement, there are some factors to consider. Note that these factors will also play a role in repairing the relationship with the EP (see T4).

Who is Asking?

There is a big difference between colleagues in work making conversation and someone closer to the situation, and while the client might feel a generalized anxiety about sharing, this should always be factored in. Who they are to the client will inform them if they are considered a threat and if the client needs to be a little more cautious in what they share. We must also bear in mind how the client might also have to contend with communicating the estrangement with a young child or teenager, which is an unenviable and often upsetting task.

Why are They Asking?

Who they are might inform their intent, i.e., why they are asking about the estrangement and if it is general curiosity versus nosiness versus trying to influence the situation. The intent is very important, although it may be hard to determine, especially if the asker is not clear or is pressing for more information. This can naturally be upsetting for a client who may have a history of having their boundaries crossed, and the professional may validate their response to this, whether it is to end the conversation abruptly or reveal an aspect they wish they had not.

What Do They Wish to Share?

Who and why they are asking about the estrangement will dictate the levels of disclosure chosen, as the client may feel obliged to share a degree of information with certain people. Again, this will be contextual but also based on any pressures the client feels. The stigma surrounding estrangement also means information management may be necessary to avoid social rejection (Gray, 2002), but there may be times the client has no choice but to disclose their estrangement. For example, if the client is struggling at work or needs time off, they may need to discuss the situation with a manager, but this does not mean they need to explain the full family history; maybe a few simple details will be enough for the manager to understand. Unfortunately, not every person in a senior position in the workplace will be compassionate, but there is only one way to find out.

How Do They Want to Respond?

The last consideration is the manner in which the client wishes to communicate and deliver their story or message. Traditional approaches, such as face-to-face conversation, text message, email, or handwritten letter, might not always be available or comfortable for the client. They may need to be creative in finding ways to do this, such as recording a video. This will add more depth to the message as the client can express more through facial expression and tone of voice. Although not everyone will be comfortable with the technology of recording or speaking to a camera, suggesting they try it and feeling no pressure to send the video might encourage them to try.

Privacy vs. Disclosure

One other consideration a client should reflect on is how comfortable they are with lying when faced with a communication challenge. This will be influenced by several factors, including personal values around truthfulness, fears around further repercussions if the lie is discovered, and/or if the client is caught off guard and put on the spot. To be clear, while I don't encourage lying, under the circumstances I would not blame anyone for doing so to protect their privacy and wellbeing, and I empathize with those in this position. As the *estrangement impact triad* highlighted, shame is not uncommon for those living with estrangement, and lying, even if it is only to protect oneself, may come at a high psychological cost. It might also come at a social cost, as a client might close their circle to avoid this scenario or fear they are now untrustworthy, especially if they feel their estrangement is a dirty secret. I say these not to make a client feel worse but to acknowledge what they might be dealing with.

With that in mind, deflection might be a better choice, where the client can subtly redirect a conversation while maintaining a polite social contract. I will discuss this more in T3.1, but deflection might not always be an option, and taking the time to discuss how a client feels about lying and how they can reconcile this scenario with themselves might be useful. This includes them staying true to the core reason of why they are lying in the first place: their right and need to protect themselves, and how, in many cases, the family situation really is no one else's business. I will now look at how a client might manage three common communication challenges.

T3.1: Planning for Uncomfortable Questions

One source of indecision is not knowing how to respond to difficult questions. These questions could come from different sources, both inside and outside the family, and revolve around different topics, either directly regarding family, such as whether the client will be visiting estranged family over the holiday period, or in a peripheral way that might require the client to mention family, such as what they will be doing over the holiday period.

What makes these scenarios uncomfortable are the potential responses from the asker, and it is understandable to dread a bad response, especially if the client has experienced judgment in the past. However, even if it is someone the client knows and trusts, they may still feel a defensive reaction and involuntarily freeze. I find reminding the client that 1) if the asker is not part of the family, this situation is not affecting them nearly as much as the client, and 2) embracing this inevitable scenario will help to maintain some control over the flow of information and reduce stress, and so the client might appreciate spending some time on this.

Scripting/Response Preparation

When preparing a response, I find it best to have a set of default answers that are quickly accessible to the client when they are put on the spot. To avoid the lying dilemma I just mentioned, it might be more useful to deflect while choosing answers that are grounded in some truth. For example, if asked if they will see their family over the holidays, they might say:

- "I'm still not sure what everyone's plans are yet."
- "We hope to pop in at some stage, but it depends on how the dinner goes."
- "We are just staying at home this year, and everyone can visit us."
- "There are too many of us to all be at home this year."

Some questions will be more sensitive, and again, in an ideal world, everyone would have a sense of boundaries and not ask these questions, but there will always be one or several. For example, if the EP were not invited to an event, some would know better than to ask, but others might not. However, despite their lack of tact, sticking to the script may still be more helpful.

- "They had to attend another family event."
- "They wanted to come but were not well."

Role-playing different scenarios might also help the client practice delivering them, although this does not need to be an intense exercise and might be done with some needed levity.

T3.2: Explaining the Situation

There may be times when the client wishes or is required to explain their estrangement, and again, this could be with anyone, such as:

- A non-estranged family member who is struggling to understand the true cause of the estrangement.
- A partner or friend who is struggling to understand the true impact of the estrangement.
- A child who is struggling to understand why they cannot see their estranged family.
- A teenager who is struggling to understand why they cannot have their own independent relationship with their estranged family.

Explaining the situation can be hard if any of the above have previously had a good relationship with the EP and cannot see the problem; or they may have no relationship with the EP, as the estrangement may predate their involvement and thus have no context. Similarly, the client's children might have had a positive relationship with one or more of the EPs. A key part of communicating with these cohorts and others in the client's *estrangement radius* is being clear about what the client needs from them and what they need from the client. This will determine how much they need to share and how much the other side needs to hear for all parties to be on the same page. I will discuss these four groups separately below.

Non-Estranged Family

This can be the most tenuous group, as there might be a further explosion within the *estrangement radius* if non-estranged family members reach out to the EP and share what they are told. At the same time, they might also be a great source of support, and the client will need to trust their own judgment on this. So firstly, the client should not presume this group knows much of the family history or if they have had similar experiences or histories with the EP. The client might need to explicitly ask this group of people not to discuss what is shared with the EP or anyone else within the family in an attempt to control the flow of information, and hopefully this request will be respected. They can also be asked not to get directly involved, although some might still feel compelled to do so, believing this is best for everyone. Even if it is, although it is hard to know who determines this due to the now broken trust and their vulnerable state, the client may be very angry, and validating this anger (see T1) while also resourcing them (see T2) might help them to work through some of these feelings and emotions.

Partner/Friends

This might be a more urgent and ongoing conversation, especially if the client is under a lot of pressure and their partner or friend is either oblivious to this or is contributing to the problem with their attitude or behavior. Even if they are somewhat aware or are not causing any issues for the client, this can still be difficult if they have very little emotional context and personal experience with family issues and thus struggle to fully empathize with the client. In these cases, patience and firmness are needed by the client to reiterate important points until they are accepted. Also note that, while many partners and friends will have a great deal of love due to their closeness, they may be very worried about the client's wellbeing and may struggle to hear aspects of the family history. Because of this, some clients will feel compelled to censor aspects to protect others, which is unfortunate as I feel they need to express themselves fully in order to heal and form healthier connections.

Children

I believe this will be the hardest conversation any estranged person will have to face, and some will defer it, but this will not always be possible or fair for the child or children affected. Plus, children have their own logic and may incorrectly attribute the family situation to something they did (Melvin & Hickey, 2021), and it is important to address this sooner rather than later.

Depending on the relationship of the child to the client, they might be angry with the EP for putting the client in this position, as well as appearing to have little regard for the impact the estrangement might have on children. Alternatively, the client may not be responsible for or even close to the child or children affected but is being forced to explain it to them as the EP refuses to take on this responsibility. For this and other reasons, some children will not get a full understanding of the situation, and this can extend into adult life when some facts are eventually shared with them, although they might not even get this.

There is a degree of common sense as to what is shared, but it will naturally be difficult due to the emotions the client is carrying and how the situation is affecting them and the child or children. Plus, if the client has found, during their own childhood, that decisions or events were never explained to them or not done in a manner that matched their age, they might start to compensate. This is about the present and not the client's history, and separating these two will be tough.

I generally find that less is more, so the client might not go into more detail than necessary. As time moves on and the estrangement evolves or remains the same, and the child becomes more aware and curious, the client might need to share more. If there are multiple children, it might be useful for the client to have a one-on-one conversation with each and then have a group discussion later. The children might start discussing it amongst themselves, which is natural, and allowing them this space might be very helpful for them. In terms of what is shared, it is important to protect them, and I would not share anything that will upset them, like abusive behaviors within the family, although I appreciate how these behaviors may prompt a need to maintain distance, both for the client and also for their children. The ET, i.e., physical vs. emotional, will also determine how much contact there is with family and how much the client needs to share.

Whatever is shared and when, the client should not attempt to get it over and done with quickly, as, like any relationship challenge, promoting effective communication takes time, despite how hard it is. Each child will need their own time to make sense of it all, and it is important to give them this. Due to black-and-white thinking, some children will not be satisfied with what they are told, and there may be an extended period where there are constant questions or the child needs more time to process their own feelings. Sometimes it is not about words but just expressions of affection, such as hugs and reminders of love, to reassure the child and make them feel safe and protected from the situation.

Teenagers

This presents a different challenge due to a teenager's developmental stage in life, meaning they are more focused on peer relationships and forming a social identity. They will also start to form strong views and beliefs, and they may feel compelled to rebel against any authoritative figures. They might then push against any requests to limit contact with the EP, as they may feel it is unfair or unwarranted. The client may have fears of secondary estrangements with their teenagers, which is understandable considering the family history, and this might influence how much the client shares with them. The teenager might have limited knowledge but feel like they know everything, and for this reason, they might need more information than younger children while holding onto the fact they are not adults.

Understanding their rebellious nature while respecting the other challenges the teenager is dealing with will help to keep the door to communication open and allow the teenager to have an independent relationship with the EP. Just focusing on their own relationship with the teenager might be the only option, but even this will be hard if the EP is influencing the relationship in any way.

T3.3: Managing Family Requests and Demands

When re-engaging with the EP (see T6), there may be situations that necessitate ongoing and stressful communication in different forms. Circumstances might mean family members expect more from each other, whether it is time, money, emotional support, or cooperation. This will be particularly relevant if there is a sickness and efforts are being made to coordinate and delegate caring responsibilities, and this can be difficult to maneuver, especially if there are antagonistic dynamics or imbalances in responsibility or expectations. Here are some suggestions to consider with the client.

Stick to the Facts

Emotion will drive the content of exchanges, and it is often best to keep everything factual and to the point to prevent getting drawn into conflict. One way to prepare for this is to use journaling time (see T2.5) to write down important details as bullet points, as if this were a professional workplace scenario, such as a business meeting. This will help the client be clear on what is relevant and ensure all important issues are addressed.

Knowing when to Compromise

Necessity may lead to compromises, and depending on the situation and its urgency, it is useful to establish what this means for the client. These sacrifices may be emotional, requiring the client to put aside personal feelings or painful experiences to tend to an issue. This is common with the aforementioned sickness in the family, such as an ailing parent, and the family must rally together to engage with healthcare providers and coordinate visits. Alas, not everyone is reasonable and willing to compromise, which can lead to resentment (or further resentment) and greater levels of stress if one or more people are left to carry the burden. There may be no way to change this dynamic, but validating the client's desire to help and ability to focus on solutions (see T1.5) might provide a reason to keep compromising when it is not appreciated or even being consciously manipulated.

Boundaries vs. Pressure

The idea of asserting boundaries and saying no to unreasonable requests sounds great on paper, but the reality is very different. In fact, the very idea of saying no to a family member can send shivers down the spines of clients who dread the repercussions. Depending on the family's individual and collective needs and priorities, these may take precedence over others, and thus, they may have no concept of what a boundary is. The client may have struggled with putting their needs first or may have lost all sense of what their needs are. For the purpose of helping the client during times when they are dealing with family requests, here are some points to consider with them.

EXPLORING PRESSURES

How the client experiences or perceives pressure will be unique and relative to their history with family. The pressures might be covert, such as disapproving remarks, sounds, or facial expressions, or more overt, such as direct criticism or judgment. The client might need these validated, especially if they were experienced behind closed doors with no other witnesses.

RESPONDING TO PRESSURE

How a client reacts to these experiences and perceived pressures will identify patterns that might not be helpful to them, such as apologizing, ruminating, shouting, or deflecting. It might be worthwhile discussing how they would like to respond going forward, and while this may seem unrealistic to them now, after a period of personal development, they might consider taking action on these changes.

FEELING PRESSURES

To take it to another level, the professional might discuss where exactly the client feels the pressure in their body, such as tightness in their chest, restlessness in their arms and legs, or tension in their back. Resourcing the client with a grounding exercise (see T2.3) might help them to stay connected to the uncomfortable sensations and observe them in order to reduce their impact.

T3.4: Asking for Help

It requires great courage to reach out to others, even if they appear to be closed to the client. Validating this courage is important, as the client might not feel courageous at all. They may have internalized so much criticism and judgment that they feel heartbroken and devastated, harbor a great deal of unexpressed anger, and carry even more shame and anxiety for feeling this anger. Because of this, asking for help will be tough for some clients, particularly if they have had no choice but to be completely self-reliant and don't believe they need help, or if they are terrified to open the box of painful emotions they have so diligently kept tightly closed. However, over time, they might start to get a better sense of how they have negatively changed over the period of estrangement, whether this comes from an observation from someone connected to the client or via their own awareness, and they now need more support. Unfortunately, if they are surrounded by people who do not have similar struggles with family, they may feel asking for help is pointless as they couldn't possibly know what they are going through. While to some extent this is possibly true, it does not mean the people around them 1) don't want to help or 2) don't know how to help.

If the client can find it in themselves to ask for help, it is useful to be clear about what exact help they need. Well-intentioned friends, family members, and even professionals may have missed the mark by not knowing what was needed, and encouraging the client to reflect on and verbalize these will save time and unnecessary stress. Based on the need(s), the client may need to actively train the helper, such as by preparing for an upcoming visit with the EP (see T6.5). Alas, the type of help they need will vary, such as some personal space or practical support, but believing they deserve this support may require regular convincing and persistence from the professional working with them.

T4: Repairing Strategies

When working with estranged adults, I always try to look past the various interpersonal and intrafamilial reasons behind an estrangement to find something more fundamental, and I consistently discover how family members appear to be removed from the inner lives and struggles of their kin. Despite the many years spent together and the many events shared, it is tragic to hear how little each person truly knows or cares to know about those they have spent literally a lifetime around. It is almost like they are house guests, just coexisting and occasionally interacting with each other. I appreciate that everyone is entitled to a private life, and it is unrealistic to expect everyone in a family to be close, but this goes beyond just living their own lives. It is equally disappointing to hear of families that were once very close and shared everything, then became strangers almost overnight, and how all the history between them seems to now mean nothing.

There are many ways families can't see or don't know each other; it could be due to a lack of context, especially if there is a large generational gap or just a lack of understanding of the personal, social, and environmental pressures a family member is experiencing; it could be the product of a rigid and possibly negative outlook, where family chose presumption over fact finding; it could be a self-protective strategy, choosing to withhold life choices away from family or wearing masks suggesting everything is fine, to avoid disapproval, conflict and/or rejection; or it could be outside influences, and how family member(s) seem to devalue their relationship with kin in favor of someone else.

At some point, a client or their EP may make the bold move of reaching out with the intention of expressing that which they could not have done previously and possibly mending the damaged or severed bond. As difficult as family life was pre-estrangement, trying to repair the relationship with this same family member might prove even more difficult, but that does not mean it is not worth trying, and below are some further considerations to discuss with the client.

T4.1: Establishing Intent

When any client suggests attempting a reconciliation, my initial response is always "What has changed to prompt this?" Whether in response to a request from others or from their own urge, it is important to explore the decision and its implications, and below are some questions that might guide this. The goal of these is not to deter or fuel uncertainty but to reflect on lessons learned and if the client feels there has been any real change in the passage of time:

- What is life currently like? Is it tough, passable, or even a little better than when they last had a relationship with the EP?
- If they are initiating a reconciliation, why are they the ones making their intentions known first? Are there past patterns of them taking the bulk of the responsibility? Do they feel the EP will be prepared to meet the client halfway?
- Are they prepared to fight for this? How much effort and energy are they prepared to invest?
- Can they strive to find the right words to align with their experiences? When it comes to explaining themselves, is there a cutoff point where enough is enough? If an apology is required, either from the client or the EP, will it be accepted? If an apology is required, are they prepared to ask for it?

- Are they prepared to re-establish the relationship's rules and boundaries? What behaviors, attitudes, and expectations will they tolerate going forward? Will they accept being made to feel bad?
- What is life like for the EP now? Have the EPs moved on with their own lives to the point where they might not make room for the client? Will they include and involve the client fully or keep them on the outer rim?
- Are they hoping the EP will change?
- Is the client capable of change? Do they feel they need to change at all? Are they the only ones trying to change?
- What happens if the reconciliation attempts are rejected or ignored? Can they live with the knowledge they tried? Do they have support in place after the attempt?
- What happens if the reconciliation attempts are initially successful? Do they have the patience and determination to persist in the face of any setbacks that might later present themselves?

Encouraging the client to journal (see T2.5) on these questions will help them to reflect on their why, i.e., the personal reasons that they attribute to the estrangement, but the why comes in two sizes. The **Big Why** represents the estrangement dynamic between the principal estranged parties, leading to one or more people consciously creating distance from each other, and is the reason many will focus on. However, the **BIGGER WHY** represents something more expansive and far-reaching, such as why estrangement exists and persists in some families more than others. While the **Big Why** will be hard to answer, the **BIGGER WHY** might feel impossible as it involves people and stories that are often lost over time or silenced, perhaps due to estrangement. So, the client may have no choice but to focus on the **Big Why** when reconnecting with some or all of the EP.

In step one of the *Estrangement Inquiry Model* we established who the EP are, and in the context of reconciliation, this can be used to establish who exactly the client wishes to reconcile with. If there are many parties involved, depending on the estrangement dynamic, the client may be unable to or not desire to reconcile with all of them. The client's *estrangement map* will reveal some factors, and taking the time to reflect on each person as a separate entity might help to focus on their perspective as much as the clients, prioritizing what issues are worth addressing and how much tact is required.

T4.2: Clarify Content

To successfully come together, the EP needs to be able to at least entertain and accept that each party has their own estrangement narrative. This does not mean they have to agree with it, but the foundation of any relationship should not crumble under the weight of disagreement or even a family crisis. Once the client is clear on their why and who, it is useful to then explore what exactly they want to say. This might feel like an impossible task if there is a lot to say; however, with research suggesting the major reason families become estranged is inadequate communication (Allen & Moore, 2016), taking the time to be clear on the language needed to relay even a small measure of the issues is worthwhile. One helpful way of doing this is to send a letter to the EP to ensure nothing is missed. This letter is not necessarily sent and only serves to provide some clarity, but I will discuss the different ways of contacting family in the next section. There are several advantages to letter writing, such as:

- Writing helps formulate clear responses to potential questions.
- Presuming the letter is read, there is no chance of interruption mid-sentence, so important points can be completed.
- There is a sense of safety in writing, as there is no immediate reactivity or threat.

Instead of sending the letter to the EP, it might be useful to first read the letter aloud directly to someone they trust, such as a professional. This is common practice in therapy; the therapist's compassion and healthy distance from the situation facilitate safe expression. The letter must be seen and heard from the place in which it was written, not just in the words but in their tone of voice, in their eyes and face, in their posture and gestures, in everything that is unique to them. Safety permits slowing down the process of reading the letter and thus allowing the client to slow down, sit with the difficult emotions in the present moment, and work through them in a way that was too difficult or impossible to do before.

This is not something to do without considering how the process of writing can leave a person feeling raw, vulnerable, and even more uncertain as to what to do next. However, reading this to a professional or someone in their support network can validate what they need to say while also making sure they are not being vague or caught up in petty issues. We can watch out for ambiguous language, which can be easily misconstrued, and focus on their desires and how they would like them to be achieved.

Some of my clients are voracious readers, especially in the fields of psychology and self-help, and adopt technical terms or lingo that might not connect with their families' level of understanding or could be perceived as condescending. I would encourage using natural, conversational language and emphasize being understood as opposed to sounding impressive. It can also be more beneficial to acknowledge their own faults or how they are in some way responsible for what happened, with the hope that the EP will reflect on the same. Acknowledging the EP's perspective might also help. For example, consciously respecting differences in beliefs and values may promote both individuality and tolerance. However, if this feels wrong, letting them know their vision of what the relationship could look like and how this comes from a place of love might be more helpful.

Some will naturally struggle to comprehend a person's subjective experiences, so I find the use of analogy can be a useful way of sparking the imagination, referencing personal stories to reach them in a way conventional dialog cannot. Framing issues around their own experiences of conflict, stress, and isolation may help the client connect with the EP emotionally more than cognitively. This is also useful to avoid anything that can be perceived as nit-picking and focus on the bigger picture, such as recurring themes of conflict and expectations and how these are contributing to the overall breakdown of relations.

T4.3: Timing and Delivery

Timing is everything, both for the client and for others. Any attempt to reach out, whether it is via letter, phone call, email, or text message, received at the wrong time could be ignored, skimmed over, or read in a haze of stress, and it might be worth considering these questions before the client does anything further.

- Do they think the EP will be more open to listening now or soon?
- Are there other issues in the EP's lives preventing them from hearing the client?
- Have circumstances in the EP's own life changed that may alter their perceptions of the client?

They may not find answers to these questions, but a bit of detective work with other family members might shed a little light. Alas, it is impossible to control the outcome, and a negative reaction can be crushing. This is why professionals should ensure the client is prioritizing self-care to mitigate against the negative repercussions of a failed reconciliation attempt. When I say self-care, I don't mean the occasional bath, workout, healthy dinner, or other ways in which people are kind to themselves temporarily. Those living with estrangement need to apply a business-like approach to self-care by consciously planning what steps they will take every day to tend to their physical and mental health, as well as ensuring they have the right accountability in place to consistently put their plan into action (see T5.2).

The way reconciliation happens must also be carefully decided to reduce the chance of misinterpretation and/or avoid a re-creation of the old dynamic. Some decide to grab the bull by the horns, so to speak, and confront the issues immediately. Some wait for what they perceive as the ideal moment. Some may begin to exchange civilities via text messages to set up a future conversation. In step five of the *Estrangement Inquiry Model*, we determined the estrangement method, and this gives us some insight into how the family communicates. This can help inform what the preferred mode of delivering information is, and it might be best to keep to this to respect boundaries and hopefully reduce the chances of it being ignored. However, these might not work if there is a lot to be shared, so it might be best to pick a medium that matches the content. Another way is to relay a message via a third party, which may be how the estrangement was communicated. This might or might not be a good thing, depending on how neutral and tactful the third party is, but the EP might not appreciate the involvement of others. There is the old-school face-to-face conversation, which can be difficult depending on the type of estrangement, which may be physical, and the estrangement approach, which may be indirect, and thus, communication quality is poor.

One last point that has come up in several conversations is whether the client should attend therapy with one or more of their EPs, and this is yet another divisive topic. I have discussed this with other therapists who had concerns about the EP colluding with the therapist against the client. This can be quite damaging and feel like another rejection, and it is a particular concern for estranged parents whose son or daughter offered this as the only option, although it can apply to any perspective. In some cases, when put in this situation, the parent declined the offer to attend therapy, and their window of opportunity to reconnect was closed, either temporarily or permanently, and this was devastating to them. My own approach has been to encourage the client to trust their own intuition but also be fully aware of the potential outcomes, whether positive or negative, and prepare for them as best as possible.

T4.4: Outcomes and Expectations

Another necessary discussion is exploring what the client's expectations are from the reconciliation attempt and if they are open to what might happen, as opposed to being locked into a specific outcome. If they have become used to disappointment due to consistently being let down or failing, they may become conditioned to give up early. I often ask my own clients to reflect on how long they are prepared to wait and what they are prepared to compromise on.

There are many ways a reconciliation attempt can be received: it may be viewed as an olive branch, an act of diplomacy, and an appreciated attempt to mend the emotional cracks; it may also be viewed as an attack or an act of dictatorship, diminishing the EP's character; or it may be met with apprehension and distrust. However, where some families are oblivious to the negative effect they have on the client, the attempt may be an eye-opener as they begin to realize their role in the client's life. The client or their EP may be asked to backup or explain words, and while they might be initially defensive, this might be driven by genuine fear, surprise, and all the other emotions triggered when confronted. Alternatively, the client may get a response of pure anger, but such is the complexity of human interaction that the client may get a confusing response, such as semi-acknowledgements, or they may get nothing at all, creating an anti-climactic sense of disappointment and/or relief. Living with this disappointment is another reality many of my own clients must face, and to work with this, we might take the time to find a bigger purpose and meaning (see T7) for their lives.

Unfortunately, some families are too fractured to rebuild a solid bridge. The truth is a very complex thing as there are many ways to tell the same story, and one person's truth may be vastly different from another's, but as I have said, this does not mean it is not worth trying. Some lessons are hard learned, and while they might have some success with the EP, perhaps another negative experience may be the necessary step in helping the client to embrace what they should do next.

The client might consider the work of other estrangement authors who explore different perspectives on reconciliations, such as Karl Pillemer's *Fault Lines: Fractured Families and How to Mend Them* (Pillemer, 2020), Joshua Coleman's *The Rules of Estrangement: Why Adult Children Cut Ties and How to Heal the Conflict* (Coleman, 2021b), Tina Gilbertson's *Reconnecting with Your Estranged Adult Child: Practical Tips and Tools to Heal Your Relationship* (Gilbertson, 2020), and Laura Davis's *I Thought We'd Never Speak Again* (Davis, 2013).

T5: Parking Strategies

An estrangement and its impact can pervade every aspect of a client's life, including work, social engagements, health and wellbeing, and time with non-estranged family. In particular, the previously mentioned rumination, which is understandable as the situation would play on their mind as they seek (and struggle) to find a resolution, can also become all-consuming and rob the client of their focus and attention. Thus, while respecting the role rumination will play in their lives, clients will benefit from learning how to effectively park their estrangement for the short, medium, or long term so they can prioritize other important areas.

To be clear, parking is not the same as running away or avoiding issues. If it is obvious that the client has exhausted every avenue in trying to make sense of the situation but still feels like they are struggling to find a place in their head to position the estrangement, this will free up some cognitive real estate that can be populated with things that matter to the client. There may be added urgency to this if others connected to the client are personally affected by this inability to be present and focus on pressing issues. For example, a partner or child may become upset that the client is constantly distracted, perhaps unhappy, and feel helpless to do anything. If this is then expressed to the client, it might add extra pressure on them to feel differently, and providing some strategies to function a little better may ease this pressure. However, the first step in parking estrangement is the most necessary, as it involves each client making an agreement with themselves to commit to showing up, both for those who need them but also for themselves, to living their lives as best as possible, and to commit to healing, irrespective of the setbacks they will inevitably face.

T5.1: Scheduling Reflective Time

The more a person is asked to stop thinking about a "thing", or in this case, their family, the harder it will be for them to not think about them. I don't believe there is any point in battling patterns of rumination, as it only dismisses the powerful bond of family. Instead, I find it more effective to assign dedicated time each day for active reflection to allow a client to work through their current thought process and then put it aside for the day. There may be trial and error for the client to find out what works best for them, but I generally suggest ten minutes at the start and then build up to a 30-minute window of dedicated reflection, either in the morning or evening, as one might suit the client more than the other. While some will prefer to do this right after they wake up or soon after, others would rather do it later as they wind down their day. There are benefits to both; morning time might help the client eventually put aside the family situation for the rest of the day, whereas evening time might help the client sleep after taking the time to reflect.

This time can be used to talk to a partner, friend, or anyone else in their support network, such as an accountability buddy (see T5.2), or to journal (see T2.5), as opposed to just ruminating in their heads. What they do with this time will depend on how the client feels as well as the support available. If they are journaling, and they only have a short time frame, it would be best if they focused on a specific challenge, emotion, memory, or anything else that is bothering them. This time might also be used to do any homework or exercises they may have been given if they are working with a professional. Letting their partner know they are taking this time and where it will happen, i.e., specifying the room, will relay the importance of this reflective time and actively involve them in the overall process. There is an element of discipline required to maintain this regularly and keep it to 30 minutes only, but knowing they have this dedicated space will be helpful if they become overwhelmed at any point in the day but still need to focus on present-moment issues.

T5.2: Finding an Accountability Buddy

We can all easily be distracted from our plans or goals when faced with setbacks, and this will be particularly true of estrangement, where setbacks are around every corner, whether they come from interactions with family or any trigger that reminds the client of the situation. These setbacks can significantly hinder a client's progress, but one way to overcome them is to encourage the client to find someone on a similar path who will motivate them to keep going. A professional might act in this capacity, but it could be anyone in the client's life, such as a friend who is aware of their struggle or even someone they met in a support group. The client might resist approaching someone because they are too embarrassed to ask, but taking a risk is a step towards growth. Plus, the person they ask may be yearning for more accountability for themselves.

Accountability may not be specific to the estrangement and is more connected to other life goals, so the accountability partner does not need to be estranged themselves but just have similar goals, and thus they can help each other. How they hold each other accountable is up to them. It could be a check-in message every few days, or they might schedule time to talk, to train, or to do whatever it is they are aspiring to do. They might share specific goals with a clear timeline, so each knows where the other hopes to be. Or they may work together to help when there is a specific upcoming event, and this might include an impending family gathering that they fear might set them back (see T6.5). Unfortunately, not everyone will have access to this type of person, and I would not push too hard as it may cause frustration for the client, but suggesting it once may keep them open to the idea of an accountability buddy and seeking one out.

T5.3: Being Busy

Another aspect of parking is helping the client keep their mind occupied, and this might involve being busy. To do this, they may naturally gravitate towards doing certain things, like regularly cleaning, baking, exercising, and other behaviors to distract themselves. These could also be considered coping mechanisms and validated as such (see T1.5). However, I find it best to plan this so the client is more directed towards personal goals and things they have always aspired to do.

When discussing how they might park their situation, a professional might also discuss what the client's priorities are. This includes exploring the different aspects of their lives, such as taking care of non-estranged family, spending time with friends, managing their health and financial responsibilities, personal projects, professional ambitions, and vacation plans. Suggesting to a client that they focus their energy on these, as difficult as it is, may be a step towards reclaiming some autonomy that may have been lost to the estrangement. It might help for the client to create a visual representation of these priorities, such as a poster, which the client can place somewhere in their line of sight and act as a reminder of where their attention could or should be. This can be done as a creative exercise (see T2.6), where the client can use different colors, images, textures, or mediums, such as hand-drawn or digital images, to make an engaging chart that they can come back to regularly and even further refine as they continue their lives.

However, it is not enough to just discuss these priorities, and I would ask the client to detail exactly how they will do this. This could involve exploring their schedule for these priorities, how much time and energy they will commit to them and who they need to share them with. They can even add these details to the above poster to add more depth and hopefully keep the client on track.

T5.4: Getting Lost

This strategy came to me one Christmas when I had the unusual opportunity to travel to Cambodia over the festive season. As mentioned, this time of the year can be particularly tough for estranged people, and that included me, which is probably why I jumped at the chance to break my own routine. Maybe it was the hot climate and the incredible culture and environment, but the shift in location allowed me to completely wind down, relax, and distance myself from the pain of my family situation. Similarly, many of my clients have made a point of being away for holiday periods, and getting lost in new environments helped them get away from the situation, if even temporarily. Not everyone will have the time, freedom, or funds to go to Cambodia or even anywhere else abroad, but I would still encourage a client to visit new places locally, create new memories and experiences, and allow these to act as a healthy distraction. There can be an excitement about seeing new places, and helping clients reconnect with this could also instill a sense of optimism for the future and connectedness with others with whom the client shares the experience.

This can start by asking the client to list places they would like to visit that are within their reach and places they would love to someday visit. If they are unsure of local sites or landmarks, suggesting websites, such as TripAdvisor (www.trip advisor.com) might help, as might searching for travel bloggers on different social media platforms who have visited their city or town and can provide more insight.

There may be resistance from the client with this, as they may just want to withdraw to their home and stay there, so it may take some willpower from them to push against any desire to hibernate, but they might surprise themselves and enjoy the experience. Even if a client has no capacity to travel, encouraging them to read books or watch movies might offer some escapism and trigger a desire to explore their environment.

T5.5: Starting a Project

If there is one thing that I insist all my clients try to do, it is to start a project. This idea came from witnessing the buildup of physical and emotional energy my clients carried that was yearning desperately to be expressed. Because of the deep wounds of estrangement and an even deeper sense of isolation, this energy has become trapped, stagnant, and even destructive, but if harnessed, it can be used productively and perhaps become transformative.

The project has to come from the client, and it might be overtly connected to their estrangement, but it might have nothing at all to do with family. It might involve creative writing, arts and crafts, the humanities and charitable work, sporting or academic achievement, or any field that engages the client and which they can use their negative experiences to drive. This project can give a client purpose, which I will discuss more in T7, but it may also motivate them to embrace each day instead of dreading it. A project will also act as a necessary distraction, and it might foster new social connections with people who are working on similar projects or are inspired by the client. Finding this project may take time as the client may have no concept of what they might do, but planting the seeds of curiosity by suggesting this may be enough to get them thinking and seeking ideas.

T6: Re-Engaging Strategies

The pressure to re-engage with the EP for the reasons previously mentioned, despite the family history, stress, and maybe lack of desire, can be powerful. Having contact with estranged family can be very distressing (Linden & Sillence, 2021), but the context of the re-engagement is important as it will dictate the level of distress. For example, visiting estranged family is not the same as being tasked with caring for them. With research highlighting the usefulness of developing strategies for future events and circumstances, such as illnesses and deaths in the family (Blake et al., 2022b), I have included some below to make the situation more manageable, both socially and emotionally, for the client.

Before I proceed, I want to state one more thing. In the event of sickness or even a funeral, I know some who chose not to visit for personal reasons, and there is no judgment from me if that is how a client feels, as it reflects the family history and how they have been treated. This might be the case if there has been zero contact with the EP and if the client feels there is no point in pretending everything is fine and would rather stay true to their own feelings. At the same time, if they feel they must attend these events, professionals can still validate the experiences and feelings that underpin their desire not to attend.

T6.1: Pre and Post-Visit Stabilization

The stress of an impending visit could begin weeks or even months before the event. This will be the case if there is a history of recurring conflict and damaging behaviors from certain family members that have left deep emotional scars and possibly trauma for the client. These traumas can be uncovered just by thinking about the source, sending the client into a heightened state of anxiety. Similarly, the aftermath of a visit may be equally difficult for a range of reasons, such as fears of repercussions. However, even if nothing happens, the client may experience symptoms of depression. Acknowledging the pre and post-impact will normalize their experience and hopefully encourage them to prepare for this by focusing on stabilizing their lives around these times. Here are some ways the professional might help the client do this.

Pre-Visit

In the days or weeks before a visit, the client may already be highly stressed in anticipation of the visit, and encouraging them to diligently drink water to stay hydrated will actively reduce this stress and its symptoms. Encouraging the client to exercise, particularly on the morning of the visit, will also help keep stress levels down.

Making post-visit plans is useful as it might give them something to look forward to and get them through this difficult event. Ideally, these plans will not be casual and should involve something the client is genuinely excited to do. Asking the client to go through these plans in detail will strengthen their importance to the client, and they might also be part of their exit strategy (see T6.4).

Letting others in the client's support network know of the impending visit, including any professionals working with them, will give them a sense that they are not alone. These people might also help the client clarify how they might plan out the other strategies in this section, as well as play an active role in the exit strategy.

Post-Visit

After each visit, acknowledging that they got through it and were able to cope better than expected might be appreciated. Taking the time to debrief with someone in their support network will give the client space to decompress emotionally while also deconstructing what did or didn't happen. They may also need their interactions with family validated, particularly if they appear to be manipulative and/or antagonistic. This analysis is not the same as rumination, although the client will eventually need to draw a line under the event and focus their attention elsewhere.

Making plans is not enough; the client must act on them, and an accountability buddy (see T5.2) will encourage this. Also important is encouraging the client to consciously recharge and focusing on reclaiming their energy via sleep, movement nutrition, and setting goals after each visit.

T6.2: Setting their Agenda

In the repairing strategies section I discuss the client's expectations (see T4.4) when making a reconciliation attempt, but this is relevant to all engagements with the EP. These expectations, whether positive or negative, although predominantly negative with my own clients, will determine the client's agenda, i.e., when they will arrive and leave, and their intention for the visit. Below are some considerations for this:

- Sticking to the agenda involves the client being very clear on why they are here, e.g., is it for the sake of the children, is it to make an appearance, is it to ease guilt, etc.
- This also involves deciding how much information they wish to share, and it might be worth reminding the client that their private life is privileged and they are not obliged to share anything if they are not comfortable doing so.
- They might need to watch out for conversation ambushes, where a simple exchange is designed to guide the client into revealing something private or create an antagonistic scenario.
- They will need to check their own defensive responses, as they may become overly friendly and agreeable under pressure and compromise boundaries to placate and reduce any tension.

An agenda may need to be flexible and based on how the visit goes. So, if family members are being civil and friendly towards each other, the client may feel relatively comfortable and decide to stay longer.

T6.3: Finding their Watchtower

Another way to maintain some control over the situation is to position themselves in a physically neutral position where they can observe some of the dynamics that may have contributed to the estrangement. These can include *triangulation*, where two people, to manage any stresses between them, direct their discomfort at a third party deemed vulnerable (Haefner, 2014), the formation of allegiances and power dynamics, subtle passive-aggressive remarks, and more obvious criticisms.

Finding this figurative watchtower can help the client avoid the crossfire and protect themselves.

Alternatively, some of my clients cognitively switch off to family and effectively keep their heads out of the game. Withdrawing from their inner world and focusing on plans or other important considerations may seem rude if someone is explicitly talking to the client, but this is purely a self-protective measure and not a conscious decision to be ignorant.

T6.4: Exit Strategies

Finding a way out of a difficult family event might be as necessary as managing the visit itself, and one way of doing this is to have an exit plan, or several, to diffuse an incendiary situation and avoid making the estrangement worse. An exit plan is effectively an excuse to leave, but one that is hard to challenge. It might involve making legitimate commitments, such as the plans made during pre-visit stabilization (see T6.1), which are impossible to cancel. There will be more conviction to leave if the reasons are real and pressing, and it also means the client does not have to lie. I have found work or child commitments will go unquestioned, and it is not uncommon to say they need to take the children home to bed.

Another exit strategy is to have someone contact the client during the visit, creating a reason to leave, which again would ideally be legitimate. This could be the person from the pre-visit strategy and is referred to as a buffer, which I will elaborate on in the next section.

T6.5: Buffer Training

If the client is fortunate enough to have support, one function this person or persons can serve is acting as a deterrent to negative behaviors during a visit and acting as a buffer between the client and the EP. However, for a buffer to be effective, they need to be told how best to help, but we must first look at the characteristics of an effective buffer.

They must be someone the client trusts and feels safe around, trusting them to maintain composure if things get heated, not overshare any aspect of their private lives, and stick to the established agenda. The buffer knows they are present to primarily support the client, and this takes precedence over all other matters that might come up during the visit, aside from obvious emergencies. The buffer doesn't explicitly need to know the details of the family history, but just enough to know its impact on the client so they can get a sense of how difficult it is and how important their presence is. If they appear doubtful or dismissive, they might not be the right choice of buffer, as they may feel the client is being excessive and perhaps even paranoid. However, if they appear to understand the situation on either a cognitive or emotional level, or preferably both, then the client might start to guide them on what exactly they need from them. This includes:

- Being clear about the agenda and letting them know the topics or information that they do not wish to be shared.
- Asking them not to let their own frustration or anger get in the way of the agenda.
- Letting them know how the client would like them to respond in certain scenarios.
- Informing them of what cues, whether verbal or non-verbal, to look for when the client feels overwhelmed and needs some grounding or even a quick exit.

Can everyone in the client's life be a buffer? Unfortunately, the answer is no, and for a range of reasons, such as their own closeness and personal history to the EP or their general predisposition to stress and worry. Only the client will know this, and it is important to trust their instincts on this. Even if the client has the right buffer, they might not be able to be physically present at events. However, just having them on standby via mobile phone is better than nothing to create an emotional safety net if the event knocks the client back.

T7: Purpose and Meaning Strategies

At some point, a client may feel hopeless and lost, and this is completely understandable when we frame their struggles around the *estrangement impact triad* as well as how the situation has endured for many years. This will be particularly relevant if the client is faced with no closure or final goodbye with the EP. The client's life may have come to be completely defined by the estrangement, and irrespective of whether there is a reason or not, if the estrangement was chosen or not, or if it was communicated or not, the professional may find them in need of help in a way that is not explicitly practical. By this, I mean the client may be seeking answers to philosophical questions, such as why they are here, why they suffered this way, and what they need to do next. Finding purpose and meaning may help them unearth answers to these, which outweigh the hopelessness they feel, but it may also inspire them to use their experiences to improve not only their own lives but the lives of others.

Having a purpose in life has also been found to be a component of psychological wellbeing, particularly in being creative and productive by setting clear and direct goals (Ryff & Singer, 1996). When coupled with good social support, this will also have a positive impact on loneliness, which will be particularly relevant to estranged adults (Hill et al., 2023). This focus on wellbeing through purpose and meaning may be more effective than focusing on happiness, which might seem impossible to the client who is still grief-stricken by the loss and feels they will never get over it. This purpose must be relative to the client, as there will be factors that influence it, including their age, gender, education, and life experience, as well as cultural, religious, and other social influences. Thus, the purpose must also come from them for it to have any meaning or act as an anchor for the client, particularly during challenging times. Below are some suggestions for discussing the bigger picture of their lives.

T7.1: Searching for Symbolism

Deriving purpose and meaning may be hard to establish at any point during the estrangement process, and the client may resist this, but it may begin by suggesting that maybe there are less obvious signs just outside of their line of sight. These signs might reveal themselves in random conversations, real-life stories of adversity on TV, powerful and thought-provoking imagery, or anything else that might have hidden meaning and can act as a symbolic compass to guide them as to why they have had to endure this struggle and what they might do next.

Active reflection is a necessary component of this, as the client might need to cross-reference current knowledge and understanding with past experiences. This level of reflection might be triggered by periods of transition, such as birthdays, acknowledging the passing of the calendar year, meeting personal goals, such as changing jobs, etc. These can come to represent a new phase in their lives and the importance of letting go. They might take this time to reflect on those they have loved and lost, but not specifically from estrangement, and honor them and their wishes for the client. By focusing on lessons learned over the previous year and what they might do differently going forward, they might make radical changes that they would not have made if there was no estrangement, such as prioritizing their health.

Acts and Gestures

Symbolism may come from specific acts and gestures that are personal to the client and represent a conscious effort to make sense of their life and experiences. These can include:

- Writing a detailed and unfiltered letter to the EP, but instead of delivering this letter as it may not serve any positive purpose, doing something with it represents closure, such as ripping it up.
- If the client has strong religious or spiritual beliefs, praying or performing other traditional rituals might help them process emotions and perhaps let go and forgive those who have hurt them or those whom the client has hurt.
- This can also include symbolic gestures, such as committing to volunteer work or even sending gifts to disadvantaged adults or children, which would have been traditionally sent to the EP.

T7.2: Finding Role Models

During times when a client is struggling to function, suggesting they seek out others who inspire them might be very helpful. These could be real people who have struggled in their own lives but found a way to move forward despite the odds being heavily stacked against them. The role model could be a sporting figure, an artist, an educator, an activist, a philosopher, a political figure, or any high-profile person who has demonstrated traits the client admires, such as intelligence, compassion, determination, integrity, and generosity. These could be traits the clients share, such as the strengths and coping mechanisms in T1.5, but have never been recognized, or traits they wish the EP had. The client might connect with the role models stories, their struggles, their losses, their perspectives, and their attitude. I was personally inspired by several athletes who struggled very much with their mental health while also having young children. I could empathize with how hard this must have been for them and possibly their children, and I admired how they managed to overcome these obstacles and turn their lives around.

There are role models around every corner if the client keeps looking. They could be family members, like a grandparent, who had a strong connection to the client and who demonstrated the above-mentioned traits. In fact, if the client is comfortable, taking time to reflect on these connections with either those alive or those who have passed might evoke positive emotions that will remind them how much they are or were loved, and this might be exactly what they need to embrace their lives and enjoy every day with no shame or guilt.

Part 4

Case Studies

Up to this point in the book, I have offered theories and ideas around families, estrangement, and how we might help, and I will now explore five stories of differing perspectives and experiences. Each narrative is shaped around the specifics of each estrangement, the accompanying *estrangement map,* the impact, and the strengths and coping mechanisms adopted. I will integrate these with the mapping process and toolbox to offer suggestions on the interventions we might use to help. These stories do not represent the gamut of estrangement experiences, but will give some ideas. For confidentiality reasons, I have chosen to avoid real people and have crafted fictional accounts; although I name the parties involved in each narrative, these families do not represent actual families, but rather aspects of stories combined to paint a picture of what an estrangement might look and feel like.

Each story represents the past dynamics, current status, and present challenges the client is facing. And each subsequent *estrangement map* is an entry into the client's immediate world, evoking a deeper conversation about their family history and how they are struggling. At times, any thoughts shared or interventions suggested are as much based on professional intuition. So, while each professional will find their own insights and interpretations, these may change, and being open to not getting it right all the time will better serve our clients.

DOI: 10.4324/9781003362203-13

Case Studies

Chapter 9

Living on the Edge (Parental/Sibling Estrangement)

It was 4 a.m. Joan woke up as usual to check her phone. A chronic worrier, she was always on high alert, unable to relax for fear that something terrible might happen to someone in the family. This time, she had reason to worry. She had missed a call from her sister, who had left a voice message crying over the phone and telling her she needed to talk. In a state of panic, Joan phoned back immediately, but it rang through. She tried ringing several times but received no call back, and she didn't get much, if any, sleep after that. She rang her sister again the next day and the day after, but there was no answer. She then tried her mother; she wasn't answering either. Christmas was slowly creeping up, and weeks before the call, Joan had made the difficult decision that she wasn't going to visit the family this year. She was in her 30s and felt she had had enough of the stress and unpredictability of her family's behavior. Following long periods of inner turmoil over what to do – the age-old battle of head vs. heart – this was a huge turning point for Joan, defying her family's expectations and fighting the hold Joan's mother and sister had over her life.

After not hearing back from her family and many sleepless nights, she re-enforced her decision by sending a text message to her mother to say directly she wouldn't be visiting for Christmas this year. Almost like magic, her sister replied immediately, pretending that everything was ok and never mentioning the late-night call. In an amazing act of synchronicity, her mother sent a similar text message minutes later, acting as if there was no issue. Joan had taken part in variations of this drama many times before, particularly when her mother sensed any shift in the power dynamic between them; however, she was oblivious to how these acts simply validated Joan's gut feeling that she was being manipulated and there would be no change unless she initiated it.

Joan's father left when she was a child, and she was never sure why or even when (ET: absent). Her mother never felt compelled to explain in compassionate terms why their marriage broke down and how it had nothing to do with her, and like many children of broken homes, she personalized his act of leaving. At such a vulnerable and emotionally dependent stage in their lives, children need to be explicitly told and constantly reminded that it was not their fault, using sensitive language that respects their age. Believing she was responsible influenced her

DOI: 10.4324/9781003362203-14

development and need for security and love from her mother, the only attachment figure who remained in her life, but her mother's parenting style could only be described as harsh and inconsistent; her moods changed from one minute to the next and expectations followed suit. Throughout her childhood and teenage years, Joan deeply craved safety and acceptance from her mother, but she didn't have it to give. Later in life, Joan felt her mother may have suffered from an undiagnosed mental health condition, but this would never be confirmed.

Although there were stable times in her life, particularly when her mother managed to hold down a steady job, Joan always felt a constant sense of impending doom. The trauma of seeing her father walk away and her mother's constant complaining about him reinforced a deep-seeded fear of rejection, which would haunt her for many years. We are all prone to being critical of those we love, not with the intent of weakening them but perhaps hoping to highlight areas of personal frustration or possible improvement. However, when this is a pathological process of consistent put-downs with the sole intention of making a person feel inadequate, the obviousness of the intent does not ease the pain. Joan's mother was critical of her life choices, which did not suit her own needs. These criticisms included insisting on doing better in school and commenting on Joan's body and general appearance. With no buffer to stop these from penetrating her mind, Joan heavily internalized her mother's words and attitude, to the point where she became incredibly self-critical. This fed into her co-dependent, approval-seeking behavior, impacting many other areas of her life, especially her intimate relationships.

Despite her mother's attitude, Joan would not allow herself to be angry. Our environment and essential relationships determine the many lessons we learn about emotions, and Joan learned it was not safe to express her anger as her mother would just explode in response. The need for survival superseded her natural and authentic responses, which illegitimatized her feelings and worth. Her sense of unimportance led to many self-imposed rules around sacrifice and conformity. She appeared to become that which her mother wanted her to be, perhaps a representation of her own past and her relationships with her own parents.

Estrangement

Tired of the expectations, the boundary violations, and the worries, and completely drained of her resources, Joan initially pulled back cautiously (EN: voluntary). Although she slowly started to share less with her mother, positioning herself at the emotional end of the *estrangement continuum*, she did not initiate a full communication cut-off just yet (ET: emotional). At times, her mother would ring and then insist Joan call her back, as her phone bill was more important to her, but Joan would push back and say she could not. Eventually it became a text-only relationship, but Joan could not bring herself to move towards the more estranged end of the *estrangement continuum* just yet (ET: physical).

Joan did not want to lose her relationship with her sister despite the distance from her mother; this was perhaps why she did not estrange earlier, and this would later become another source of great pain for her (ET: secondary). Joan's mother treated her younger daughter completely differently, perhaps seeing more of herself in her and more of her husband in Joan. Her mother was considerably more concerned for her sister but was equally controlling of her. I could imagine a later estrangement between them as her sister's desire for independence grew, but there was nothing Joan could do to influence this.

With her sister's birthday looming, her mother ensured that all arrangements were made through her and would remind Joan of how she was letting her little sister down if she wasn't there. Joan was not yet ready to completely walk away, although I've never met anyone who was truly ready for this. She would wait until after the birthday to take a more permanent stance. It wasn't until several months had passed with no word from Joan that her mother realized what was happening.

Joan's mother began to influence her sister, alienating Joan and prompting the sister to collude. This started with small antagonistic remarks and demands for money from her sister, which Joan struggled to say no to, but eventually it accumulated in the Christmas phone call from the start of the chapter. Joan came to realize this was not a genuine call for help but rather an attempt at control, possibly instigated by her mother. It must have been hard for her sister to be part of this drama, but she might have felt like she had no choice.

Psychological Impact

One of the many ambiguities of estrangements is the paradoxical desire for both closeness and distance and the dance of re-connecting and re-estranging. Like many of my clients, Joan would spend years trying to resolve this invisible inner struggle. She knew she had to find a different way of living and relinquish the control her mother had over her; however, anxiety was Joan's cellmate in life. She had become conditioned to predict worst-case scenarios, compromise her boundaries, and avoid unnecessary conflict in her adult relationships to protect against a phantom menace. After pulling back from her mother and sister, her life was an emotional rollercoaster on which she felt trapped. The build up to the Christmas exchange with her mother had been long in the making and took its toll.

The initial physical distance did not help as she was still in a perpetual state of waiting for something, for anything, to happen, and resourcing (see T2) or parking strategies (see T5) might be helpful to Joan at this point. However, simply validating (see T1) her experiences and defensive need for preparedness in the context of her relationship with her mother might help to normalize her feelings while emphasizing safety in the present moment.

Despite how she felt, Joan held firm to her decision, fighting the urge to call or text and striving for a semblance of peace, however short-lived it might be. Over time, she heard nothing from them; perhaps they changed their approach and tried punishing her with silence, or maybe they were just getting on with their lives (EN: voluntary/mutual). The vigilance she felt was not just in relation to her outer world but also the oppressive internal presence of her mother; she did a good job of making sure Joan felt incompetent as the memories of judgment and criticism lingered. She did try to "fix" herself, finding ways to stabilize her distress and manage her worry. Another layer of estrangement ambiguity is how some seek independence by shutting out others and insisting on doing it themselves, when the real healing happens through interdependence and leaning on the love and support of those who really care about you.

Relational Struggles

Due to her lack of confidence, Joan did not make many friends in her hometown during her teenage years. Later, when she attended college in a different city and felt a measure of freedom, she began to reveal more of herself and make some friends. She eventually worked even further away and made more friends. Many were oblivious to her situation and would occasionally inquire about her family. This was always very difficult for Joan, as she already felt like she was hiding a dirty secret, didn't enjoy lying, but equally feared their judgment. She chose to say nothing for a long time, pretending everything was fine; although when she was in contact with her mother, she did reflect on the strangeness of how she lived two lives: one with friends, work, and hobbies, and a second with her mother, who seemed removed from her other world. Her mother didn't even know the names of Joan's friends, rarely asked about her career, and just presumed everything without ever asking. Joan was also aware of her own contribution to this by sharing very little information that could be used against her.

One saving grace was how her mother was also estranged from her own siblings, and thus there was no pressure from aunts and uncles to reconcile. However, any closeness with them was destroyed by Joan's mother's attitude and the need to pick a side, preventing her from accessing support from those who had first-hand experience and could possibly validate her decision. As we explored earlier, when trust is broken, it takes time and courage to let anyone back in. Joan would have to dig deep to find this courage and take huge personal risks in sharing her inner world with others, and in her own time, when she was ready, she would.

Other Social Challenges

Joan was hard working and diligent but, perhaps in response to her anxious attachment style with her mother, she often worried about losing her job, especially if she perceived a boss to be unhappy with her work, and yet this scenario would never become a reality.

Another hurdle Joan had to face was overcoming the hump of birthdays and Christmas. She struggled to allow herself to enjoy these periods as she clung to nostalgic memories of time gone by. She would spend several Christmases alone, as she did not feel comfortable telling friends she had no plans, and they presumed she would be with her family. However, one sensitive friend sensed there was something wrong and, without prying, asked her if she would like to spend the festive season with her, and it eventually became a tradition they would enjoy for years after.

Strengths and Coping Mechanisms

Joan had many strengths, but what was immediately obvious was her ability to relate to others. She was an excellent listener and could see past words to get to the essence of a problem or the point a person was making. She was also compassionate and protective of others. Despite many of my clients being reared in quite dispassionate homes, it amazes me how they retain their own warmth and capacity for love. Joan could have gone down a different path, becoming cynical and uncaring, but her desire to help and put others first was a gift that her family could not value. Like a rare find in a thrift shop, the right person can see value in something someone else views as just taking up space.

Long before her estrangement, she would occasionally need to escape her family, and walking became her way of achieving this. She would explore every corner of her hometown to get away, and she later developed a passion for travel. It is easy to dismiss the smallest of resources as insignificant, but their importance cannot be overstated. Something as simple as a long walk in nature can have a profoundly positive effect on emotional wellbeing (Bratman et al., 2019) and is considerably healthier than leaning on substances such as alcohol to reduce stress. The same goes for strengths that we pass off as inconsequential, and yet it often feels like compassion and unbroken attention have become rare commodities not easily found. Reinforcing their role in an individual's life through validation (see T1.5) can help empower the client as they realize they are not as weak as they thought. An important aspect of healing is balancing a positive attitude and perspective while acknowledging the very real negative impact of the situation hanging over them. Joan acknowledged she had more freedom now and was grateful for everything she had in life, including the steady group of friends around her.

The sheer terror of making a mistake and getting it wrong can present a huge personal crisis, and it was important for Joan to focus on bringing safety into her life (see T2.1). One way of doing this was by consciously spending time around people she trusted, where boundaries were clear and the agenda was transparent. She also needed to know that others would not ask about the situation, so she could drop her guard and relax. She eventually discussed the situation with her friends (see communication strategies in T3), and thankfully they were sensitive to how she might be struggling, but others are not so lucky and intrusive questions can be commonplace.

Joan had avoided conflict for many years due to her concern for how she would be perceived, but she became frustrated with how others would take advantage of her "nice person" persona and would occasionally speak condescendingly to her. She had to risk external judgment by standing up for herself, which was something she would constantly have to work on, but she was surprised at how some people responded. Naturally, there were those who reacted defensively but over time respected her more, and there were others who didn't respect her efforts at all, but she was seeing a side to them that she had no interest in being close to and so stopped chasing their approval.

Part of her journey was saying no to her mother at Christmas, and this became a defining moment in her life. Despite how cold walking away from family may appear, it is never easy, and irrespective of any potential positive outcomes of an estrangement, grief is unavoidable (see T1.4) and often silenced by shame. But by facing her shame, Joan disrupted a pattern that had existed for much of her adult life, and this would not be just another revolution in the cycle of estrangement. None of us can predict the future, and the uncertainty Joan felt didn't disappear, but she could no longer accept the old dynamic and knew it was time to focus on building her new life, despite not having the family support she yearned for.

Estrangement Map

Table 9.1 Joan's Estrangement Map

Client Name: Joan

EP	ET	EN	EA	EM	ED	ER	Notes
Mother	Initially Emotional, then Physical	Voluntary/Non-Mutual	Initially indirect but eventually direct	Text message	5 Years	Controlling behaviours, manipulation, and constant criticism. Possible mental health struggles	Joan slowly created distance by not sharing details of college and her financial situation with her Mother. She never felt comfortable expressing her feelings as her Mother would react with anger, so despite the initial text message, there is much unsaid between them
Sister	Secondary/Self-Protective	Voluntary/Non-Mutual	Direct	Text message	5 Years	Pressurizing Joan to reconcile, association with Mother	Her sister felt she was in the middle and had no choice but to insist on reconciliation. The client felt she was colluding with her Mother
Father	Absent	Involuntary	Indirect	No contact	25 Years	Divorce	She wasn't sure how old she was when her father left and was too afraid to ask her Mother. She had no contact with him after he left

General Notes/Observations

Validating Joan's decision to estrange and the type of distance required would be useful, especially if she is constantly ruminating over the situation. Joan is quite anxious and we might validate the experiences which created this and as well as focus on resourcing strategies to help her feel grounded. She is afraid her job will be impacted by her situation and how it plays on her mind, we might clarify her fears and start looking at parking strategies. She is currently single and would like to meet someone, but is unsure how to explain her situation, and it might be helpful to discuss how much she needs to share and at what point, whilst maintaining her boundaries. She worries about the future, her mother getting sick and how she will manage the situation, so we might explore different scenarios and how to respond to them.

Chapter 10

The People vs. Estrangement (Adult Son Estrangement)

"How can you not talk to your [**insert family member**]*?"* | *"You haven't seen* [**insert family member**] *in how long?"* | *"That's a bit harsh, isn't it? Maybe you need to forgive* [**insert family member**] *and forget!"*

Many people struggle to get their heads around estrangements. Even if they have had first-hand experience in their own family or have witnessed the behaviors that led to the estrangement of others, they still may not have the emotional context needed to fully grasp either the reasons or the impact of those behaviors. This might extend to regularly inquiring about the relationship, even though the client has repeatedly explained the situation in detail. The disenfranchised nature of estrangement from family leads many to suffer in silence. Being cut off from one's family is often seen as being cut off from what is considered normal, and many will react uncomfortably with the very notion that a client is not currently speaking to or may never speak to a family member again. It is quite telling that 68% of the participants in a 2015 study (Blake et al., 2015) felt there was a stigma associated with family estrangement. Specifically, they spoke of "feeling as if they were contradicting societal expectations and felt there was a general lack of understanding about estrangement" (Blake et al., 2015, p. 7). The idea of not having a close, or any, relationship with family can conflict with the idealized view of family as a respectful and supportive unit.

Setting an often-impossible standard, films and TV programs regularly offer an entertaining perspective on even the most dysfunctional families, as they laugh off certain behaviors, throw in a witty response to a dramatic situation, and then get back to the normal day-to-day way of life. In reality, not every family can or will be close; not every family will communicate effectively; and not every family and its members will have the coping mechanisms to deal with the many challenges life throws at them. For some, an estrangement might represent their only coping mechanism; however, irrespective of who is estranged or why, there will always be those who, at best, just won't get it and, at worst, will judge the estranged person for it.

Christine, who was estranged from her only son, Peter, was a victim of this stigma. She and Peter had been very close and were a great source of emotional support for each other. They would spend countless hours together just hanging out,

DOI: 10.4324/9781003362203-15

and he felt comfortable telling her his own fears and dreams. However, the relationship changed after he met and quickly married his wife, Elaine, who injected the emotional chaos of her own family into the relative calm of Christine's. Peter's relationship appeared to be a whirlwind romance which surprised his parents, as he had had relationships before and did not seem in a hurry to settle down. Despite this, they were very welcoming of his new partner but did not know what to expect. Unfortunately, there were issues from the beginning, as Elaine established herself as a difficult person. She was argumentative and unreasonable, which was something neither Christine nor Peter had any experience with in the family context. This included insisting on changing family plans at short notice as it did not suit her, making condescending remarks to Christine regarding her parenting abilities, and not expressing any gratitude for the efforts Christine made, including generous gifts at birthdays. This came up in an early conversation between Christine and her son, but due to their patient nature, they were quick to excuse her behaviour: "she's under a lot of pressure", "she had a difficult relationship with her own parents", and "she is really very loving but finds it hard to express it". Despite the issues, Peter continued with the relationship and eventually married Elaine. Although his parents were not happy, they accepted his choice and his feelings for his new wife; however, Elaine was less accepting.

Estrangement

Elaine appeared to view her husband's parents as an inconvenience and a source of frustration. Any effort Christine made to include and involve Elaine was initially met with dismissal, and then with contempt. Over a period of years, Christine felt Elaine slowly nipping away at Peter's confidence by emphasizing innocent mistakes he made and challenging his competence. She also questioned his loyalty to her and the closeness between himself and his mother. He had never had to defend himself in this way before, and was not prepared for the psychological attacks she made. This was made harder when they started a family, and after having two children, I wondered if he feared they would be negatively affected if he fought back with his wife.

Christine could see what was happening and was quick to stand up for her son, but this created a tense dynamic between them as Elaine was threatened by her directness and began to alienate Peter from her more. Aware of Elaine's rifts within her own family and friends, it still never dawned on them that she would turn on them. The biggest issue Christine had was her son's passive attitude and how he consciously distanced himself from the uncomfortable dynamic to avoid further stress. She trusted him to be reasonable and not allow any issues to get in the way of their relationship; however, the seemingly inevitable occurred. A relatively minor issue around dates for an event turned into an argument and complete communication breakdown, where he chose, or was pressurized, to side with his wife and cut contact with his mother completely (ET: physical). There was no build up, just a brief phone call, and then nothing else for many years (EN: involuntary;

EA: direct; EM: phone). She tried calling him on many occasions after this, but the phone was never answered. She would also continue to send cards and presents for the children, but she received no response from them. During one Christmas, she had presents for the children delivered to their house, but they were not home, and they refused to go to the postal depot to collect them, and this naturally hurt Christine deeply.

Christine would never know exactly why Elaine was the way she was. She would never meet her family, not that she particularly wanted to, but it might have explained what she was carrying over. Maybe Elaine harbored a great deal of unresolved anger and unconsciously projected it. Maybe she was jealous of what Christine and her son had, or maybe she just thrived on drama. There would be plenty of theories, but no insight or counsel would give Christine peace.

Psychological Impact

Like so many who are suddenly removed from the lives of those they love, Christine struggled to understand how her son could devalue their bond and the lovely times spent together. Years would go by as she analyzed what she did wrong, but no answer ever presented itself. Clarifying the family history might help, but validating the senseless nature of the estrangement might be more necessary (see T1). What pained her the most was knowing the impact this would have had on her own loving and supportive parents, had they been alive. They were just as close to Peter as she was, and in some way, she was grieving for them as much as herself. One tragic loss can emphasize another. It was hard enough losing her parents, even though they passed years ago, but to lose her only son in the way she did sent her into an avalanche of sadness and regret. She was also aware of the passing of time and how she had less of it, and she was particularly worried if her grandchildren would even remember her and her husband in the future. While everyone contributes in some way to the issues in a family, much of the situation was outside of her control, and part of healing was acknowledging the unfairness and legitimate anger she felt towards her son and daughter-in-law. From my experience, validation (see T1) is the only intervention possible in this incredible tough situation, but having someone to talk openly with will still be helpful in its own way.

Relational Struggles

I have only briefly mentioned Christine's husband, as she never spoke of the impact on him in any depth. Interestingly, there is a general disparity between male and female participation in estrangement research, with more women coming forward than men (Agllias, 2017; Allen & Moore, 2016; Blake et al., 2015; Carr et al., 2015; Scharp, 2014). This is also reflected in my clinical practice, where more women sought help for estrangement issues, as well as within the various estrangement support groups I have assisted, which have been predominantly attended by women. This unfortunately reduces our understanding of how fathers could be affected by an estrangement with their adult children and the type of assistance or support they need.

I refuse to believe Christine's husband was not affected by this as he lost his connection to his son, but each parent-child attachment is unique, and maybe he was less close than Christine. Nonetheless, while he was very supportive and protective of her, he was equally infuriated by the situation and the hurt her son and daughter-in-law had caused. But his anger gave her no comfort, and the last thing she wanted was more conflict. Despite this, I wondered had he approached the son directly this have been more helpful. Often families suffer in silence, choosing to complain to everyone except those who need to hear it. However, there are times when avoiding conflict can do more damage than good, and I appreciate that it is tough to know the best decision to make (see T1.3).

Eventually, she took a risk and shared the true impact of the situation with her friends (see T3.2). The fear of disclosing is often much worse than the actual reality, but even though they had no personal context to frame an understanding of her situation, the warmth of their empathy and respect for her privacy shone forth. They would never pry or ask about the situation, knowing that bringing it up would only make her feel uncomfortable, and they were inclusive and made efforts to make her feel valued and supported. She later regretted not telling them sooner and not having more faith in them.

Other Social Challenges

Estrangement does not touch every family. There are lots of healthy, loving families out there, and spending time around them and the safety and emotional support they offer each other can be enriching. It can also act as a reminder of what the client does not have, and Christine found it hard to be around her husband's family at times, as they were close and connected; it fueled the deep yearning she had to relive similar times with her son and grandchildren. But she also felt she could not tell them about the situation. Estrangement is so alien to such families, especially when talking out differences is a given. It is easy to have an opinion on any issue when not directly impacted by it, and it is equally easy to reduce complex situations into overly simplistic black-and-white views. To genuinely want to understand an estrangement and how it is impacting a person requires putting aside rigid ideas about family. It also requires being open to subtle dynamics that are beyond current awareness as well as cultural and generational differences. Unfortunately, many are not motivated to do this and would rather maintain a subjective and sometimes stigmatizing view of how and why distance exists in families.

After about a year, Christine did try on occasion to disclose, initially with an elderly aunt whose only wisdom was to tell her to just accept the situation. Others in the family, including her sisters, would ask her how her son was, knowing how close they once were. They would inquire about her grandchildren as well. She struggled to tell anyone that she had not seen them in some time and chose to be sparse with details to avoid getting into conversations about it. We could work on communication approaches (see T3) to help find the best way to explain every-thing, but perhaps helping her find support (see Part 2: The Support Dilemma) would be more useful.

Eventually, they found out the details but were caught in the middle and left in the difficult position of coordinating family events around this. Ultimately, as her son's children were so young, they felt it was best to prioritize them. So, on one family birthday, they chose to exclude Christine completely. This felt to her as if she were being punished despite having done nothing wrong, and although she would eventually reason with their decision, it did nothing to ease the loneliness she already felt. It is difficult to know if the decision to exclude any estranged family member for the sake of children is the right one or the wrong one. Past expe-riences will dictate this, but the consequences may cause further rifts, and I envy no one in this predicament. For clients in this situation, we can only advise them to take the time to weigh up the options (see T1.3) and trust their intuition in taking the best course of action.

To expect someone to move on from this or even find any positives would be an insult. Over time, she might allow herself to forget, even temporarily, but there were reminders of the good times around every corner. From watching a TV program of a family having fun to casual conversations over nothing specific to family, any-thing could trigger her sense of loss. Christine would then withdraw from friends as she became enveloped by her pain. Other times, she would have some drinks, drop the mask, and allow the sadness to exist publicly. Her friends would worry very much about her in this state, as they were used to seeing her composed but did not know what was driving it. Their pity only emphasized how her son could never fully grasp the full impact of his actions.

Strengths and Coping Mechanisms

Christine had strong morals and compassion for others. She was also solution-focused, had a sharp wit, and knew how to listen. She inherited these from her own mother, but her negative bias towards herself positioned them in her blind spot. And yet these traits, which her daughter-in-law would never have, eventually became a source of strength as she focused on helping others whenever and how-ever she could.

Staying true to her mother's way was also important. In times of hurt, it is important to stay connected to the strong attachments that have had a positive impact on us, both past and present, and she knew she must honor her mother by respecting herself. Redefining what a normal life is now is necessary and involves forging new memories and not allowing the situation to be so all-consuming. Christine maintained her love of travel (see T5.4) and would always plan her next adventure with her husband. Although her son and grandchildren were never far from her mind, she would allow herself to get lost in the culture and architecture of each place.

Christine's loving nature brought her great comfort. She chose to remain optimistic, hopeful that maybe things would change and she would be open to a reconnection with her son and his family. She was even prepared to take on board their issues with her, however unreasonable they might be. But she knew she couldn't spend her life waiting for this to happen. She would never stop loving her only son and grandchildren, but she would have to learn to live with the heartbreak, learn to live with the tragedy, and learn to love herself. A key part of this was honoring the energy she put into carrying, birthing, and raising her son to be the healthy person he is today, irrespective of how her hard work appeared to mean nothing to him.

Estrangement Map

Table 10.1 Christine's Estrangement Map

Client Name: Christine

EP	ET	EN	EA	EM	ED	ER	Notes
Adult-Son	Physical	Involuntary	Direct	Phone Call	Unclear exactly but several years	Unreasonable expectations/attitude, prioritizing feelings of his wife over his parents	She was devastated that she could not talk to son, although even if he did, he always sided with his wife. She could never understand why he devalued their relationship over something she felt was very small
Grandchild #1	Inherited/Physical	Involuntary	Indirect	No Contact	Unclear exactly but several years	Association with adult-son/daughter-in-law	She was equally devastated about the loss the relationship with her grandchildren, and would become overwhelmed with sadness on birthdays and holiday periods. There may also be feelings of shame but need to clarify this. She also feared the influence and perception her daughter-in-law might have over them
Grandchild #2	See above	See above	See above	See above	See above	See above	See above
Daughter-In-Law	Physical	Involuntary	Indirect	No Contact	Unclear exactly but several years	Not known, but the client feels resentment plays a part	She reached a point where so no longer cared why her daughter-in-law adopted her attitude

General Notes/Observations

Validating Christine's anger would be necessary as she may struggle to accept these feelings. Acknowledging the depth of her grief will also be necessary. Resourcing her during birthdays and holidays might be useful if she is anxious around these times and chooses to just withdrawn. Due to her sister's decision to exclude her, she may need help with future exchanges or events, i.e. re-engagement. There is the potential for secondary estrangements with her sisters which might upset her even more so we must be conscious and sensitive to this.

Chapter 11

The Long Goodbye (Parental Estrangement)

The build up to and initiation of an estrangement can act as a critical anchor in an individual's life. Time appears to stand still, and the internal clock stops as the EP becomes imprisoned in their own reality, constantly reimagining what, why, when, and how certain events played out, desperately hoping to find an answer to a problem that may have existed long before they were born, and yet time can often be a contentious topic when it comes to estrangement (see Points of Contention in Part 3: The Model/Step 6). While there will be some who might not be able to pinpoint exactly when the distancing process began, others will be convinced the estrangement began sooner or later than others in the family, perhaps furthering any on-going tensions.

In the case of Paul, he knew the exact date and time he last spoke with his father, and despite 15 years having passed since then, he still becomes distressed by the oppressive memories of him blaming Paul for all the issues within the family. As far back as he could remember, his father would blow up over the most trivial matter, and as a child and later in adult life, Paul would try to empathize with why his father was this way. Perhaps he was bullied as a child and could not stand up for himself. Was he now initiating a battle of wills to reclaim what he lost during those experiences? Or did he choose the easiest target available, the vulnerable son who loved him greatly? Paul spent much of his life caught in two places: one part of him wanted to attach to his father, terrified of losing his love, and yet another part felt the love simply wasn't there. In many ways, it sounded like his father was emotionally stuck, refusing to grow up and accept his role as a father. As the days became weeks, months, and years, Paul's father remained exactly where he always was. Later, when Paul found it difficult to move forward in life, he realized he was equally stuck.

Paul's parents had separated just before he was born, and he lived with his mother, who was empathic and acted as an important emotional buffer to the challenges he faced. Unfortunately, she could not buffer the biggest and most painful challenge. Like many children of broken homes, Paul had an irregular relationship with his father. After any parent leaves the home permanently, it can be tough to maintain a consistent relationship on either side, parent or child, but Paul, aware of

DOI: 10.4324/9781003362203-16

how close his friends were with their own fathers, would do anything to keep his own in his life.

There were good times between them, and his father had a wicked sense of humour, which would always make Paul laugh. But over a period of decades, he could see a subtle change in their relationship; he was no longer being treated or viewed as a son. As Paul became a young man, he was expected to provide excessive emotional support, and he would burden Paul with many of his problems. He also expected financial support, and never once did his father worry if this was taking its toll on him. He later learned his father was jealous of his career successes, despite all the sacrifices he made for their love and the hard work he put into his own education.

Paul spent much of his life trying to make sense of his father's many contradictions. For example, he would say he loved him but only demonstrate outwardly loving behavior when Paul was performing his duties; he would tell Paul he was welcome in his new family home but then criticize him for visiting too much; and he would say he missed Paul, but the thought of ringing him or even replying to a text message never crossed his mind. The dishonesty and unfairness of the entire relationship led to resentment building up in Paul, but unable to express himself, he would replay unresolved arguments with his father in his mind and what he wished he had said at the time. Eventually, he internalized his anger, finding reasons to hate himself.

It appeared the issues were not exclusive to his relationship with his son. Paul shared how his father was in a constant state of conflict with others and could go years fighting with them. Paul wasn't wired that way. Whenever his father was struggling, Paul would get a call looking for help, and naturally, whenever he declined, which wasn't often, he would not hesitate to resort to emotional blackmail to pressurize him or relay disappointment through passive-aggressive sighs of disappointment or prolonged silence. He could imagine the angry glare in his father's eyes had they been in the same room. He worked hard to hold onto his father – in fact, too hard. He had tried reasoning, pleading, and shouting, and now, for the sake of his own mental health, his only option was withdrawing completely (ET: physical). Pulling back was tough, but staying away was even tougher, as his urge to protect others and make peace was powerful, prompting him to pick up the phone and reconnect, thus walking back into the pain (ET: cyclical).

Estrangement

Initially, he would limit his interactions to phone calls and fight the urge to involve himself in his father's problems (EA: indirect). Paul shared how his father would only contact him if he needed something, and as soon as he realized his son would not enable this, he had no other reason to call him again except for the occasional redirection and attempts to antagonize him into reconnecting. Paul had walked this path many times before and knew where it led; however, the pressure his father placed on him was just too great, and he had no choice but to directly tell his father to leave him alone (EA: direct). A powerful part of Paul still held on, waiting and hoping that his father might find his own courage and do some authentic work on himself.

Despite everything, Paul still loved him very much, and his father's birthdays were particularly hard as he always felt compelled to call him. Since becoming a young adult, he would budget all year to save for family birthdays and Christmas and genuinely enjoyed helping, but this did not register with his father as he was not connected to Paul in such a way as to see the effort he was making.

Paul never heard from his father again. Even though he thought about him every day, he feels he was barely on his father's mind at all. Of course, he would never know the truth of this; even if he were in contact with him and told him this was how he felt, his father might simply deny it. But trust has broken by now, and Paul knows his father's words no longer carry any weight.

Psychological Impact

Paul blamed himself for the estrangement. He thought he was maintaining stability by constantly compromising, and when his father went too far, demanded too much of him, and expected him to always make peace, he blamed himself for not speaking up years ago. Validating (see T1) the dynamic between them and how it necessitated the estrangement would be important.

Paul felt he was only worthy if he was doing, giving, and caring. He identified as being a good person because just being a person wasn't good enough. To achieve this, he had to repress the real anger he felt. In fact, he became terrified of his anger, as the price of expression would be too great. Resourcing him so he could work through his anger, such as through the grounding exercise (see T2.3), might help him become less afraid of his emotions.

Despite pulling back, Paul was haunted by his father. Traumatized by the constant rejections, his inner world became a constant game of emotional shadow-boxing as he attempted to predict how his father might act and find an appropriate counter, but this was a fight he could never win, and his focus now was finding safety in whatever way he could (see T2.1).

Relational Struggles

Paul had a few intimate relationships in his life and was caring towards all of his partners; perhaps his healthy attachment to his loving and respectful mother carried forward to his relationships with other women. This does not mean he was perfect, and he acknowledged his own selfishness in his youth, but he punished himself enough for those times. Despite being very considerate and caring, there was a harsh impatience in him. Perhaps his father was the same when he was a child, unable to accept Paul's natural needs. He could see this in himself, where he would become frustrated with the dependency of others. He hated that side of himself; the part that was angry when he didn't need to be and the part that was critical when it was time to be compassionate. He had to battle with it and keep himself in check, but the self-punishment would not stop it; finding tenderness in the harsh internal terrain would perhaps be his greatest challenge. Finding compassion through resourcing, such as conscious breathing, could be useful (see T2.2).

When he eventually found the right partner, they were perfect for each other. Her template for a relationship was based on love, fun, and teamwork; she believed in commitment, had a solid career, and had a family orientation. His mother heavily contributed to his own template, and it was very much aligned with his partner, but no relationship is without its struggles. There were patterns of conflict over seemingly insignificant issues. The "thing" that caused the conflict was generally symbolic of something deeper, something fundamentally important to each person, but presented as an overreaction in the present. Thankfully, they were both committed to working through their distress, establishing when to speak up and when to turn a blind eye.

Like others who are living with estrangement, there were times he was distant when consumed with grief (see T1.4), and a cloud of depression would engulf him. This was very evident when he was surrounded by his partner's family, whose focus was on enjoying each other's company. Over time, his partner became used to him disappearing into his own world, but this was not a good place, and now more than ever, he needed someone who could pull him out of this state. "It is no loss anyway." Paul's partner, who had never met his father and had only heard bad things about him, would struggle to understand the complex nature of his grief. She could see the positive aspects of his life and felt this was all that mattered; however, Paul was grateful for what he had and was quick to recognize how others have it harder, but this does not nullify the pain of estrangement. This lack of understanding would be a source of frustration for Paul and his partner; they would need to be patient with each other and see past their own experiences while holding onto a healthy level of intimacy. Eventually, they would start their own family, and he would be the best dad he could be. His broken heart never left him, but he wore it with dignity. The rejections he experienced were never far away, but I hoped someday he could connect with himself in a way his father never could, from a place of acceptance without the old conditions he had no choice but to abide by.

Other Social Challenges

While his father was alive, Paul was always afraid of bumping into him or his family, as they did not live far away. He knew his father would either ignore him or feign politeness to draw him back in, both of which caused great distress and a desire to just run away. This carried through to his dreams, as he often had vivid images of his father. Interesting, in his dreams he also ran away from him, suggesting this is something he desired to do, perhaps for a long time, but felt he could not. His father's eventual passing and funeral years later were always going to be tough. He had anticipated this inevitability, and in his mind, he auditioned many ways the funeral would play out. In particular, he was conscious of how there were people in his father's life who had never met him and were probably influenced by whatever victim narrative his father had spun. This proved true, as strangers described him as a loving person who did everything for his family but was simply unlucky in life. Paul was less affected by this than he felt he would be, as he had embraced his own truth and experiences (see T1.2). This involved being vulnerable around those who did love him and using their emotional support to complete his childhood grief. There were times he sobbed uncontrollably, but he didn't withdraw to his bedroom alone like he did in the past and instead let the grief be in the present. This was something he would continue to do for several years, and eventually he reached a place where he didn't seek external validation, but healing would be a lifelong endeavor.

As Paul's father was estranged from his own siblings and thus their families, he inherited estrangements from aunts and cousins (ET: inherited; EN: involuntary; EA: indirect). Over the years, at the rare times when they were under the same roof, his father would say he didn't care if he spoke to them, but Paul knew he would turn on him later for being disloyal. Recognizing his extended family as healthy and close, he felt an urge to reconnect (see T4) with them but feared they would insist on reconciliation. It was years before they did reach out to him, and there were some polite exchanges via email. Maybe in time, he will re-connect with them fully.

Strength and Coping Mechanisms

Paul was direct in his language, thoughtful, and interested in others, being extra conscientious of their feelings. His social skills were strong, and he developed a solid group of friends, but they all had solid relationships with their own families, and there were times he questioned if they could ever understand the impact his relationship with his father had on him. However, he was taken aback one time when, during a particularly low period of depression, an empathetic friend commented on how he seemed to want to smile but something was holding him back. This acknowledgement disarmed him but eased the isolation he felt.

We all need ways to switch off and escape reality, and for Paul, it was reading. Some of the happiest memories of his childhood were of losing himself (see T5.4) in bookshops and libraries, and now he would listen to endless podcasts discussing new writers and published works. Plus, the stories and characters acted as motivation to keep going (see T7.2), something to look forward to, and something to associate with happier times.

The battle of wills with his father instilled in him discipline and focus; once he committed to something, he saw it through. Practical and solution-focused, perhaps these were adaptations as his father's life would be hit with many self-made problems, and Paul's codependent need for everything to be fine would drive him to step up and look for ways to fix the issue. He would think things through in detail, although some of this was driven by a deep fear of getting into trouble and of the consequences of making a mistake. This would become an issue later when he felt pressured to solve the estrangement and his relationship with his father. Ultimately, there was no solution, or rather, it was not his job to find one. Paul had to stop trying to fix what he didn't break and put his energy into re-establishing relationships based on the interdependence and trust we all need to grow as human beings.

Estrangement Map

Table 11.1 Paul's Estrangement Map

Client Name: Paul

EP	ET	EN	EA	EM	ED	ER	Notes
Father	Physical/Cyclical	Voluntary/Mutual	Initially indirect and then direct	Phone	15 years	Unreasonable expectations/Neglect/Emotional Abuse	Much time would be spent understanding why his father was the way he was and the impact of their relationship, separating who he really is from his father's projection. Rebuilding self-worth by focusing on his strengths will be important. Connecting both with his anger and grief would an ongoing process. He could carry attachment trauma, so resourcing would be helpful
Aunt #1	Inherited/Physical	Voluntary/Non-Mutual	Indirect	Not attending events	Unclear exactly but several years	Pressure from father	Considered voluntary although it was the product of issues with his father and not Paul, and he did not want to anger his father. Paul might have considered reconnecting with them as there was no negative history between them
Uncle #1	See above	See above	See above	See above	See above	See above	See above
Aunt #2	See above	See above	See above	See above	See above	See above	See above
Aunt #2	See above	See above	See above	See above	See above	See above	See above
Multiple Cousins	See above	See above	See above	See above	See above	See above	See above

General Notes/Observations

A map can change after reflection; in this case, Paul initially only listed his father as the EP but once he reflected on the bigger family structure and relational dynamics, he decided to add his aunts/uncles and cousins. He might later consider reconnecting with them as there was no specific issues between them. Exploring patterns of compromising might be helpful, as well as resourcing him ahead of anxious times when he might need to speak up and put his own needs first. Paul's grief would be complicated as he never had a final moment to make peace with his father and validating this and giving him space to express his hurt might help.

Chapter 12

Perpetually Sorry (Sibling Estrangement)

Perspective is everything when it comes to relationships. Perspective shapes how we view individual personalities, the source of specific issues, and how we respond to these issues. Within the context of estrangement, perspective determines if it is warranted or unnecessary, a blessing or a curse, or something in between. When perspectives are worlds apart, family members can feel blindsided, as an estrangement was the very last thing they would consider, and despite how difficult the relationship may have been, they cannot believe someone they have known for most of their lives would respond this way.

Susan was one such person who was left devastated when her sister Rose cut her out of her life. Despite them never having a close relationship, they had circled in and out of estrangements several times, and each time it would hit her to the core. As she shared stories of Rose's sudden aggressive responses to a seemingly insignificant remark and how she appeared to be punishing Susan by cutting all contact, I wondered if maybe devastated was the only appropriate word to use. Susan came from a big family and was the middle child of two older and two younger siblings, with a gap of only a few years between them. To an outsider looking in, there were no apparent issues with her parents and siblings, and over the course of her young adult life, she would describe them all as being a happy unit, projecting an image to friends that they were a supportive, healthy family. Years later, she would question if this was true; the bond between her and the family was not particularly strong, except for her father, who was kind and showed an interest in all of the siblings' hobbies. For many years, Susan's mother was career-focused and part of a senior management team in a large firm, which meant working long hours and not being physically present a lot of the time. When she was at home, she seemed distracted or generally elsewhere in her mind. Her goals took priority over everything else within the family, and each sibling had to fend for themselves to avoid being a nuisance. Her husband was there, but he didn't seem to be able to handle the challenges of looking after five kids, so strict rules were put in place around conflict, and no fighting was allowed, irrespective of who initiated the fight and why. There were rules around communication as well, such as that children were never to be seen or heard; however, as is the case in many families, the rules did not apply to everyone.

DOI: 10.4324/9781003362203-17

Susan was calm and compliant, but she described how Rose was less so, as she felt no pressure to abide by her parents instructions. Over the course of their relationship, she would blow up over trivial matters that others might disregard and generally seemed to be constantly at odds with different family members. Susan got the brunt of it, though, as casual exchanges between them led to explosive arguments and periods of complete communication cut off, all instigated and maintained by her sister. Rose would never back down or apologize, appearing to be very different from everyone else in the family, who just wanted peace. To achieve this peace, there was only one solution: Susan had to apologize every single time there was a fight. She didn't want to do this but was given no choice by her parents. Due to her mother's focus and her father's inability to cope with any stress in the house, this took precedence over other family issues, including the dynamic between Susan and her sister, and her parents would never support her or take her side.

There is no way to control how an apology is received, but nonetheless, an apology is an important part of repairing any damage if it is authentic and appropriate. Not everyone is prepared to give one, though, and not everyone is prepared to accept one either, although they may begrudgingly do so to appear the bigger person. Susan's sister would humbly accept her apology, and Rose's husband would remind Susan of how grateful she should be for this. After later estrangements, Susan would have to fight this urge to apologize and contain the part of her that still wished for things to be better between them. It would not be hard to see Rose being resentful of Susan's natural ability to lead and succeed, especially if she allowed herself to do so. Maybe Rose had no clue about the profound impact she was having, or maybe she was afraid to due to her pride.

Estrangement

The ability to be a completely different person toward different people can be baffling. Rose seemed to be a caring, compassionate mother and wife, but anything Susan said or did would trigger her. How someone could be kind and calm in one context and then enraged in another can lead many to doubt themselves and personalize the change as something they did wrong. This, coupled with guilt over the effect this was having on their aging father, prompted Susan to always say sorry. A truce would then be made, but the potential for another blowup was never far away, and each time, the pattern of shock and devastation continued (ET: cyclical). Another interesting relationship dynamic is how those brought into the family not only adopt but propagate existing patterns. Susan's brother-in-law, perhaps driven by his own emotional dependencies, would never challenge his wife and, in fact, would encourage the need for an apology. Susan never had time to create a separate relationship with him, to offer her side of the overall story, or to share its impact on her.

As Susan grew older, she slowly discovered a new level of strength and awareness, and it was not a coincidence that this aligned with the birth of her first child and then her second two years later. Children have an amazing gift of teaching us about love; it is harder to hate ourselves when a precious little person gives us a gentle smile. Through their pure innocence, we get to see who we are and not what others project. For once in her life, she had a reason to love herself, to stop apologizing, and to question what she was prepared to accept. This does not mean her estrangement would be less challenging, and in the absence of her sister, she would constantly need to tend to the wounds of her own childhood.

As with the previous estrangements, the most recent one involved her sister cutting contact with her after an explosive row over the planning of a very rare holiday with all five siblings (ET: physical). As usual, she was being reasonable and transparent, but Rose saw something else. Susan could feel it coming as she sent a message to the family message group offering a suggestion to the situation, and that is exactly what Rose did, sending an essay of accusations of Susan being awkward and selfish (EN: involuntary; EA: direct; EM: WhatsApp message). Her siblings were equally shocked and would defend Susan, but it fell on deaf ears. After the explosion, there was no repair attempt or open discussion; it was just over.

Susan's sister had no concept of the many struggles Susan faced in her life and the impact she had on her worth, as it seemed she was too caught up in her own internal representation to really get to know her. When Susan did struggle in other aspects of life, including her health, Rose would express no interest or concern, which only compounded the divide between them. When siblings estrange, it often highlights massive differences in personality, and despite being essentially reared in the same environment, there may be subtle differences that influence the formation of each unique person. How come Susan was calm and reasonable, and yet Rose was angry and resentful? Was Rose born with a certain temperament? Did she feel Susan's words were personal attacks, igniting her own defensive need to lash out to protect herself? Susan would never fully find out, but as time went by, her own perceptions of her sister would change.

Psychological Impact

Like many who are suddenly and completely cut out, Susan was initially very angry. This was not her natural state, and unlike her sister, she did not let bitterness rule. This was something she would later acknowledge as being a huge positive for her own health (see T1.5), but nonetheless, she was emotionally shattered by the fact that Rose could be so quick to discard their relationship. The instant sense of loss can also contribute to this, as almost overnight and sometimes with little provocation, a client can lose several of the most important people in their life (see T1.4).

The psychological damage of a client repeatedly having to apologize for something they did not do cannot be overstated. Having to compromise worth, personal values, and emotional expression at the expense of the family unit shapes a person's sense of self and their ability to establish a secure and independent identity away from the familial unit. Without providing a solid foundation of empathy and personal responsibility, her parents gave Rose no reason to question herself or how she was treating Susan. Rose grew to believe she was justified in her responses and valid in putting her feelings first. It took Susan many years to realize it wasn't her at all, but these experiences taught her how to "be" in relationships, particularly with other women. Her way of living was enmeshed in her sister's reality and the family's response to her, creating patterns where she hid aspects of herself. A talented entrepreneur and business coach, she withheld her successes for fear of offending Rose. This loss of positive self-image may have prompted the development of a positive family image, which she had to hold on to. Over the course of her life, she felt she wasn't herself and, at times, almost didn't know herself. Was this the trauma of her sister's attitude toward her? Was it the product of a lack of healthy individualism within the family, where cohesiveness had been pushed on her? This became a source of great sadness and regret for her, which needed to be validated (see T1).

Relational Struggles

Children can remind us of what unconditional love feels like; however, they can also compound an already complex and difficult situation. Susan's estrangement was not just about the loss of her sister but also the loss of her connection to Rose's three children. She was very close to her niece and nephews, particularly as during the initial estrangements she did not have children herself. She loved them very much and would try to maintain some remnants of a relationship with them by sending gifts on birthdays and Christmas. She would ask permission from her brother-in-law to visit, and her sister would arrange to not be there during this time. She treated Susan like she was a truly horrible human being, and even the strongest person would be affected by this.

By the time of her last estrangement, Susan and her husband had two sons, whom they naturally adored. She was so happy to have created a family of her own that she was still driven to include her sister in her life and have cousins for her sons to play with. She naturally introduced her sons to the entire family, including her sister, a decision she would come to regret during their penultimate estrangement (see T1.3). There was literally nothing that Susan could do to change how her sister viewed her, including having children. Despite having got to know her sons, Rose would not pause to reflect before cutting Susan out again. She feared her sons would miss their aunt and cousins, but she also worried they might ask why they were not part of their lives anymore. Now she was tasked with the difficult job of trying to explain the estrangement to two little people who know only love and dependency (see T3.2). It is hard to know how children will be affected by this, but I chose to believe Susan's children would be fine as they were cushioned by the constant presence and unconditional love of their two parents. As they grow, maybe they will find their own logic; children can be creative and magical in their perspectives, provided this logic does not result in incorrectly assigning blame to themselves.

Other Social Challenges

Re-engaging with family is often a challenge during estrangement, as it can be a minefield of awkward exchanges and subtle pressures (see T3.3 and T6). If there has been a history of abusive behavior, the safety of distance is compromised, reversing years of hard work to bring emotional stability into their lives. Susan dreaded bumping into her sister when she visited the family home; in fact, everyone within the family did, and with so much negative history between them, something as simple as a look or passing remark from her would be perceived as an attack, and from what she shared, it probably was.

Later, after a sudden illness, her mother passed tragically, and Susan was expected to make all the funeral arrangements, probably due to her reasonable nature. Susan requested that all siblings help out equally, but Rose viewed this as an attempt on her part to control and manipulate the situation. The funeral was tense as well as heart breaking and took its toll on their father. As he aged, his health declined rapidly, and it became increasingly harder for Susan to avoid interacting with Rose as she needed to be involved in important medical decisions, and as expected, she was difficult. Susan didn't want to lose her father but relished a time when she would no longer have to depend on her sister.

Strengths and Coping Mechanisms

It never ceases to amaze me how reasonable and well-adjusted my clients are, despite the real struggles and difficult upbringings they faced. They rarely seek conflict and understand the importance of personal responsibility. Even though there may be times when they feel like pushing those they care about away due to the intensity of the closeness, they try hard to resist this impulse. Maybe being well-adjusted was part of Susan's mask, part of her survival adaptation, or maybe it was an unconscious decision to be different from her sister. This is something that should always be validated (see T1), as she could have gone down a different path, becoming bitter and resentful.

One thing that struck me was Susan's ability to communicate effectively. It can be hard to find the right words to match our unique interpretations of family and life, but not for Susan. She was deeply reflective and became an incredibly strong narrator of her own life. She was also determined and independent in many aspects of her life, and this resilience should be validated as not everyone has this trait (see T1.5).

Among Susan's strengths, loyalty and honesty were perhaps the most honorable, and because of this, she was a great mother. These assets were most valued by her friends, with whom she was very close, and they played an instrumental role in overcoming her damaged self-worth. Susan trusted her friends, and she knew they had her back (see T2.1). They knew who she was and, more importantly, who she was not, and although they were her friends and thus likely biased in her favour, this doesn't make their views invalid.

Her passion for social enterprise became an important outlet for Susan to make sense of her world, and she embraced it fully. The act of helping others follow their dreams through her coaching business was powerful and helped her maintain a positive and optimistic attitude. Aside from work, which was an important resource for parking the estrangement (see T5), she embraced other wellness tools, such as yoga (see T2.5), mindfulness, and breathing approaches (see T2.2), to catch moments of impulse in real-time that she might regret later. For example, if she became overwhelmed with sadness, she learned to centre herself by focusing on deep-diaphragm breathing (see T2.2) and staying connected to her inner world until the feelings subsided.

Life presents many opportunities for transformation, but none are as powerful as having children. Having a small person or people to take care of and nurture can help gain new perspectives and reappraise priorities. Carrying two vulnerable children in her arms allowed her to connect with her own vulnerability as well as motivate her to become the best role model she could be for her sons. To start loving herself, she needed to distance herself internally from the false narrative her sister had scripted, own her own talents and strengths, and take pride in how she came through so much and yet asked for so little. When reflecting on how Susan grew despite her situation, one ponders whether this would have happened had she not become estranged from her sister. Maybe it was a combination of her age and stage in life, the sense of having had enough of the cycle of estrangement, or the decision to create something better for her sons, but enough was enough (EN: voluntary/mutual); she deserved better and would no longer compromise on who she was and how she was treated.

Estrangement Map

Table 12.1 Susan's Estrangement Map

Client Name: Susan

EP	ET	EN	EA	EM	ED	ER	Notes
Sister	Cyclical/ Physical	Initially Involuntary, now Voluntary/ Mutual	Direct	Text Message	The current iteration was 1 year, but the issue began 10 years ago	Unreasonable expectations/ verbal and emotional abuse/ personality differences/ perhaps favouritism	The inability to reason with her sister might need to be validated and the anxiety she felt when interacting with her. We might explore the estrangement pattern, and what previously prompted her to reconnect. Validating the transition from Involuntary to Voluntary/Mutual might identify what changed in her
Brother-In-Law	Secondary/ Physical	Involuntary	Indirect	No Contact	The current iteration was 1 year, but the issue began before then	Association with the client's sister	Validating her views on her brother-in-law's motivations and dependencies might be helpful
Niece	Inherited/ Physical	Involuntary	Indirect	No Contact	See above	Association with mother and father	This would be a great source of pain as her own sons and her niece\nephews were friends but would no longer see each other. Validating the guilt Susan might feel as well as exploring how to communicate the situation to her sons might be helpful
Nephew	See above	See above	See above	See above	See above	See above	See above
Nephew	See above	See above	See above	See above	See above	See above	See above

General Notes/Observations

Much time will be devoted to validating her need to apologize, even though she did nothing wrong. Also validating why she introduced her sons to her sister, her kind nature and genuine desire for them to have a better relationship. We might explore her relationship with women and discuss breaking patterns of people pleasing. She never mentioned anger towards her parents for not recognising her feelings, or protecting her from her sister, and I wondered was this something to explore with her. Validating her strengths and achievements in life would be important as few others may have done this before.

Chapter 13

Grief and Grievances (Adult Daughter Estrangement)

Estrangement might not be the result of an obvious life-changing event or sequence of events. It could be a much more silent and slow process of making and receiving fewer phone calls, transitioning to text messages or email only to facilitate basic exchanges, or not sharing anything personal and keeping exchanges civil but superficial. That's not to say there is anything wrong with privacy and choosing to withhold aspects of your life, but when this lack of sharing becomes the norm, family members will be left to piece together what happened between them.

Tina had a son and a daughter, but her relationship with her daughter Louise was always a little different. When Louise was a child, they were close, although they did not have a stereotypical mother-daughter bond. They were both strong-willed, which led to occasional disagreements between them, but Tina's compassion and genuine love for her kids were always her primary focus, and this love got them through tough moments and the day-to-day challenges of family life. As Louise grew older and her world opened up to different influences and ideas, their personalities began to clash on a more regular basis. Their beliefs on politics and general social issues were poles apart, and while these differences seemed insignificant at the time, the dynamic between them took a more painful turn when Louise started her own family.

Tina and her husband created a fun and warm home; their marriage was stable, and despite some losses within the family, including her own ailing parents due to ill-health, nothing stood out as traumatic or a cause for concern. Her other son, Richard, was a couple of years younger than Louise, and there was rarely any conflict between them. The siblings had their own friends, interests, and goals in life, and they had all the support they could ask for. Tina was naturally a worrier, protective of both her children, and perhaps a little overbearing, something she would readily admit. However, despite Tina's attempts to consciously not pressurize Louise to be who she needed or wanted her to be, nothing could prepare her for what was to come between them later. Although she seemed to have more in common with her son, she was conscious of any perceived favoritism. Like any son or daughter, they both leaned on their parents for financial aid but were relatively independent and focused, although Louise seemed a little less settled than her brother and impulsive in life decisions, such as dropping out of college

DOI: 10.4324/9781003362203-18

and switching careers several times. She was outspoken about many issues and was prepared to debate with anyone on topics she felt strongly about. No one was exempt from this, including Tina, who said: "I could never win". These words struck me; the notion of a competitive relationship with a child, trying to overcome each other. This dynamic is not uncommon during the teenage years but can become a bigger problem if it continues into young adult life and there is no other way to resolve differences. Although Tina managed to maintain a consistent relationship with Louise, this power struggle between them would frequently make it a tense one. I have spoken about the expectations parents place on their children, but these expectations can sit on both sides. At times, Tina felt Louise expected too much of her; to give into her whims and to accept her sporadic life choices without question. It is only natural that Tina would be concerned and need to express her reservations, but this was from a place of love and concern and not from a need to control or negatively influence.

Estrangement

As the years went by, Louise met her husband, and they eventually married. Early in the relationship, Louise seemed to prioritize her husband's family, and this was particularly noticeable when planning their wedding. Tina was told she could not invite several close friends who had known Louise since she was a child and generally did not involve her in any of the preparations. Tina felt Louise was embarrassed by them. Things further changed when her daughter started her own family, and a power shift was formed when Louise started to use her child for leverage. Tina was told she could only see her granddaughter when permitted, at specific places and times. She often excluded her from events, and Louise did not hide this on social media. The situation came to a head when, out of the blue, she received a letter with a detailed list of ways her mother had hurt her. Her grievances included 1) not respecting her opinions, 2) not meeting the standards of her friends' parents, and 3) a wide variety of incidents that did not register with Tina at all but that her daughter seemed to harbor.

When family members are slow to forgive and cling to every grievance, it can rock a person's perceptions of reality and the relationship itself. While Tina agreed with some of the issues, her views were not on the same scale. She felt like she was being painted as an abusive mother, which went against her very nature. She tried to have a reasonable conversation with Louise to find a better understanding between them, but Louise wasn't interested in this. Tina felt her hands were now bound, as if she challenged these issues, she would be accused of gaslighting and perhaps be deprived of any future contact with her granddaughter. She outwardly put up with this, accepting her daughter's terms, but knew things may never recover.

Psychological Impact

For the longest time, Tina questioned what she had done wrong. Was Louise being unfair? Did Tina not express her love enough? Was she in some way abusive and didn't see it? Such thoughts were as punishing as the attitude of her daughter. "I feel guilty over everything". This became Tina's truth and culminated in her searching for reasons to hate herself. I sometimes wonder if some family members see their kin, whether it is parents, siblings, adult children, or any other family member, as emotionally bullet-proof and impervious to pain. Maybe Louise had an internal image of Tina being strong, like an immovable object, and not like a real person with feelings. Tina's guilt was closely followed by worry, mostly manifesting as concern for what other people would think. Much time would be needed for Tina to clarify and decipher the complex family history (see T1.2) with both her daughter and with her own parents to understand the lessons she absorbed about parenting and relationships.

One contentious issue with estrangement is whether to keep photos of the EP around to be viewed daily. Alas, there are many reasons why someone might decide to take down these pictures: it could be too painful to regularly look at them as they act as reminders of happier times long gone; they might be a constant source of anxiety; or they may be a trigger for anger. During one visit, Tina noticed her picture was taken down from their living room wall, and she would never know why. She cried for some time as soon as she realized this; one of many times sadness got the better of her. Validating this grief (see T1.4) would be essential, as would any doubts she might have.

Several months after receiving the grievance letter from Louise, Tina noticed the signs of what she felt was depression and what she described as an inescapable dark cloud sitting above her head that followed her everywhere. She found it hard to get out of bed, asking herself, "What was the point?" but her husband pushed her to keep going. Her doctor suggested she try an anti-depressant, but she did not feel comfortable taking it. She knew what the root of her suffering was and felt no medication would change it. She would find it hard to sit still and was always in motion: cleaning, cooking, working; doing anything to avoid feeling the emptiness inside. Any mental health issues are very serious and must be treated as such. Although we can suggest resources (see T2) to help her manage her struggles, I always advise my own clients to continue to seek medical advice alongside other therapeutic approaches.

The birthday and Christmas visits would be a mix of joy and dread. She would be excited to see her granddaughter, but being around her daughter became increasingly difficult as there was no way to predict how she would receive Tina. Sometimes she would greet her with a hug and they would be ok, and other times she would completely ignore her. Thus, on occasion, Tina would feel hopeful for positive change, only to be crushed with disappointment when nothing changed at all. She might need re-engagement strategies (see T6) to help prepare her for these visits.

Relational Struggles

Tina's husband was furious with their daughter and did not accept any of the grievances on her list. He was particularly angry when he looked back at the efforts they both made in rearing their children: the sleepless nights, the countless nappies, the times of stress on their relationship, the sacrifices, and how all of this was forgotten. Add to this the helplessness he felt seeing his wife clearly suffer and not knowing what to do to help. Although he was more inclined to confront the issue head-on and take a firm stance against Louise, Tina knew this would not help and would run the risk of never seeing her grandchildren again. It is my personal belief that using a child in this manner will have long-term repercussions on the parental relationship, as the child may realize they are being used. Tina chose to remain quiet and went along with her daughter's conditions, and each time she would return home distraught and heartbroken. Such was his anger that her husband suggested taking their daughter off the will as some symbolic gesture to let her know of their pain, and occasionally, during tough times, she considered it. Exploring this decision (see T1.3) might be suggested. It might also be worthwhile exploring if there is a better way to communicate with her husband and acknowledge each other's subjective perceptions and feelings as well as their needs. Despite what they were going through, Tina and her husband were grateful to be able to maintain a relationship with her son, who sided with them and was equally baffled by his sister's attitude. While holding onto a relationship with her son was reaffirming, it was also a reminder of what was missing, and she had to force herself to remain present and leave no space for the dark cloud to reappear.

Other Social Challenges

What further compounded her struggles was the ongoing nature of the COVID-19 pandemic. This unprecedented situation brought a level of complexity to difficult family relations across the globe and amplified existing challenges. In some cases, it forced families to spend time together in their respective bubbles, adding pressure to an already repressive containment unit. For others, it added a layer of urgency to the ambiguous desire to connect and check on the welfare of family members. For Tina, it just gave her another thing to worry about, namely, whether her daughter and granddaughter were doing ok. She could not call them to find out, as her call would probably be ignored or met with a cutting remark. What equally upset her was how her daughter expressed no concern if Tina was affected by the pandemic. Because of her age and previous health conditions, she was at high risk and just wanted one demonstration of love, but there was none.

Finding support can be a challenge, but after some research, Tina engaged with several estrangement online groups to share her experiences. While she was met with a lot of support, one disgruntled person reacted with judgment, and this was enough for her to question whether sharing her inner world on social media was wise or safe. What particularly upset her, when searching for practical advice on what to do next, was how she would regularly see a common theme of "just walk away" from family as the solution to the situation, like the biases discussed in Part 2: Challenges and Roadblocks. Apart from the fact that this is neither easy nor appropriate for every family or estrangement, for those involuntarily estranged it might appear as if their pain is being dismissed. In particular, she would see terms such as "toxic" or "narcissist" used to describe estranged parents, but they did not match the specific details of her own relationship with her daughter or her very nature, which is far from destructive or uncaring. However, over time, Tina found the courage to stand up for herself by challenging such labels and one-sided views, insisting she was not abusive, had no desire to gaslight anyone, and simply wanted to know how to make it better. Thankfully, Tina found a safe group led by a compassionate facilitator who made sure everyone felt heard and supported.

Strengths and Coping Mechanisms

Control was essential for Tina to manage her inner reality, and this included planning every detail of her life, such as spending her days cleaning her home to cope with the overwhelming emotions she felt. This might seem obsessive, but it served an important purpose for her, and maybe it was her own coping mechanism (see T1.5) and facilitated parking the situation in her mind (see T5). I feel there are much more destructive ways of using the energy she carried around, provided she understood this and did not force her self-imposed ways and cleaning standards onto her partner and create tension between them.

Questioning the necessity of her guilt was essential to her own growth, and those close to her would remind her that there was no need for it and that she deserved happiness. Like others in this book, I believe Tina's compassion was her greatest strength, and I admire how, despite the depression she felt, her love never faded into apathy. Remaining optimistic and hopeful was tough, but like many who are struggling with estrangement, she pushed forward. There would be resentment towards her daughter, which may flit in and out, but she also knew to not let it interfere with her own self-esteem and relationships with others.

Despite this, Tina's grief would endure. This is a reality many estranged people must face, and I personally think it is disingenuous to insist some will get over an estrangement. To be truthful, I don't believe anyone fully gets over such a loss, irrespective of whether it is voluntary or involuntary, or whether it is a mother or father, son or daughter, brother and sister, or other family relative. This does not mean our clients can't heal in many ways, accept the situation, and find some peace despite their losses.

Was there something Tina could have done differently with her daughter to prevent this situation? Even with hindsight, it is tough to identify how exactly she could have approached their differences and not let them interfere with their bond. There is an argument that Tina could exert more influence and let Louise know the impact her behavior was having. If she felt this might help, it is worthwhile discussing how and when she might reconnect (see T4). This might also involve deciding if her husband should be involved in this process and the various potential outcomes, and if she reached a point where she felt the relationship could not get worse, this might be a last effort and at least give her some peace knowing she tried.

While some relationships are irreparable, part of me feels there is some potential for Tina and Louise to have a better relationship in the future, but only if they can find a common language and values that bind them and establish a new baseline based on respect for individuality combined with a desire for something better. For now, both feet should remain on the ground, and Tina has had to accept the loss of time, the loss of peace, and the loss of the future she had hoped for and keep on living despite this.

Estrangement Map

Table 13.1 Tina's Estrangement Map

Client Name: Tina

EP	ET	EN	EA	EM	ED	ER	Notes
Adult-Daughter	Physical although occasionally Emotional	Involuntary	Direct	Letter	Tina is unsure of the timeframe	Unreasonable expectations/ Personality Differences	It is not uncommon to struggle to identify when an estrangement began and validating this might be helpful, although the date Joan received the letter might act as milestone. It might be worthwhile asking her to read the letter in the session and express her feelings. Another suggestion would be for her to write her own letter, to express her side as well as her intentions/desire to have a better relationship
Grandchild	Inherited/ Physical although occasionally Emotional	Involuntary	Indirect	No Communication	Tina is unsure of the timeframe	Association with Mother	This would naturally be very painful for Joan as it was her only grand-child and she loved being a grand-parent
Son-In-Law	Secondary/ Physical although occasionally Emotional	Involuntary	Indirect	No Communication	Tina is unsure of the timeframe	Association with Wife	Tina was frustrated that he appeared to have no input and just went along to keep his wife happy

General Notes/Observations

Helping Tina recognise her grief and the symptoms, including feelings of Depression, might validate and normalise this for her. Focusing on her relationship with her son might motivate her to look after herself, and take control of her physical and mental health. Prioritising her relationship with her husband and parking the situation by making plans together might help them bring more fun and experiences into their lives.

Conclusion

Widening the Estrangement Lens

Without trying to sound alarmist, after hearing so many stories of estrangement from families who never thought for a second their relationship would end up this way, I slowly came to the painful conclusion that this phenomenon has the potential to affect every family in some capacity. Because of this, my hope for this book is to encourage society at large to view estrangements from a different lens and ask those who struggle to empathize, irrespective of their perspectives, genders, faiths, and the various other ways we identify, to place themselves in the proverbial shoes of those who are unfortunate in family relations. But there are mitigating factors that prevent this level of understanding.

I am frequently asked if I personally feel there is a stigma regarding the topic of family estrangement, and despite what is highlighted in the research, my honest answer is that it depends heavily on whom the client shares their story with. While there are countless accounts of negative experiences from clients who disclosed their situation with others and were "disqualified from full social acceptance" (Goffman, 1963, preface), I have equally heard many discuss how they were met with acceptance. These reactions may reflect the varied stereotypical views of estranged individuals, such as estranged adult children, who were predominately viewed negatively ("childish/immature" and "ungrateful"), although there were some positive views ("independent" and "strong") and one neutral ("out of options") (Rittenour et al., 2018). This contrasts with the stereotypes for estranged parents, which were exclusively negative and included "abusive" and "absent/disinterested" (Rittenour et al., 2018). These create walls of disapproval, which serve to imprison those on the wrong end of this judgement.

It would seem personal estrangement experience might influence this, and those who viewed estranged people with warmth and competency had first-hand knowledge as opposed to those with none (Rittenour et al., 2018). The reality is that if an individual or group has only ever had a close relationship with most of their family, they may struggle to conceive why or even how someone else would not have a similar relationship. If their family dynamics have been manageable, even in difficult times, they might oversimplify similar dynamics in other families, or the notion of being estranged may threaten their engrained beliefs about the unbreakable bond of family and how loyalty is unquestionable.

DOI: 10.4324/9781003362203-19

Alas, there are different sides to this, including those who, like our clients, equally do not have a good relationship with one or more family members but are not comfortable with the idea of putting distance between them. In fact, if a client's estrangement is voluntary, these people might even resent the client's attempts to pull away, as they feel they never could, and there are those who are themselves estranged but whose perspective and estrangement approach differ from the client's and place them in contentious positions. Such is the multiplicity of estrangement that there are times I question if it is possible to communicate fully to others why and how it happens; trying to capture the subtlety of moments of distrust and disagreement that accumulate over a long and protracted period can feel like an uphill struggle. Even with all the relevant information, "stereotyping exists adjacently to facts" (Rittenour et al., 2018, p. 3).

Discovering how the stigma of estrangement is expressed or manifests itself can be just as challenging, as it might not be an obvious statement or act but rather a more subtle disapproving look, remark, or behaviour, such as excluding a person known to be estranged from a conversation or event. What particularly interests me is the distinction between 'felt stigma', where discrimination is anticipated, and 'enacted stigma' (Gray, 2002), where discrimination is actually experienced. Was the perception of stigma influenced more by past rejection or other factors highlighted in the *estrangement impact triad*? These will naturally place a client in a vulnerable state and make them highly sensitive to potential rejection elsewhere. Coupled with the sense of shame they might have to carry, clients may seek out signs of disapproval even though that is not the intention of the person they are engaging with. This will obviously be hard to verify as each professional will only have the client's testimony, but the purpose is to identify roadblocks to a healthy connection, safety, and support.

In fact, such is the stigma that one estrangement study seeking participants chose to avoid the terms "estrangement" and "estranged" in case it deterred anyone from taking part (Scharp, 2017). This stigma is clearly not preventing estrangement from happening and might beg the question: Is this societal disapproval contributing to the desire or need for estrangement? At the very least, this stigma is compounding the already damaging impact of estrangement on individuals and families who feel isolated and alone, but it may also lead to broader societal challenges, creating a vicious feedback loop.

With the WHO (World Health Organization) estimating that, as of 2022, nearly one billion people globally are suffering from a mental health disorder (Freeman, 2022), we cannot ignore how, littered throughout the estrangement literature, are similar stories of mental health and illness struggles in various forms (Agllias, 2015; Blake et al., 2015, 2019, 2022b; Carr et al., 2015; Conti, 2015; Scharp et al., 2015; Schoppe-Sullivan et al., 2023). These can have a ripple effect across society, including potential engagement with already under-resourced addiction and health care services, police and legal services, and welfare and unemployment services, as well as propagating the cycle of estrangement for future generations. As stated in a 2022 WHO mental health report highlighting why change is badly needed: "At any one time, a diverse set of individual, family, community and structural factors may combine to protect or undermine our mental health and shift our position on the mental health continuum" *World Mental Health Report: Transforming Mental Health for all* (Freeman, 2022). It is great to see the WHO acknowledge the important role family plays in mental health struggles, but as professionals who regularly or occasionally work with estranged adults, we also have a role to play in promoting open discussion on this topic and hopefully reducing the stigma associated with it. This does not mean we are promoting or normalizing estrangement, nor does it mean we need to compromise our core beliefs around family, abuse, etc., but rather to firstly reflect on our individual and collective contribution to the stigma and how it plays out in our interactions with others, and secondly, commit to creating and engaging with different communicative platforms to discuss the nuances that are often lost in conversations. From this, society at large might slowly start to respect that which they don't understand and replace judgment and minimizing with curiosity and compassion. This might subsequently prevent estrangements for future generations, as those affected by such family issues will now feel safer engaging with support services and accessing the resources they need to recover, and perhaps even reconnecting with estranged family if they feel doing so would be for the good of everyone. In fact, the number of support services might increase as more people are prepared to avail themselves of them. On social media, I regularly see new family estrangement support groups forming, which are led by individuals who have had their own experiences and now generously commit time and effort to lead them. Such is the scale of estrangement that health service departments within respective governments might embrace this phenomenon, create targeted groups led by trained healthcare professionals, and provide funding for those leading these groups.

We can't change the world in a day, but we can start questioning the stigma of estrangement, such as: Why can so few empathize with estrangement and minimize the issues in a family? Why are people so quick to form an opinion with so little information? Why are people automatically drawn to one side over another? To overcome these, I believe we must strongly challenge the overly simplistic presumptions and stereotypes, particularly when based on negative bias and without even the most basic inquiry, which only reduce a person or entire families to caricatures as opposed to complex human beings. Judging an estranged person or persons based solely on their familial relationship status has the power to penetrate deeply; it can touch their very identity and place in the world.

Earlier, I discussed the idea of the *subjective blur*, where individuals use a very narrow lens to view a very wide issue and thus cannot see past their own beliefs, feelings, and experiences about their own family, blurring the line between their own estrangement (or lack of one) and others. To me, it is clear that further education around this topic is essential, particularly aimed at not only the general public but policymakers and leaders across the globe, to expand not just their estrangement understanding but also their vocabulary so we have a common language to relay and frame viewpoints. It takes time and many conversations for individuals to be prepared to reflect on new ideas and absorb them, which is why we must be patient while also injecting as much compassion as possible into the conversation. It also means being bold and pushing against the opinions and beliefs of others, which may evoke strong criticism, dismissal, or even judgement. Such responses can be distressing, but having the courage to preserve and hold our intentions, to listen to opinions we are opposed to, and to share our own is necessary if our society is to grow. In time, maybe more will embrace their own vulnerability and see past the public masks estranged people wear to hide the private and painful burden they silently and protectively carry. They may also see past any grievances they might have for their own non-estranged family and place more love and appreciation for what they have and what many others can only dream of.

If there is one message I would like to give to anyone reading this book, it is that we should never take our family or anyone else's family for granted. There are always going to be tough times when family members become consumed with their own struggles and there are ongoing conflicts, pressures, and personality clashes, but these should never come at the complete expense of relationships with kin. There is only so much stress a person or persons can and will take, and recognizing the human limits in all of us may help us find other ways of expressing ourselves and of connecting. This applies to everyone, not just the ones who feel wronged, who may equally need to turn inward and re-evaluate their place in the hierarchy of issues.

Perhaps this inward reflection is all we can ask of each other, but if everyone were to embrace it, a new closeness may develop and negate the need for estrangements at all. Professionals and estranged individuals alike may not be able to promote a desire to reflect within families, but we do have a role to play in promoting global awareness and compassion, and with time, hopefully this will create a ripple effect across society, reaching those who desperately need it.

Bibliography

Adler, A. B., LeardMann, C. A., Roenfeldt, K. A., Jacobson, I. G., & Forbes, D. (2020, July 27). Magnitude of problematic anger and its predictors in the Millennium Cohort. *BMC Public Health, 20*(1). https://doi.org/10.1186/s12889-020-09206-2.

Agllias, K. (2011a, January). No Longer on Speaking Terms: The Losses Associated with Family Estrangement at the End of Life. *Families in Society: The Journal of Contemporary Social Services, 92*(1), 107–113. https://doi.org/10.1606/1044-3894.4055.

Agllias, K. (2011b, April 4). Utilizing Participants' Strengths to Reduce Risk of Harm in a Study of Family Estrangement. *Qualitative Health Research, 21*(8), 1136–1146. https://doi.org/10.1177/1049732311405065.

Agllias, K. (2013, July 11). The Gendered Experience of Family Estrangement in Later Life. *Affilia, 28*(3), 309–321. https://doi.org/10.1177/0886109913495727.

Agllias, K. (2015, March 24). Disconnection and Decision-making: Adult Children Explain Their Reasons for Estranging from Parents. *Australian Social Work, 69*(1), 92–104. https://doi.org/10.1080/0312407x.2015.1004355.

Agllias, K. (2016, October 6). *Family Estrangement: A Matter of Perspective.* Routledge.

Agllias, K. (2017, May 11). Missing family: the adult child's experience of parental estrangement. *Journal of Social Work Practice, 32*(1), 59–72. https://doi.org/10.1080/02650533.2017.1326471.

Agllias, & Gray. (2013). Secrets and Lies: The Ethical Implications of Family Estrangement. In *Practical Social Work Ethics: Complex Dilemmas within Applied Social Care* (1st ed., pp. 43–61). Routledge.

Allen, J., & Moore, J. (2016, December 2). Troubling the Functional/Dysfunctional Family Binary Through the Articulation of Functional Family Estrangement. *Western Journal of Communication, 81*(3), 281–299. https://doi.org/10.1080/10570314.2016.1250156.

An, N., & Chuo, J. (2022, March 14). Walking and Activeness: The First Step toward the Prevention of Strokes and Mental Illness. *Computational Intelligence and Neuroscience, 2022*, 1–7. https://doi.org/10.1155/2022/3440437.

APA Dictionary of Psychology. (n.d.). American Psychological Association. Retrieved March 10, 2023, from https://dictionary.apa.org/.

Ardito, R. B., & Rabellino, D. (2011). Therapeutic Alliance and Outcome of Psychotherapy: Historical Excursus, Measurements, and Prospects for Research. *Frontiers in Psychology, 2*. https://doi.org/10.3389/fpsyg.2011.00270.

Arnow, B. A., & Steidtmann, D. (2014, October). Harnessing the potential of the therapeutic alliance. *World Psychiatry, 13*(3), 238–240. https://doi.org/10.1002/wps.20147.

Arránz Becker, O., & Hank, K. (2021, August 19). Adult children's estrangement from parents in Germany. *Journal of Marriage and Family*, *84*(1), 347–360. https://doi.org/10.1111/jomf.12796.

Balban, M. Y., Neri, E., Kogon, M. M., Weed, L., Nouriani, B., Jo, B., Holl, G., Zeitzer, J. M., Spiegel, D., & Huberman, A. D. (2023, January). Brief structured respiration practices enhance mood and reduce physiological arousal. *Cell Reports Medicine*, *4*(1), 100895. https://doi.org/10.1016/j.xcrm.2022.100895.

Blake, L. (2017, November 15). Parents and Children Who Are Estranged in Adulthood: A Review and Discussion of the Literature. *Journal of Family Theory & Review*, *9*(4), 521–536. https://doi.org/10.1111/jftr.12216.

Blake, L., Bland, B., & Golombok, S. (2015). Hidden Voices: Family Estrangement In Adulthood. In https://www.stand-alone.org.uk. Stand-Alone. https://www.stand-alone.org.uk/wp-content/uploads/2015/12/HiddenVoices.FinalReport.pdf.

Blake, L., & Bland, B. (2018). Hidden Voices: Family estrangement in students. In https://www.stand-alone.org.uk. Stand-Alone. https://www.stand-alone.org.uk/wp-content/uploads/2018/02/STAND-ALONE-HIDDEN-VOICES-SINGLE-PAGES-1-2.pdf.

Blake, L., Bland, B., & Imrie, S. (2019, October 9). The Counseling Experiences of Individuals Who Are Estranged From a Family Member. *Family Relations*, *69*(4), 820–831. https://doi.org/10.1111/fare.12385.

Blake, L., Bland, B., & Imrie, S. (2020). Family Estrangement and the Covid-19 crisis. In https://www.stand-alone.org.uk. Stand-Alone. https://www.stand-alone.org.uk/wp-content/uploads/2020/06/Standalone_Report_v7.pdf.

Blake, L., Bland, B., & Gilbert, H. (2022a, December). The efficacy of a facilitated support group intervention to reduce the psychological distress of individuals experiencing family estrangement. *Evaluation and Program Planning*, *95*, 102168. https://doi.org/10.1016/j.evalprogplan.2022.102168.

Blake, L., Rouncefield-Swales, A., Bland, B., & Carter, B. (2022b, December 12). An interview study exploring clients' experiences of receiving therapeutic support for family estrangement in the UK. *Counselling and Psychotherapy Research*, *23*(1), 105–114. https://doi.org/10.1002/capr.12603.

Bland, B., & Blake, L. (2019, October 16). The difficulty in evidencing family estrangement to attain statutory finance in UK Higher Education. *Higher Education Quarterly*, *74*(4), 531–542. https://doi.org/10.1111/hequ.12232.

Bland, B., & Stevenson, J. (2018). Family Matters. An exploration of the role and importance of family relationships for students in UK higher education. In https://www.stand-alone.org.uk. Stand-Alone. https://www.stand-alone.org.uk/wp-content/uploads/2018/06/Family Matters.-Final.pdf.

Boss, P., & Yeats, J. R. (2014, May 4). Ambiguous loss: a complicated type of grief when loved ones disappear. *Bereavement Care*, *33*(2), 63–69. https://doi.org/10.1080/02682621.2014.933573.

Bratman, G. N., Anderson, C. B., Berman, M. G., Cochran, B., de Vries, S., Flanders, J., Folke, C., Frumkin, H., Gross, J. J., Hartig, T., Kahn, P. H., Kuo, M., Lawler, J. J., Levin, P. S., Lindahl, T., Meyer-Lindenberg, A., Mitchell, R., Ouyang, Z., Roe, J., . . . Daily, G. C. (2019, July 5). Nature and mental health: An ecosystem service perspective. *Science Advances, 5*(7). https://doi.org/10.1126/sciadv.aax0903.

Carr, K., Holman, A., Abetz, J., Kellas, J. K., & Vagnoni, E. (2015, April 2). Giving Voice to the Silence of Family Estrangement: Comparing Reasons of Estranged Parents and Adult

Children in a Nonmatched Sample. *Journal of Family Communication*, *15*(2), 130–140. https://doi.org/10.1080/15267431.2015.1013106.

Churchill, R., Riadi, I., Kervin, L., Teo, K., & Cosco, T. (2021, May 7). Deciphering the role of physical activity in stress management during a global pandemic in older adult populations: a systematic review protocol. *Systematic Reviews*, *10*(1). https://doi.org/10.1186/s13643-021-01678-6.

Cocker, F., & Joss, N. (2016, June 22). Compassion Fatigue among Healthcare, Emergency and Community Service Workers: A Systematic Review. *International Journal of Environmental Research and Public Health*, *13*(6), 618. https://doi.org/10.3390/ijerph13060618.

Coleman, J. (2008, August 26). *When Parents Hurt: Compassionate Strategies When You and Your Grown Child Don't Get Along*. William Morrow Paperbacks.

Coleman, J. (2021a). A shift in American family values is fueling estrangement. https://www.Theatlantic.Com. https://www.theatlantic.com/family/archive/2021/01/why-parents-and-kids-get-estranged/617612/.

Coleman, J. (2021b, March 4). *Rules of Estrangement: When Adult Children Cut Ties and How to Heal the Conflict*. Sheldon Press.

Conti, R. P. (2015). Family Estrangement: Establishing a Prevalence Rate. *Journal of Psychology and Behavioral Science*, *3*(2). https://doi.org/10.15640/jpbs.v3n2a4.

Dattilio, F. M., & Nichols, M. P. (2011, February 28). Reuniting Estranged Family Members: A Cognitive-Behavioral-Systemic Perspective. *The American Journal of Family Therapy*, *39*(2), 88–99. https://doi.org/10.1080/01926187.2010.530169.

Davis, L. (2013, April 30). *I Thought We'd Never Speak Again*. Harper Collins.

Dorrance Hall, E. (2016, December 22). The communicative process of resilience for marginalized family members. *Journal of Social and Personal Relationships*, *35*(3), 307–328. https://doi.org/10.1177/0265407516683838.

Engel, G. L. (1961, January). Is Grief a Disease? *Psychosomatic Medicine*, *23*(1), 18–22. https://doi.org/10.1097/00006842-196101000-00002.

Fenn, K., & Byrne, M. (2013, September). The key principles of cognitive behavioural therapy. *InnovAiT: Education and Inspiration for General Practice*, *6*(9), 579–585. https://doi.org/10.1177/1755738012471029.

Freeman, M. (2022, September 8). The World Mental Health Report: transforming mental health for all. *World Psychiatry*, *21*(3), 391–392. https://doi.org/10.1002/wps.21018.

Gair, S. (2016, June 6). Missing Grandchildren: Grandparents' Lost Contact and Implications for Social Work. *Australian Social Work*, *70*(3), 263–275. https://doi.org/10.1080/0312407x.2016.1173714.

Gilbertson, T. (2020, April 28). *Reconnecting with Your Estranged Adult Child*. New World Library.

Gilligan, M., Suitor, J. J., & Pillemer, K. (2015, May 14). Estrangement Between Mothers and Adult Children: The Role of Norms and Values. *Journal of Marriage and Family*, *77*(4), 908–920. https://doi.org/10.1111/jomf.12207.

Gilligan, M., Suitor, J. J., & Pillemer, K. (2021, September 22). Patterns and Processes of Intergenerational Estrangement: A Qualitative Study of Mother–Adult Child Relationships Across Time. *Research on Aging*, *44*(5–6), 436–447. https://doi.org/10.1177/01640275211036966.

Goffman, E. (1963, January 1). *Stigma: Notes on the Management of Spoiled Identity*. Touchstone.

Gotlib, I. H., Goodman, S. H., & Humphreys, K. L. (2020, February 24). Studying the Intergenerational Transmission of Risk for Depression: Current Status and Future

Directions. *Current Directions in Psychological Science, 29*(2), 174–179. https://doi.org/ 10.1177/0963721420901590.

Gray, A. J. (2002, February 1). Stigma in psychiatry. *JRSM, 95*(2), 72–76. https://doi.org/ 10.1258/jrsm.95.2.72.

Haefner, J. (2014, October 29). An Application of Bowen Family Systems Theory. *Issues in Mental Health Nursing, 35*(11), 835–841. https://doi.org/10.3109/01612840.2014.921257.

Hank, K., & Steinbach, A. (2022, November 17). Sibling estrangement in adulthood. *Journal of Social and Personal Relationships, 40*(4), 1277–1287. https://doi.org/10.1177/ 02654075221127863.

Hax, C. (2016). Family estrangement is not necessarily a bad thing, for parents or children. https://www.Washingtonpost.Com. https://www.washingtonpost.com/lifestyle/style/fam ily-estrangement-is-not-necessarily-a-bad-thing-for-parents-or-children/2016/03/10/ cc63494c-e24d-11e5-9c36-e1902f6b6571_story.html.

Hill, P. L., Olaru, G., & Allemand, M. (2023, June). Do associations between sense of purpose, social support, and loneliness differ across the adult lifespan? *Psychology and Aging, 38*(4), 345–355. https://doi.org/10.1037/pag0000733.

Ipsos MORI & Stand-Alone. (2014). Family Estrangement Survey for Stand-Alone. In https://www.stand-alone.org.uk. https://www.stand-alone.org.uk/wp-content/uploads/ 2013/08/StandAlonePrevalenceRESEARCH3.pdf.

IACP. (n.d.). Irish Association for Counselling and Psychotherapy. Retrieved August 28, 2023, from http://www.iacp.ie/.

Jerrome, D. (1994, August). Family estrangement: parents and children who "lose touch." *Journal of Family Therapy, 16*(3), 241–258. https://doi.org/10.1111/j.1467-6427.1994.00793.x.

Kalmijn, M., & Leopold, T. (2018, July 11). Changing Sibling Relationships After Parents' Death: The Role of Solidarity and Kinkeeping. *Journal of Marriage and Family, 81*(1), 99–114. https://doi.org/10.1111/jomf.12509.

Katz-Wise, S. L., Rosario, M., & Tsappis, M. (2016, December). Lesbian, Gay, Bisexual, and Transgender Youth and Family Acceptance. *Pediatric Clinics of North America, 63*(6), 1011–1025. https://doi.org/10.1016/j.pcl.2016.07.005.

Khalil, R., Godde, B., & Karim, A. A. (2019, March 22). The Link Between Creativity, Cognition, and Creative Drives and Underlying Neural Mechanisms. *Frontiers in Neural Circuits, 13*. https://doi.org/10.3389/fncir.2019.00018.

Khodyakov, D., & Carr, D. (2009, May 22). The Impact of Late-Life Parental Death on Adult Sibling Relationships. *Research on Aging, 31*(5), 495–519. https://doi.org/10.1177/ 0164027509337193.

der Kolk, B. V. (2015, September 8). *The Body Keeps the Score: Brain, Mind, and Body in the Healing of Trauma*. Penguin Books.

Linden, A. H., & Sillence, E. (2021, July). "I'm finally allowed to be me": parent-child estrangement and psychological wellbeing. *Families, Relationships and Societies, 10*(2), 325–341. https://doi.org/10.1332/204674319x15647593365505.

Mahon, D., Minami, T., & Brown, G. J. (2023, April 25). The variability of client, therapist and clinic in psychotherapy outcomes: A three-level hierarchical model. *Counselling and Psychotherapy Research, 23*(3), 761–769. https://doi.org/10.1002/capr.12652.

Ma, X., Yue, Z. Q., Gong, Z. Q., Zhang, H., Duan, N. Y., Shi, Y. T., Wei, G. X., & Li, Y. F. (2017, June 6). The Effect of Diaphragmatic Breathing on Attention, Negative Affect and Stress in Healthy Adults. *Frontiers in Psychology, 8*. https://doi.org/10.3389/fpsyg.2017.00874.

Melvin, K., & Hickey, J. (2021, August 31). The Changing Impact and Challenges of Familial Estrangement. *The Family Journal, 30*(3), 348–356. https://doi.org/10.1177/10664807211035490.

Mennen, F. E., Kim, K., Sang, J., & Trickett, P. K. (2010, September). Child neglect: Definition and identification of youth's experiences in official reports of maltreatment. *Child Abuse & Neglect, 34*(9), 647–658. https://doi.org/10.1016/j.chiabu.2010.02.007.

Moors, F., & Zech, E. (2017, October 31). The Effects of Psychotherapist's and Clients' Interpersonal Behaviors during a First Simulated Session: A Lab Study Investigating Client Satisfaction. *Frontiers in Psychology, 8.* https://doi.org/10.3389/fpsyg.2017.01868.

Ogden, P., & Fisher, J. (2015, May 29). *Sensorimotor Psychotherapy: Interventions for Trauma and Attachment.* W.W. Norton

Pillemer, K. (2020, September 8). *Fault Lines: Fractured Families and How to Mend Them.* Avery.

Rittenour, C., Kromka, S., Pitts, S., Thorwart, M., Vickers, J., & Whyte, K. (2018, October 20). Communication Surrounding Estrangement: Stereotypes, Attitudes, and (Non) Accommodation Strategies. *Behavioral Sciences, 8*(10), 96. https://doi.org/10.3390/bs8100096.

Rogers, C. (2004). *On Becoming a Person: A therapist's view on psychotherapy.* Robinson.

Ryff, C. D., & Singer, B. (1996). Psychological Well-Being: Meaning, Measurement, and Implications for Psychotherapy Research. *Psychotherapy and Psychosomatics, 65*(1), 14–23. https://doi.org/10.1159/000289026.

Scharp, K. (2014). (De)constructing family: exploring communicative practices in accomplishing and maintaining estrangement between adult children and their parents. *Doctor of Philosophy (PhD), University of Iowa.* https://doi.org/10.17077/etd.rpvu7hul.

Scharp, K. M. (2017, June 22). "You're Not Welcome Here": A Grounded Theory of Family Distancing. *Communication Research, 46*(4), 427–455. https://doi.org/10.1177/0093650217715542.

Scharp, K. M., & Dorrance Hall, E. (2017, January 2). Family marginalization, alienation, and estrangement: questioning the nonvoluntary status of family relationships. *Annals of the International Communication Association, 41*(1), 28–45. https://doi.org/10.1080/23808985.2017.1285680.

Scharp, K. M. (2019, November 10). Taking sides and feeling caught: Communicative complications for immediate family members of estranged parent–child dyads. *Journal of Social and Personal Relationships, 37*(4), 1053–1072. https://doi.org/10.1177/0265407519886360.

Scharp, K. M., & McLaren, R. M. (2017, March 22). Uncertainty issues and management in adult children's stories of their estrangement with their parents. *Journal of Social and Personal Relationships, 35*(6), 811–830. https://doi.org/10.1177/0265407517699097.

Scharp, K. M., Thomas, L. J., & Paxman, C. G. (2015, October 2). "It Was the Straw that Broke the Camel's Back": Exploring the Distancing Processes Communicatively Constructed in Parent-Child Estrangement Backstories. *Journal of Family Communication, 15*(4), 330–348. https://doi.org/10.1080/15267431.2015.1076422.

Schneiderman, N., Ironson, G., & Siegel, S. D. (2005, April 1). Stress and Health: Psychological, Behavioral, and Biological Determinants. *Annual Review of Clinical Psychology, 1*(1), 607–628. https://doi.org/10.1146/annurev.clinpsy.1.102803.144141.

Schoppe-Sullivan, S. J., Coleman, J., Wang, J., & Yan, J. J. (2023, September). Mothers' attributions for estrangement from their adult children. *Couple and Family*

Psychology: Research and Practice, 12(3), 146–154. https://doi.org/10.1037/cfp0000198.

Schwartzman, G. (2006, December). The subjectivity of the mother in the mother–son relationship. Attachment, separation, and autonomy. *International Forum of Psychoanalysis, 15*(4), 226–232. https://doi.org/10.1080/08037060601082252.

Sichel, M. (2004, February 1). *Healing from Family Rifts: Ten Steps to Finding Peace after Being Cut off from a Family Member.* McGraw Hill.

Sims, M., & Rofail, M. (2014). Grandparents with Little or No Contact with Grandchildren-Impact on Grandparents. *Journal of Aging Science, 02*(01). https://doi.org/10.4172/2329-8847.1000117.

Sohal, M., Singh, P., Dhillon, B. S., & Gill, H. S. (2022, March). Efficacy of journaling in the management of mental illness: a systematic review and meta-analysis. *Family Medicine and Community Health, 10*(1), e001154. https://doi.org/10.1136/fmch-2021-001154.

Suter, E. A., Kellas, J. K., Webb, S. K., & Allen, J. A. (2016, May 24). A Tale of Two Mommies: (Re)Storying Family of Origin Narratives. *Journal of Family Communication, 16*(4), 303–317. https://doi.org/10.1080/15267431.2016.1184150.

Therapeutic Alliance. (n.d.). In https://dictionary.apa.org/. https://dictionary.apa.org/therapeutic-alliance.

Thomas, P. A., Liu, H., & Umberson, D. (2017, November 1). Family Relationships and Well-Being. *Innovation in Aging, 1*(3). https://doi.org/10.1093/geroni/igx025.

Ulrichová, M. (2014). *Ethical Aspects of Psychotherapy: The ethical training and self-training of the therapist with a focus on logotherapy and existential analysis* (1st ed.). EL-PRESS.

Varker, T., Brand, R. M., Ward, J., Terhaag, S., & Phelps, A. (2019, November). Efficacy of synchronous telepsychology interventions for people with anxiety, depression, posttraumatic stress disorder, and adjustment disorder: A rapid evidence assessment. *Psychological Services, 16*(4), 621–635. https://doi.org/10.1037/ser0000239.

Verhaar, S., Matthewson, M. L., & Bentley, C. (2022, March 30). The Impact of Parental Alienating Behaviours on the Mental Health of Adults Alienated in Childhood. *Children, 9*(4), 475. https://doi.org/10.3390/children9040475.

Vicario, C. M., & Felmingham, K. L. (2018, January 10). Slower Time estimation in Post-Traumatic Stress Disorder. *Scientific Reports, 8*(1). https://doi.org/10.1038/s41598-017-18907-5.

Wampold, B. E. (2015, September 25). How important are the common factors in psychotherapy? An update. *World Psychiatry, 14*(3), 270–277. https://doi.org/10.1002/wps.20238.

Weinberg, H., & Rolnick, A. (2019, July 4). *Theory and Practice of Online Therapy: Internet-Delivered Interventions for Individuals, Groups, Families, and Organizations.* Routledge.

Wilkins, P. (2015). *Person-Centred Therapy: 100 Key Points* (2nd ed.). Routledge.

Worden, J. W. (2009, December 2). *Grief Counselling and Grief Therapy: The Mental Health Practitioner.* Routledge.

Yaribeygi, H., Panahi, Y., Sahraei, H., Johnston, T. P., & Sahebkar, A. (2017). The impact of stress on body function: A review. *EXCLI Journal, 16*, 1057–1072. https://doi.org/10.17179/excli2017-480.

Zaccaro, A., Piarulli, A., Laurino, M., Garbella, E., Menicucci, D., Neri, B., & Gemignani, A. (2018, September 7). How Breath-Control Can Change Your Life: A Systematic

Review on Psycho-Physiological Correlates of Slow Breathing. *Frontiers in Human Neuroscience, 12.* https://doi.org/10.3389/fnhum.2018.00353.

Zhao, R., Tang, Z., Lu, F., Xing, Q., & Shen, W. (2022, January 17). An Updated Evaluation of the Dichotomous Link Between Creativity and Mental Health. *Frontiers in Psychiatry, 12.* https://doi.org/10.3389/fpsyt.2021.781961.

Zhu, Z., Chen, H., Ma, J., He, Y., Chen, J., & Sun, J. (2020, November 27). Exploring the Relationship between Walking and Emotional Health in China. *International Journal of Environmental Research and Public Health, 17*(23), 8804. https://doi.org/10.3390/ijerph17238804.

Zisook, S., & Shear, K. (2009, June). Grief and bereavement: what psychiatrists need to know. *World Psychiatry, 8*(2), 67–74. https://doi.org/10.1002/j.2051-5545.2009.tb00217.x.

Index